EVERYDAY
Slow Cooker
& ONE DISH RECIPES

Taste of Home
TRUSTED MEDIA BRANDS, INC • MILWAUKEE, WI

PICTURED ON FRONT COVER:
Slow Cooker Beef Tips Burgundy, page 21; Pineapple-Glazed Pork Tenderloin, page 52; Slow Cooker Tequila Poached Pears, page 78; Asian BBQ Pork Buns, page 72.

PICTURED ON BACK COVER:
Beef Brisket Tacos, page 22; One-Pot Meaty Spaghetti, page 110; Crispy Fish & Chips, page 224.

PICTURED ON TITLE PAGE:
Shredded Beef Burrito Filling, page 18.

CONTENTS

Slow Cooker

Stovetop Suppers

Oven Entrees

Bonus Chapter:

GET SOCIAL WITH US

 **LIKE US**
facebook.com/tasteofhome

 **PIN US**
pinterest.com/taste_of_home

 **FOLLOW US**
@tasteofhome

 **TWEET US**
twitter.com/tasteofhome

To find a recipe tasteofhome.com

To submit a recipe tasteofhome.com/submit

To find out about other *Taste of Home* **products** shoptasteofhome.com

Everyday Dinners
have never been **easier!**

You win with 369 simple, family-pleasing Slow Cooker, Stovetop and Oven recipes in this handy three-in-one cookbook.

There's always time to set a hot homemade meal on the table using this beautiful collection. Keep the comfort food coming all year with 369 amazing make-again specialties from home cooks like you!

Simmer up 120+ slow-cooked dishes, perfect for potlucks, parties and busy workdays. Toss together 110 stovetop suppers, such as tacos, pork chops and sloppy joes. And 105+ oven favorites are guaranteed to warm hearts: Potpies, meat loaves and casseroles are just the beginning.

Every dish in this big volume is another home cook's cherished favorite.
So grab an apron and make them your own!

HANDY ICONS IN THIS BOOK

EAT SMART Recipes are lower in calories, fat and/or sodium, as determined by a registered dietitian. Consider these when you're cooking for someone following a special diet or you just want to eat lighter.

FREEZE IT Freeze It recipes may be stored in the freezer if you choose. These fix-ahead dishes include directions for freezing and reheating.

ITALIAN TURKEY
MEATBALLS
PAGE 28

Slow-Cook with Confidence
Follow these tips for **slow-cooking success every time.**

PLAN AHEAD TO PREP AND GO.
In most cases, you can prepare and load ingredients into the slow cooker insert beforehand and store it in the refrigerator overnight. But an insert can crack if exposed to rapid temperature changes. Let the insert sit out just long enough to reach room temperature before placing in the slow cooker.

USE THAWED INGREDIENTS.
Although throwing frozen chicken breasts into the slow cooker may seem easy, it's not a smart shortcut. Foods thawing inside the slow cooker can create the ideal environment for bacteria to grow, so thaw frozen meat and veggies ahead of time. The exception is if you're using a prepackaged slow-cooker meal kit and follow the instructions as written.

LINE THE CROCK FOR EASE OF USE.
Some recipes in this book call for a **foil collar** or **sling**. Here's why:

▶ A **foil collar** prevents scorching of rich, saucy dishes, such as *Potluck Bacon Mac & Cheese,* near the slow cooker's heating element. To make, fold two 18-in.-long pieces of foil into strips 4 in. wide. Line the crock's perimeter with the strips; spray with cooking spray.

▶ A **sling** helps you lift layered foods, such as *Slow Cooker Cheesy White Lasagna,* out of the crock without much fuss. To make, fold one or more pieces of heavy-duty foil into strips. Place on bottom and up sides of the slow cooker; coat with cooking spray.

TAKE THE TIME TO BROWN.
Give yourself a few extra minutes to brown your meat in a skillet before placing in the slow cooker. Doing so will add rich color and more flavor to the finished dish.

KEEP THE LID CLOSED.
Don't peek! It's tempting to lift the lid and check on your meal's progress, but resist the urge. Every time you open the lid, you'll have to add about 30 minutes to the total cooking time.

ADJUST COOK TIME AS NEEDED.
Live at a high altitude? Slow cooking will take longer. Add about 30 minutes for each hour of cooking the recipe calls for; legumes will take roughly twice as long.

Want your food done sooner? Cooking one hour on high is roughly equal to two hours on low, so adjust the recipe to suit your schedule.

SLOW COOKER CHICKEN & DUMPLINGS, PAGE 27

BUTTERMILK-MUSHROOM PORK CHOPS, PAGE 61

Stovetop Suppers Are Super Convenient

Stovetop cooking is quick and easy. Many stovetop meals in this book are **ready in just one pot**, which makes cleanup a breeze. These tips will help you enjoy cooking on the stove.

CHOOSE THE RIGHT PAN FOR THE JOB.

The right cookware can simplify meal preparation when cooking on the stovetop. The basic skillets every kitchen needs include a 10- or 12-in. skillet with lid and an 8- or 9-in. saute/omelet pan.

Good quality cookware conducts heat quickly and cooks food evenly. The type of metal and thickness of the pan affect its performance. There are pros and cons to each of the most common cookware metals:

Copper conducts heat the best. However, it is expensive, it tarnishes (and usually requires periodic polishing), and it reacts with acidic ingredients, which is why the interior of a copper pan is usually lined with tin or stainless steel.

COPPER

Aluminum is a good conductor of heat and is less expensive than copper. However, aluminum reacts with acidic ingredients.

Anodized aluminum has the same positive qualities as aluminum, but the surface is electrochemically treated so it will not react to acidic ingredients. The surface is resistant to scratches and is nonstick.

Cast iron conducts heat very well. It is usually heavy. Cast iron also needs regular seasoning to prevent sticking and rusting.

Stainless steel is durable and retains its new look for years. It isn't a good conductor of heat, which is why it often has an aluminum or copper core or bottom.

STAINLESS STEEL

Nonstick is especially preferred for cooking delicate foods, such as eggs, pancakes or thin fish fillets. It won't scorch foods if you're cooking in batches. It can be scratched easily and has maximum temperature limitations.

MASTER THESE COMMON STOVETOP COOKING TECHNIQUES.

Sauteeing
Add a small amount of oil to a hot skillet and heat over medium-high heat. For best results, cut the food into uniformly sized pieces before adding. Don't overcrowd. Stir frequently while cooking.

Searing
Heat oil in a large skillet over medium-high heat until it almost begins to smoke. Pat food dry. Cook the food until a deeply colored crust has formed, being careful not to crowd the pan. Reduce heat if food browns too quickly.

Braising
Season meat; coat with flour if recipe directs. In Dutch oven, brown meat in oil in batches. To ensure nice browning, do not crowd. Set meat aside; cook vegetables, adding flour if recipe directs. Add broth gradually, stirring to deglaze pan and to keep lumps from forming. Return meat to pan and stir until mixture comes to a boil.

Steaming
Place a steamer basket or bamboo steamer in a pan with water. Bring water to a boil (boiling water should not touch the steamer) and place food in basket; cover and steam. Add more boiling water to pan as necessary, making sure pan does not run dry.

COD WITH HEARTY TOMATO SAUCE, PAGE 154

ASPARAGUS HAM DINNER, PAGE 132

SUNDAY ROAST CHICKEN, PAGE 186

ORANGE-GLAZED PORK LOIN PAGE 207

Oven Entrees Bake Hands-Free

And they **warm up the kitchen on a chilly day,** too! Follow these tips for success every time.

CHOOSE THE RIGHT BAKEWARE.

Metal baking pans

These great conductors of heat create nice browning on rolls, coffee cakes and other baked goods. Metal is a safe, smart choice for under the broiler. It may react with acidic foods such as tomato sauce or cranberries and create a metallic taste or discoloration.

Glass baking dishes

Glass provides slower, more even baking for egg dishes, custards and casseroles. It takes longer to heat than metal, but once heated, the dish holds the heat longer. This is undesirable for many desserts, because a sugary batter may overbrown in glass. If you wish to bake in a glass dish even though the recipe calls for a metal pan, decrease the oven temperature by 25°.

Other baking dishes

Ceramic or stoneware baking dishes generally perform like glass, but are more attractive. They may also be safe for higher temperatures than glass; refer to the manufacturer's instructions.

CONFIRM THE OVEN'S TEMPERATURE.

Use an oven thermometer to check. Preheat the oven to the desired temperature; place an oven thermometer on the center rack. Close the oven door and leave the oven on at the set temperature. Keep the thermometer in the oven for 15 minutes before reading. Adjust the temperature accordingly to ensure the best baking results.

NEGATE HOT OR COOL SPOTS.

To test your oven for uneven temperatures, try a bread test. Heat the oven to 350° while arranging six to nine slices of white bread on a large cookie sheet. Place in oven for 5-10 minutes; check if slices are starting to brown or burn. If some slices are noticeably darker or lighter than others, the oven may have hot or cool spots. To negate this, rotate your pans while baking.

ELIMINATE SPILLS—THE SMART WAY.

Line a rimmed baking sheet with foil and place it on the bottom oven rack directly below the dish you are using to bake a recipe. Any drips or spills from the recipe will fall onto the foil-lined pan instead of the oven bottom.

We don't recommend lining the bottom of your oven with aluminum foil or other liners, as there's a chance that they could melt and stick to or damage the oven.

Want to clean up a drip while it's still hot? Grab your oven mitt, a pair of tongs and a damp dishcloth. Using the tongs to move the cloth will help prevent burns.

BEEF BRISKET ON BUNS, PAGE 169

MEATBALLS IN HONEY
BUFFALO SAUCE, PAGE 24

Slow Cooker

One of the **greatest** things about a slow cooker is that it turns affordable cuts of beef, such as top round and chuck roast, into tender, scrumptious meals. From hearty brisket to **succulent** short ribs, there's no better way to enjoy **full-bodied** flavor than with these recipes!

Beef & Ground Beef

SLOW COOKER LASAGNA

Lasagna is a popular meal, and its slow cooker version allows you to serve up a hearty family favorite without spending too much time in the kitchen.

—**KATHRYN CONRAD** MILWAUKEE, WI

PREP: 25 MIN.
COOK: 4 HOURS + STANDING
MAKES: 8 SERVINGS

- 1 **pound ground beef**
- 1 **tablespoon olive oil**
- ½ **cup chopped onion**
- ½ **cup chopped zucchini**
- ½ **cup chopped carrot**
- 1 **jar (24 ounces) marinara sauce**
- 2 **teaspoons Italian seasoning**
- ½ **teaspoon crushed red pepper flakes, optional**
- 2 **cartons (15 ounces each) part-skim ricotta cheese**
- 1 **cup grated Parmesan cheese**
- 4 **large eggs**
- ½ **cup loosely packed basil leaves, chopped**
- 12 **no-cook lasagna noodles**
- 3 **cups shredded part-skim mozzarella cheese**
   Quartered grape tomatoes and additional chopped fresh basil, optional

1. Cut three 25x3-in. strips of heavy-duty foil; crisscross so they resemble spokes of a wheel. Place strips on bottom and up sides of a 5-qt. slow cooker. Coat strips with cooking spray.
2. In a 6-qt. stockpot, cook beef over medium heat 6-8 minutes or until beef is no longer pink; drain. Set beef aside.
3. In same pot, heat oil over medium-high heat. Add the onion, zucchini and carrot; cook and stir 2-3 minutes or until just tender. Stir in beef mixture, marinara sauce, Italian seasoning and if desired, crushed red pepper. In a large bowl, combine the ricotta, Parmesan, eggs and basil.
4. Spread ½ cup meat sauce into the bottom of the slow cooker. Layer with four noodles, breaking as needed to fit. Top with 1½ cups meat mixture, 1⅔ cups cheese mixture and 1 cup mozzarella cheese. Repeat layers twice. Cook it, covered, on low 4 hours or until noodles are tender. Let stand 30 minutes. If desired, sprinkle with grape tomatoes and additional basil.

STOUT & HONEY BEEF ROAST

Here's a heartwarming meal that's ideal for chilly days and hectic nights. Honey, beer and seasonings make the sauce different and so good.

— *TASTE OF HOME* **TEST KITCHEN**

PREP: 15 MIN. • **COOK:** 8 HOURS
MAKES: 12 SERVINGS

- 12 **small red potatoes (about 1½ pounds), scrubbed**
- 6 **to 7 medium carrots (about 1 pound), peeled and cut into ½-inch pieces**
- 2 **medium onions, quartered**
- 1 **boneless beef chuck roast (4 pounds), trimmed**
- 1 **can (14½ ounces) beef broth**
- 1 **cup beer or additional beef broth**
- ½ **cup honey**
- 3 **garlic cloves, minced**
- 1 **teaspoon dried marjoram**
- 1 **teaspoon dried thyme**
- ½ **teaspoon salt**
- ½ **teaspoon pepper**
- ¼ **teaspoon ground cinnamon**
- 2 **tablespoons cornstarch**
- ¼ **cup cold water**

1. Place potatoes, carrots and onion in a 5-qt. slow cooker. Cut roast in half; transfer to slow cooker. In a small bowl, combine next nine ingredients; pour over top. Cook, covered, on low until meat and vegetables are tender, 8-10 hours.
2. Slice beef and keep warm. Strain the cooking juices, reserving vegetables and 1 cup liquid. Skim fat from reserved liquid; transfer liquid to a small saucepan. Bring to a boil. Combine the cornstarch and water until smooth; gradually stir into the juices. Bring to a boil; cook and stir until thickened, about 2 minutes. Serve with beef and vegetables.

TOP TIP

BEAT THE CLOCK

Save time with a jar of minced garlic from the produce department. Simply measure out ½ teaspoon of the garlic for every fresh garlic clove called for in a recipe.

CARRIE'S
CINCINNATI CHILI

STEPHANIE'S SLOW COOKER STEW

Start this warming one-pot meal before you head out for the day. By the time you get home, the well-seasoned meat will be tender and ready to devour.

—STEPHANIE RABBITT-SCHAPP
CINCINNATI, OH

PREP: 20 MIN. • **COOK:** 7½ HOURS
MAKES: 5 SERVINGS

- 1 **pound beef stew meat**
- 2 **medium potatoes, peeled and cubed**
- 1 **can (14½ ounces) beef broth**
- 1 **can (11½ ounces) V8 juice**
- 2 **celery ribs, chopped**
- 2 **medium carrots, chopped**
- 1 **medium sweet onion, chopped**
- 3 **bay leaves**
- ½ **teaspoon salt**
- ½ **teaspoon dried thyme**
- ½ **teaspoon chili powder**
- ¼ **teaspoon pepper**
- 2 **tablespoons cornstarch**
- 1 **tablespoon cold water**
- ½ **cup frozen corn**
- ½ **cup frozen peas**

1. In a 3-qt. slow cooker, combine the first 12 ingredients. Cover and cook on low for 7-8 hours or until meat is tender. Discard bay leaves.
2. In a small bowl, combine cornstarch and water until smooth; stir into stew. Add corn and peas. Cover and cook on high for 30 minutes or until thickened.
Per 1⅓ cups: 273 cal., 7g fat (2g sat. fat), 56mg chol., 865mg sod., 31g carb. (9g sugars, 4g fiber), 22g pro.
Diabetic Exchanges: 3 lean meat, 2 vegetable, 1 starch.

FREEZE IT

CARRIE'S CINCINNATI CHILI

Every time we had company or a family gathering, folks would request this. My husband convinced me to enter it in a local chili contest, and I won third place! It's quick and easy. If I don't have fresh garlic, I use minced garlic in the jar.
—CARRIE BIRDSALL DALLAS, GA

PREP: 20 MIN. • **COOK:** 6 HOURS
MAKES: 6 SERVINGS

- 1½ **pounds ground beef**
- 1 **small onion, chopped**
- 1 **can (29 ounces) tomato puree**
- 1 **can (14½ ounces) whole tomatoes, crushed**
- 2 **tablespoons brown sugar**
- 4 **teaspoons chili powder**
- 1 **tablespoon white vinegar**
- 1 **teaspoon salt**
- ¾ **teaspoon ground cinnamon**
- ½ **teaspoon ground allspice**
- ½ **teaspoon pepper**
- 1 **garlic clove, crushed**
- 3 **bay leaves**
  Hot cooked spaghetti
  Shredded cheddar cheese, optional
  Additional chopped onion, optional

1. In a large skillet over medium heat, cook beef and onion, crumbling meat, until beef is no longer pink and onion is tender, 6-8 minutes; drain. Transfer to a 3- or 4-qt. slow cooker. Add the next 11 ingredients.
2. Cook, covered, on low 6-8 hours. Discard the garlic clove and bay leaves. Serve on hot cooked spaghetti; if desired, top with shredded cheddar cheese and additional chopped onion.
Freeze option: Before adding toppings, cool the chili. Freeze the chili in freezer containers. To use, partially thaw it in the refrigerator overnight. Heat through in a saucepan, stirring occasionally and adding a little water or broth if necessary. Serve as directed.

"This faux prime rib roast is delicious served with regular or horseradish mashed potatoes. It can even be baked in the oven in a covered Dutch oven at 350° for about 1½ hours or until 165°."

—**KIMBERLY KUHLMAN** BRYAN, TX

SLOW COOKER FAUX PRIME RIB ROAST

SLOW COOKER FAUX PRIME RIB ROAST

PREP: 20 MIN. • **COOK:** 8¼ HOURS
MAKES: 8 SERVINGS

- 2 **pounds small Yukon Gold or medium red potatoes, quartered**
- 3 **tablespoons water, divided**
- 1 **pound fresh baby carrots**
- 8 **tablespoons butter, softened, divided**
- 6 **tablespoons prepared horseradish**
- 5 **to 6 garlic cloves, minced**
- 2 **teaspoons dried rosemary, crushed**
- 2 **teaspoons dried thyme**
- 2 **teaspoons pepper**
- ¾ **teaspoon salt**
- 1 **boneless beef chuck roast (4 to 5 pounds)**
- 2 **cups beef broth**
- ½ **cup white wine or additional beef broth**
- 1 **tablespoon all-purpose flour**

1. Microwave the potatoes with 2 tablespoons water, covered, on high until potatoes just begin to soften, about 7-10 minutes, stirring occasionally. Transfer to a 6-qt. slow cooker; add the carrots. Meanwhile, mix 6 tablespoons softened butter with the horseradish, garlic and seasonings; then refrigerate half of the butter mixture.

2. In a Dutch oven, heat the remaining 2 tablespoons plain butter over medium heat. Brown roast on all sides; transfer to slow cooker. Add broth and wine to Dutch oven; cook 2-3 minutes, stirring to loosen browned bits from pan. Pour over meat. Spread butter mixture over roast; cook, covered, on low until beef is tender, 8-10 hours.

3. Remove roast and vegetables to a serving platter; tent with foil. Mix flour and remaining water until smooth; gradually stir into cooking juices. Cook, covered, on high until thickened, about 15-20 minutes.

4. Cut roast into thick slices. Top with the remaining butter mixture; drizzle with 1 cup gravy. Serve with potatoes, carrots and remaining gravy.

BARBACOA

My husband adores this beef roast simmered in lime juice, chipotle and cumin. I serve it over rice flavored with cilantro and more zippy lime.

—AUNDREA MCCORMICK DENVER, CO

PREP: 45 MIN. • **COOK:** 7 HOURS
MAKES: 8 SERVINGS

- ¼ **cup lime juice**
- ¼ **cup cider vinegar**
- 3 **chipotle peppers in adobo sauce**
- 4 **garlic cloves, thinly sliced**
- 4 **teaspoons ground cumin**
- 3 **teaspoons dried oregano**
- ¾ **teaspoon salt**
- 1½ **teaspoons pepper**
- ½ **teaspoon ground cloves**
- 1 **cup reduced-sodium chicken broth**
- 1 **boneless beef chuck roast (3 to 4 pounds)**
- 3 **bay leaves**

RICE
- 3 **cups water**
- 2 **cups uncooked jasmine rice, rinsed and drained**
- 3 **tablespoons butter**
- 1½ **teaspoons salt**
- ½ **cup minced fresh cilantro**
- 2 **tablespoons lime juice**

1. Place the first nine ingredients in a blender; cover and process until smooth. Add broth; pulse to combine.

2. Place roast and bay leaves in a 4- or 5-qt. slow cooker; pour sauce over top. Cook, covered, on low 7-9 hours or until meat is tender.

3. Prepare rice about 30 minutes before serving. In a large saucepan, combine water, rice, butter and salt; bring to a boil. Reduce heat; simmer, covered, 12-15 minutes or until liquid is absorbed and rice is tender. Remove from heat; gently stir in cilantro and lime juice.

4. Remove roast from slow cooker; cool slightly. Discard bay leaves and skim fat from cooking juices. Shred beef with two forks; return beef to slow cooker. Serve with the rice.

ITALIAN BOW TIE SUPPER

For a family-pleasing Italian dinner, you can't go wrong with this all-in-one meal featuring bow tie pasta. Any leftovers taste just as good the next day.

—JOY FREY KELSO, MO

PREP: 10 MIN. • **COOK:** 7¼ HOURS
MAKES: 6 SERVINGS

- 1½ **pounds ground beef**
- 1 **medium onion, chopped**
- 1 **garlic clove, minced**
- 2 **cans (8 ounces each) tomato sauce**
- 1 **can (14½ ounces) stewed tomatoes, chopped**
- 1 **teaspoon dried oregano**
- 1 **teaspoon Italian seasoning Salt and pepper to taste**
- 1 **package (16 ounces) bow tie pasta, cooked and drained**
- 1 **package (10 ounces) frozen chopped spinach, thawed and squeezed dry**
- 1½ **cups shredded part-skim mozzarella cheese**
- ½ **cup grated Parmesan cheese**

1. In a large skillet, cook the beef and onion over medium heat until meat is no longer pink. Add the garlic; cook for 1 minute longer. Drain.

2. Transfer to a 3-qt. slow cooker. Stir in the tomato sauce, tomatoes and seasonings. Cover and cook on low for 7-8 hours or until bubbly.

3. Increase heat to high; stir in pasta, spinach and cheeses. Cover and cook 10 minutes longer or until it is heated through and cheese is melted.

TOP TIP

STRIKING OIL?

Some cooks like to add a bit of oil to the water when they cook pasta because it stops the pasta from sticking together. Our test kitchen believes oil is not needed when pasta is stirred into a slow cooker because the sauce will likely prevent the pasta from sticking.

APPLE & ONION TIP ROAST

I thicken the cooking juices from this roast to make a pleasing apple gravy that's wonderful over beef and onions.

—**RACHEL KOISTINEN** HAYTI, SD

PREP: 30 MIN.
COOK: 5 HOURS + STANDING
MAKES: 8 SERVINGS

- 1 **beef sirloin tip roast (3 pounds), cut in half**
- 1 **cup water**
- 1 **teaspoon seasoned salt**
- ½ **teaspoon reduced-sodium soy sauce**
- ½ **teaspoon Worcestershire sauce**
- ¼ **teaspoon garlic powder**
- 1 **large tart apple, quartered**
- 1 **large onion, sliced**
- 2 **tablespoons cornstarch**
- 2 **tablespoons cold water**
- ⅛ **teaspoon browning sauce**

1. In a large nonstick skillet coated with cooking spray, brown roast on all sides. Transfer to a 5-qt. slow cooker. Add water to the skillet, stirring to loosen any browned bits; pour over roast. Sprinkle the roast with seasoned salt, soy sauce, Worcestershire sauce and garlic powder. Top with apple and onion.

2. Cover and cook on low for 5-6 hours or until the meat is tender.

3. Remove roast and onion; let stand for 15 minutes before slicing.

4. Strain cooking liquid into a saucepan, discarding apple. Bring liquid to a boil; cook until reduced to 2 cups, about 15 minutes. Combine cornstarch and cold water until smooth; stir in the browning sauce. Stir into cooking liquid. Bring to a boil; cook and stir for 2 minutes or until thickened. Serve with beef and onion.

Per serving: 242 cal., 8g fat (3g sat. fat), 108mg chol., 256mg sod., 7g carb. (3g sugars, 1g fiber), 34g pro.
Diabetic Exchanges: 4 lean meat, ½ starch.

POT ROAST WITH ASIAN BLACK BEAN SAUCE

You can't beat a fork-tender pot roast combined with a black bean sauce. Yum!

—**JUDY LAWSON** CHELSEA, MI

PREP: 25 MIN. • **COOK:** 6 HOURS
MAKES: 10 SERVINGS

- 1 **boneless beef chuck roast (3 to 4 pounds)**
- ½ **teaspoon salt**
- ½ **teaspoon pepper**
- 1 **tablespoon olive oil**
- 1 **medium onion, cut into 1-inch pieces**
- ¾ **cup Asian black bean sauce**
- ¼ **cup reduced-sodium beef broth**
- ½ **pound sliced fresh mushrooms**
- 8 **ounces fresh snow peas, trimmed**
- 1 **tablespoon cornstarch**
- 1 **tablespoon cold water**
  Hot cooked rice
- 4 **green onions, sliced**

1. Sprinkle roast with salt and pepper. In a large skillet, heat oil over medium-high heat. Brown roast 3-4 minutes on each side. Transfer to a 6-qt. slow cooker. Add onion. Whisk together black bean sauce and broth; pour over roast. Cook, covered, on low 5-6 hours.

2. Add mushrooms and snow peas; continue cooking on low until meat is tender, about 30 minutes.

3. Remove roast and vegetables to a serving platter; keep warm. Transfer the cooking juices to a small saucepan; skim fat. Bring the cooking juices to a boil. In a small bowl, mix the cornstarch and cold water until smooth; stir into the cooking juices. Return to a boil; cook and stir for 1-2 minutes or until thickened. Serve the roast with hot cooked rice and sauce. Sprinkle with green onions.

Per serving: 281 cal., 14g fat (5g sat. fat), 89mg chol., 602mg sod., 8g carb. (4g sugars, 1g fiber), 29g pro.
Diabetic Exchanges: 3 lean meat, ½ starch.

POT ROAST WITH ASIAN BLACK BEAN SAUCE

CREAMY CELERY
BEEF STROGANOFF

CREAMY CELERY BEEF STROGANOFF

Cream of celery soup adds richness to this dish that's a family favorite. Besides the delicious flavor, the meal is a breeze to toss together!

—**KIMBERLY WALLACE** DENNISON, OH

PREP: 20 MIN. • **COOK:** 8 HOURS
MAKES: 6 SERVINGS

- 2 pounds beef stew meat, cut into 1-inch cubes
- 1 can (10¾ ounces) condensed cream of celery soup, undiluted
- 1 can (10¾ ounces) condensed cream of mushroom soup, undiluted
- 1 medium onion, chopped
- 1 jar (6 ounces) sliced mushrooms, drained
- 1 envelope onion soup mix
- ½ teaspoon pepper
- 1 cup (8 ounces) sour cream
  Hot cooked noodles

In a 3-qt. slow cooker, combine the first seven ingredients. Cover and cook on low for 8 hours or until beef is tender. Stir in sour cream. Serve with noodles.

SOUTHWEST BEEF & BEANS

My spicy steak and beans over rice will have your family and friends asking for more. It's a go-to in my recipe collection.

—**MARIE LEAMON** BETHESDA, MD

PREP: 10 MIN. • **COOK:** 6½ HOURS
MAKES: 8 SERVINGS

- 1½ pounds boneless round steak
- 1 tablespoon prepared mustard
- 1 tablespoon chili powder
- ½ teaspoon salt
- ¼ teaspoon pepper
- 1 garlic clove, minced
- 2 cans (14½ ounces each) diced tomatoes, undrained
- 1 medium onion, chopped
- 1 teaspoon beef bouillon granules
- 1 can (16 ounces) kidney beans, rinsed and drained
  Hot cooked rice

Cut the steak into thin strips. Combine mustard, chili powder, salt, pepper and garlic in a bowl; add the steak and toss to coat. Transfer to a 3-qt. slow cooker; add tomatoes, onion and bouillon. Cover and cook on low for 6-8 hours. Stir in beans; cook 30 minutes longer. Serve over rice.

Per cup without rice: 185 cal., 3g fat (1g sat. fat), 47mg chol., 584mg sod., 16g carb. (5g sugars, 5g fiber), 24g pro.
Diabetic Exchanges: 2 lean meat, 1 starch, 1 vegetable.

MEAT LOAF &
MASHED RED
POTATOES

MEAT LOAF & MASHED RED POTATOES

Satisfy the meat-and-potatoes lovers in your house with this satisfying meal in one that cooks up in one pot! Talk about classic comfort food!

—FAITH CROMWELL SAN FRANCISCO, CA

PREP: 30 MIN.
COOK: 4 HOURS + STANDING
MAKES: 8 SERVINGS

- 3 pounds small red potatoes, quartered
- 1½ cups beef stock, divided
- 3 slices white bread, torn into small pieces
- 2 large portobello mushrooms (about 6 ounces), cut into chunks
- 1 medium onion, cut into wedges
- 1 medium carrot, cut into chunks
- 1 celery rib, cut into chunks
- 3 garlic cloves, halved
- 2 large eggs, lightly beaten
- 1¼ pounds ground beef
- ¾ pound ground pork
- 2 tablespoons Worcestershire sauce
- 2 teaspoons salt, divided
- 1 teaspoon pepper, divided

GLAZE
- ½ cup ketchup
- 2 tablespoons tomato paste
- 2 tablespoons brown sugar

POTATOES
- 3 tablespoons butter

1. Using a large microwave-safe bowl, combine potatoes and 1 cup beef stock. Microwave, covered, on high just until softened, 12-15 minutes. Transfer potato mixture to a 6-qt. slow cooker. Combine the bread and remaining stock in a large bowl; let stand until liquid is absorbed.

2. Meanwhile, pulse the mushrooms, onion, carrot, celery and garlic in a food processor until finely chopped. Then add the vegetable mixture, eggs, beef, pork, Worcestershire sauce, 1¼ teaspoons salt and ¾ teaspoon pepper to bread mixture; mix lightly but thoroughly. Place the meat mixture on 18x12-in. piece of heavy-duty foil; shape into a 10x6-in. oval loaf. Lifting with foil, place in slow cooker on top of the potatoes; press foil up the sides and over the edges of slow cooker, creating a bowl to contain the meat loaf juices. Mix together the glaze ingredients; spread over meat loaf.

3. Cook it, covered, on low until a thermometer reads 160°, 4-5 hours. Using a turkey baster, remove and discard the liquid contained in foil; lifting with foil, remove the meat loaf to a platter (or carefully remove the meat loaf using foil, draining liquid into a small bowl). Let it stand 10 minutes before cutting.

4. Drain potatoes, reserving cooking liquid; transfer potatoes to a large bowl. Mash, gradually adding butter, remaining salt and pepper and enough reserved cooking liquid to reach the desired consistency. Serve with meat loaf.

EAT SMART

BEEF & RICE STUFFED CABBAGE ROLLS

My family runs to the table when I serve my cabbage rolls. The meal is quick to put together and really satisfies without being too fattening.

—LYNN BOWEN GERALDINE, AL

PREP: 20 MIN. • **COOK:** 6 HOURS
MAKES: 6 SERVINGS

- 12 cabbage leaves
- 1 cup cooked brown rice
- ¼ cup finely chopped onion
- 1 large egg, lightly beaten
- ¼ cup fat-free milk
- ½ teaspoon salt
- ¼ teaspoon pepper
- 1 pound lean ground beef (90% lean)

SAUCE
- 1 can (8 ounces) tomato sauce
- 1 tablespoon brown sugar
- 1 tablespoon lemon juice
- 1 teaspoon Worcestershire sauce

1. In batches, cook cabbage in boiling water 3-5 minutes or until crisp-tender. Drain; cool slightly. Trim the thick vein from the bottom of each cabbage leaf, making a V-shaped cut.

2. In a large bowl, combine rice, onion, egg, milk, salt and pepper. Add beef; mix lightly but thoroughly. Place about ¼ cup beef mixture on each cabbage leaf. Pull together cut edges of leaf to overlap; fold over filling. Fold in sides and roll up.

3. Place six rolls in a 4- or 5-qt. slow cooker, seam side down. In a bowl, mix sauce ingredients; pour half of the sauce over cabbage rolls. Top with remaining rolls and sauce. Cook, covered, on low for 6-8 hours or until a thermometer inserted in the beef reads 160° and the cabbage is tender.

Per 2 cabbage rolls: 204 cal., 7g fat (3g sat. fat), 83mg chol., 446mg sod., 16g carb. (5g sugars, 2g fiber), 18g pro.
Diabetic Exchanges: 2 lean meat, 1 starch.

BEEF & RICE STUFFED CABBAGE ROLLS

SLOW-COOKED
SWISS STEAK

SHREDDED BEEF BURRITO FILLING

FREEZE IT

Offer a taco or burrito bar at your next party! Set out the beef in the slow cooker on warm, along with tortillas and bowls of shredded cheese, salsa and sour cream. For a variation, I also make beefy bean burritos by mixing a can of refried beans into 3 or 4 cups of the cooked beef filling.
—**HOPE WASYLENKI** GAHANNA, OH

PREP: 20 MIN. • **COOK:** 7 HOURS
MAKES: 12 SERVINGS

- 5 **pounds boneless beef chuck roast, cut into 4 pieces**
- ½ **cup beef broth**
- 2 **tablespoons canola oil**
- 1 **medium onion, finely chopped**
- 2 **jalapeno peppers, seeded and finely chopped**
- 2 **garlic cloves, minced**
- 2 **tablespoons chili powder**
- 1 **tablespoon ground cumin**
- ⅛ **teaspoon salt**
- 1 **can (28 ounces) crushed tomatoes in puree**
- 1 **jar (16 ounces) salsa verde Flour tortillas, taco shells, shredded cheddar cheese, sour cream, guacamole, salsa and fresh cilantro leaves, optional**

1. In a 6-qt. slow cooker, combine beef and broth. Cook, covered, on low until meat is tender, 6-8 hours. Remove meat; discard juices. When cool enough to handle, shred with two forks. Return to slow cooker.

2. In a large skillet, heat oil over medium heat. Add the onion and jalapenos; cook and stir until softened, 3-4 minutes. Add the garlic and seasonings; cook 1 minute longer. Stir in the crushed tomatoes and salsa; bring to a boil. Pour the mixture over the shredded beef; stir to combine. Cook, covered, on high until it is heated through, about 1 hour.

3. Using tongs, serve on tortillas for burritos or taco shells for tacos; add toppings as desired.

Freeze option: Freeze cooled meat mixture in freezer containers. To use, partially thaw in refrigerator overnight. Heat the meat through in a saucepan, stirring occasionally.

SLOW-COOKED SWISS STEAK

This is a favorite of mine because I can flour and season the round steak and refrigerate it overnight. In the morning, I just put all the ingredients in the slow cooker, and I have a delicious dinner waiting when I arrive home.
—**SARAH BURKS** WATHENA, KS

PREP: 10 MIN. • **COOK:** 6 HOURS
MAKES: 6 SERVINGS

- 2 **tablespoons all-purpose flour**
- ½ **teaspoon salt**
- ¼ **teaspoon pepper**
- 1½ **pounds beef round steak, cut into six pieces**
- 1 **medium onion, cut into ¼-inch slices**
- 1 **celery rib, cut into ½-inch slices**
- 2 **cans (8 ounces each) tomato sauce**

1. Using a large resealable plastic bag, combine the flour, salt and pepper. Add the steak; seal bag and shake to coat.

2. Place the onion in a greased 3-qt. slow cooker. Top with the steak, celery and tomato sauce. Cover and cook on low for 6-8 hours or until the meat is tender.

CRANBERRY MEATBALLS

Whether you serve them as appetizers or the main course, these tasty meatballs are going to be popular. Cranberry and chili sauces give them extra sweetness.
—**NINA HALL** SPOKANE, WA

PREP: 20 MIN. • **COOK:** 6 HOURS
MAKES: 6 SERVINGS

- 2 **large eggs, beaten**
- 1 **cup dry bread crumbs**
- ⅓ **cup minced fresh parsley**
- 2 **tablespoons finely chopped onion**
- 1½ **pounds lean ground beef (90% lean)**
- 1 **can (14 ounces) jellied cranberry sauce**
- 1 **bottle (12 ounces) chili sauce**
- ⅓ **cup ketchup**
- 2 **tablespoons brown sugar**
- 1 **tablespoon lemon juice**

1. In a bowl, combine the eggs, bread crumbs, parsley and onion. Crumble beef over mixture and mix well. Shape into 1½-in. balls. Place in a 3-qt. slow cooker.

2. Using another bowl, combine the cranberry sauce, chili sauce, ketchup, brown sugar and lemon juice. Pour over meatballs. Cover and cook on low for 6-7 hours or until meat is no longer pink.

SHREDDED BEEF
BURRITO FILLING

SLOW COOKER
BEEF TIPS BURGUNDY

SLOW COOKER BEEF TIPS BURGUNDY

Here's a heartwarming classic made simple thanks to a slow cooker. Mushrooms, red wine and tender beef make an elegant supper that's so easy.

—**DEANNA ZEWEN** UNION GROVE, WI

PREP: 15 MIN. • **COOK:** 6¾ HOURS
MAKES: 10 SERVINGS

- 1 **boneless beef chuck roast (3 pounds), trimmed and cut into 1-in. pieces**
- 2 **medium onions, halved and sliced**
- ½ **pound sliced fresh mushrooms**
- 4 **garlic cloves, minced**
- 3 **cups beef stock**
- ½ **cup dry red wine or additional beef stock**
- 2 **tablespoons Worcestershire sauce**
- 2 **tablespoons red wine vinegar**
- 1¼ **teaspoons salt**
- 1 **teaspoon crushed red pepper flakes**
- ½ **teaspoon pepper**
- ⅓ **cup cornstarch**
- ⅓ **cup cold water**
  Hot cooked egg noodles
  Minced fresh parsley

1. In a 5-qt. slow cooker, combine beef, onions, mushrooms and garlic. In a small bowl, mix next seven ingredients; pour over beef mixture. Cook, covered, on low until meat is tender, 6-8 hours.

2. Skim fat from juices. In a small bowl, mix cornstarch and water until smooth; gradually stir into slow cooker. Cook it, covered, on high until thickened, about 45 minutes. Serve with noodles; sprinkle with parsley.

Freeze option: Omitting parsley, freeze the cooled meat mixture, sauce and egg noodles in freezer containers. To use, partially thaw the food in the refrigerator overnight. Microwave it, covered, on high in microwave-safe dishes until it is heated through, stirring gently and adding a little water if necessary. Sprinkle with parsley.

MUSHROOM POT ROAST

Packed with wholesome veggies and tender beef, this is one company-special entree all ages will like. Serve with mashed potatoes to soak up every drop of gravy.

—**ANGIE STEWART** TOPEKA, KS

PREP: 25 MIN. • **COOK:** 6 HOURS
MAKES: 10 SERVINGS

- 1 **boneless beef chuck roast (3 to 4 pounds)**
- ½ **teaspoon salt**
- ¼ **teaspoon pepper**
- 1 **tablespoon canola oil**
- 1½ **pounds sliced fresh shiitake mushrooms**
- 2½ **cups thinly sliced onions**
- 1½ **cups reduced-sodium beef broth**
- 1½ **cups dry red wine or additional reduced-sodium beef broth**
- 1 **can (8 ounces) tomato sauce**
- ¾ **cup chopped peeled parsnips**
- ¾ **cup chopped celery**
- ¾ **cup chopped carrots**
- 8 **garlic cloves, minced**
- 2 **bay leaves**
- 1½ **teaspoons dried thyme**
- 1 **teaspoon chili powder**
- ¼ **cup cornstarch**
- ¼ **cup water**
  Mashed potatoes

1. Sprinkle roast with salt and pepper. In a Dutch oven, brown the roast in oil on all sides. Transfer to a 6-qt. slow cooker. Add the mushrooms, onions, broth, wine, tomato sauce, parsnips, celery, carrots, garlic, bay leaves, thyme and chili powder. Cover and cook on low for 6-8 hours or until meat is tender.

2. Remove the meat and vegetables to a serving platter; keep warm. Discard bay leaves. Skim fat from the cooking juices; transfer to a small saucepan. Bring liquid to a boil. Combine cornstarch and water until smooth; gradually stir into the pan. Bring it to a boil; cook and stir it for 2 minutes or until thickened. Serve with mashed potatoes, meat and vegetables.

Per 4 ounces cooked beef with ⅔ cup vegetables and ½ cup gravy: 310 cal., 14g fat (5g sat. fat), 89mg chol., 363mg sod., 14g carb. (4g sugars, 3g fiber), 30g pro.

Diabetic Exchanges: 4 lean meat, 2 vegetable, 1½ fat.

GLAZED CORNED BEEF DINNER

This recipe is so tasty, it is now the only way my family will eat corned beef. The glaze is the real kicker!

—**SHANNON STRATE** SALT LAKE CITY, UT

PREP: 20 MIN. • **COOK:** 8¼ HOURS
MAKES: 8 SERVINGS

- 8 **medium red potatoes, quartered**
- 2 **medium carrots, sliced**
- 1 **medium onion, sliced**
- 1 **corned beef brisket with spice packet (3 pounds)**
- 1½ **cups water**
- 4 **orange peel strips (3 inches)**
- 3 **tablespoons thawed orange juice concentrate**
- 3 **tablespoons honey**
- 1 **tablespoon Dijon mustard**

1. Place the potatoes, carrots and onion in a 5-qt. slow cooker. Cut brisket in half; place over vegetables. Add the water, orange peel and contents of spice packet.

2. Cover and cook on low for 8-9 hours or until meat and vegetables are tender.

3. Using a slotted spoon, transfer corned beef and vegetables to a 13x9-in. baking dish. Discard the orange peel.

4. Combine orange juice concentrate, honey and mustard; pour over the meat. Bake it, uncovered, at 375° for 15-20 minutes, basting occasionally.

TOP TIP

WHAT IS CORNED BEEF?

Corned beef is most often beef brisket that has been cured in a brine. The brine often contains spices, and quite often an additional spice packet accompanies the beef when packaged.

BEEF BRISKET TACOS

Brisket is my meat of choice because it can be made in the slow cooker or oven.

—YVETTE MARQUEZ LITTLETON, CO

PREP: 15 MIN. + MARINATING
COOK: 8 HOURS
MAKES: 10 SERVINGS

- 1 bottle (12 ounces) beer or nonalcoholic beer
- 1 cup brisket marinade sauce or liquid smoke plus 1 tablespoon salt
- 2 bay leaves
- ½ teaspoon salt
- ½ teaspoon pepper
- 1 fresh beef brisket (3 to 4 pounds), fat trimmed
- 20 corn tortillas (6 inches), warmed
  Shredded cheddar cheese, media crema table cream, fresh cilantro leaves, thinly sliced green onions, avocado slices and salsa, optional

1. Using a large resealable plastic bag, combine the first five ingredients. Add the brisket; seal bag and turn to coat. Refrigerate overnight.

2. Transfer the brisket and marinade to a 6-qt. slow cooker. Cook, covered, on low until tender, 8-10 hours. Remove meat; discard bay leaves. Reserve juices in slow cooker. When cool enough to handle, shred meat with two forks. Return to the slow cooker.

3. Using tongs, serve shredded brisket in tortillas. Add toppings as desired.

Freeze option: Freeze cooled meat mixture and juices in freezer containers. To use, partially thaw in refrigerator overnight. Heat through in a saucepan, stirring occasionally.

Test Kitchen Note: This is a fresh beef brisket, not corned beef. The recipe was tested with Claude's Barbeque Brisket Marinade Sauce.

ROUND STEAK SAUERBRATEN

My easy version of an Old World classic takes just minutes to prepare for the slow cooker. The flavorful beef is also great with white rice or dirty rice.

—LINDA BLOOM MCHENRY, IL

PREP: 20 MIN. • **COOK:** 6½ HOURS
MAKES: 10 SERVINGS

- 1 envelope brown gravy mix
- 2 tablespoons plus 1½ teaspoons brown sugar
- 2½ cups cold water, divided
- 1 cup chopped onion
- 2 tablespoons white vinegar
- 2 teaspoons Worcestershire sauce
- 2 bay leaves
- 2½ pounds beef top round steak, cut into 3-inch x ½-inch strips
- 2 teaspoons salt
- 1 teaspoon pepper
- ¼ cup cornstarch
- 10 cups hot cooked egg noodles

1. In a 5-qt. slow cooker, combine the gravy mix, brown sugar, 2 cups water, onion, vinegar, Worcestershire sauce and bay leaves.

2. Sprinkle beef with salt and pepper; stir into gravy mixture. Cover and cook on low for 6-8 hours or until meat is tender.

3. Combine cornstarch and remaining water until smooth; stir into beef mixture. Cover and cook on high for 30 minutes or until thickened. Discard bay leaves. Serve with noodles.

WHAT'S THE BEEF WITH SAUERBRATEN?

The German roast sauerbraten is a main course in which beef is seasoned with vinegar and bay leaves. Many versions also include garlic and/or peppercorns. The robust entree is traditionally served with egg noodles or potatoes.

BEEF BRISKET TACOS

SLOW COOKER
JERKED SHORT RIBS

FIESTA BEEF BOWLS

This easy entree will knock your socks off. Zesty ingredients turn round steak, beans and rice into a phenomenal meal.

—DEBORAH LINN VALDEZ, AK

PREP: 25 MIN. • **COOK:** 8½ HOURS
MAKES: 6 SERVINGS

- 1½ pounds boneless beef top round steak
- 1 can (10 ounces) diced tomatoes and green chilies
- 1 medium onion, chopped
- 2 garlic cloves, minced
- 1 teaspoon dried oregano
- 1 teaspoon chili powder
- 1 teaspoon ground cumin
- ¼ teaspoon salt
- ¼ teaspoon pepper
- 2 cans (15 ounces each) pinto beans, rinsed and drained
- 3 cups hot cooked rice
- ½ cup shredded cheddar cheese
- 6 tablespoons sliced ripe olives
- 6 tablespoons thinly sliced green onions
- 6 tablespoons guacamole

1. Place the round steak in a 3-qt. slow cooker. In a small bowl, combine the tomatoes, onion, garlic and seasonings; pour over steak. Cover and cook on low for 8-9 hours or until meat is tender.
2. Remove meat from slow cooker. Add beans to tomato mixture. Cover and cook on high for 30 minutes or until beans are heated through. When cool enough to handle, slice meat.
3. In individual bowls, layer the rice, meat and bean mixture. Top with the cheese, olives, onions and guacamole.

SLOW COOKER JERKED SHORT RIBS

Sweet and spicy jerk seasonings give these saucy ribs an unforgettable flavor! They're great in the summer because they don't heat up the kitchen.

—SUSAN HEIN BURLINGTON, WI

PREP: 15 MIN. • **COOK:** 6 HOURS
MAKES: 10 SERVINGS

- 1 tablespoon ground coriander
- 2 teaspoons ground ginger
- 2 teaspoons onion powder
- 2 teaspoons garlic powder
- 1 teaspoon salt
- 1 teaspoon pepper
- 1 teaspoon dried thyme
- ¾ teaspoon ground allspice
- ¾ teaspoon ground nutmeg
- ½ teaspoon ground cinnamon
- 10 bone-in beef short ribs (about 5 pounds)
- 1 large sweet onion, chopped
- ½ cup beef broth
- 1 jar (10 ounces) apricot preserves
- 3 tablespoons cider vinegar
- 3 garlic cloves, minced

1. Combine the first 10 ingredients, reserving 2 tablespoons. Rub remaining seasoning mixture over ribs. Place onion and broth in a 6-qt. slow cooker; cover with ribs. Cook, covered, on low until ribs are tender, 6-8 hours.
2. Meanwhile, combine preserves, vinegar, garlic and reserved seasoning mixture. Serve with the ribs.

CUBE STEAKS WITH GRAVY

Here's a hearty, home-style dinner that your family will love after a busy day. The slow-cooked beef is wonderful served over mashed potatoes or noodles.

—JUDY LONG LIMESTONE, TN

PREP: 15 MIN. • **COOK:** 8½ HOURS
MAKES: 6 SERVINGS

- ⅓ cup all-purpose flour
- 6 beef cube steaks (4 ounces each)
- 1 tablespoon canola oil
- 1 large onion, sliced and separated into rings
- 3 cups water, divided
- 1 envelope brown gravy mix
- 1 envelope mushroom gravy mix
- 1 envelope onion gravy mix
  Hot mashed potatoes or cooked noodles

1. Place flour in a large resealable plastic bag. Add the steaks, a few at a time, and shake until completely coated.
2. In a skillet, cook the steaks in oil until lightly browned on each side. Transfer to a 3-qt. slow cooker. Add the onion and 2 cups water. Cover and cook on low for 8 hours or until meat is tender.
3. In a bowl, whisk together gravy mixes with remaining water. Add to the slow cooker; cook 30 minutes longer. Serve over mashed potatoes or noodles.

TOP TIP

THE REST IS GRAVY

Can't find the mushroom or onion gravy mixes called for in the cube steak recipe? Just replace either or both with additional packets of brown gravy mix. Consider tossing a handful of chopped fresh mushrooms into the slow cooker with the onion or a little minced garlic.

SLOW COOKER TAMALE PIE

Canned beans and corn bread/muffin mix speed up the prep on this crowd-pleasing main dish. It's perfect for potlucks and carry-in dinners.

—JILL POKRIVKA YORK, PA

PREP: 25 MIN. • **COOK:** 7 HOURS
MAKES: 8 SERVINGS

- 1 pound ground beef
- 1 teaspoon ground cumin
- ½ teaspoon salt
- ½ teaspoon chili powder
- ¼ teaspoon pepper
- 1 can (15 ounces) black beans, rinsed and drained
- 1 can (14½ ounces) diced tomatoes with mild green chilies, undrained
- 1 can (11 ounces) whole kernel corn, drained
- 1 can (10 ounces) enchilada sauce
- 2 green onions, chopped
- ¼ cup minced fresh cilantro
- 1 package (8½ ounces) corn bread/muffin mix
- 2 large eggs
- 1 cup shredded Mexican cheese blend
  Sour cream and additional minced fresh cilantro, optional

1. In a skillet, cook beef over medium heat until no longer pink; drain. Stir in the cumin, salt, chili powder and pepper.
2. Transfer to a 4-qt. slow cooker; stir in the beans, tomatoes, corn, enchilada sauce, onions and minced cilantro. Cover and cook on low for 6-8 hours or until heated through.
3. In a small bowl, combine muffin mix and eggs; spoon over the meat mixture. Cover and cook 1 hour longer or until a toothpick inserted near the center comes out clean.
4. Sprinkle with cheese; cover and let stand for 5 minutes. Serve with sour cream and additional cilantro if desired.

MEATBALLS IN HONEY BUFFALO SAUCE

PREP: 45 MIN. • **COOK:** 2 HOURS
MAKES: ABOUT 2½ DOZEN

- 2 large eggs, lightly beaten
- 15 Ritz crackers, crushed
- ½ medium onion, finely chopped
- ¼ cup 2% milk
- 4 teaspoons brown sugar
- ½ teaspoon garlic powder
- ½ teaspoon ground chipotle pepper
- ¼ teaspoon smoked paprika
- ¼ teaspoon salt
- ⅛ teaspoon pepper
- ½ pound ground beef
- ½ pound ground pork
- ½ pound ground veal

SAUCE
- ½ cup honey
- ¼ cup Buffalo wing sauce
- ¼ cup packed brown sugar
- 2 tablespoons orange marmalade
- 2 tablespoons apricot spreadable fruit
- 2 tablespoons reduced-sodium soy sauce
- ¼ teaspoon crushed red pepper flakes
  Hot cooked rice or pasta
  Sliced celery, optional

1. Preheat oven to 400°. Combine first 10 ingredients. Add meat; mix lightly but thoroughly. Shape the meat mixture into 1½-in. balls; bake on a greased rack in a 15x10x1-in. baking pan lined with foil until lightly browned, 12-15 minutes
2. Meanwhile, in a small saucepan over medium heat, whisk together sauce ingredients until brown sugar is dissolved.
3. Transfer meatballs to a 3-qt. slow cooker; add sauce. Cook, covered, on low until meatballs are cooked through, about 2 hours. Serve with hot cooked rice or pasta and, if desired, sliced celery.
Freeze option: Freeze cooled meatballs and sauce in freezer containers. To use, partially thaw in refrigerator overnight. Heat through in a covered saucepan, stirring gently and adding a little water or broth if necessary. Serve as directed.

MEATBALLS IN HONEY BUFFALO SAUCE

Poultry

TARRAGON
CHICKEN

TARRAGON CHICKEN

I tried this one night when I had friends coming over for dinner and I was amazed at how deliciously fresh-tasting it was. Even my picky husband liked it! Serve it with crusty French bread to soak up the delicious sauce.

—SHANELLE LEE EPHRATA, PA

PREP: 30 MIN. • **COOK:** 6 HOURS
MAKES: 6 SERVINGS

- 1 **pound fresh baby carrots**
- ½ **pound medium fresh mushrooms, halved**
- 1 **small onion, chopped**
- 6 **bone-in chicken thighs (about 2¼ pounds), skin removed**
- 1 **cup chicken broth**
- 1 **teaspoon dried tarragon**
- ½ **teaspoon salt**
- ¼ **teaspoon pepper**
- 2 **tablespoons cornstarch**
- ½ **cup heavy whipping cream**

1. In a 5-qt. slow cooker, combine carrots, mushrooms and onion. Top with chicken. In a small bowl, combine broth, tarragon, salt and pepper; pour over the chicken. Cook, covered, on low until the chicken is tender, 6-8 hours. Remove chicken; when cool enough to handle, shred with two forks. Transfer chicken and vegetables to a serving platter; keep warm.
2. Pour cooking juices into a small saucepan. Skim fat. In a small bowl, mix cornstarch with ½ cup cooking juices until smooth. Whisk into pan. Bring to a boil; cook and stir 1-2 minutes or until thickened. Add cream; heat through. Serve with chicken and vegetables.

SLOW COOKER
CHICKEN & DUMPLINGS

3. For dumplings, whisk together flour, baking powder, salt and pepper in a large bowl. Stir in milk and butter to form a thick batter. Drop by ¼ cupfuls over the chicken mixture. Cook, covered, on low until bubbly and dumplings are set, 6-8 hours. Discard bay leaves. Remove insert and let stand, uncovered, for 15 minutes.

LEMON DILL CHICKEN

The lemon and dill in this recipe give the chicken a bright, fresh taste. Pair this entree with a side of noodles or a mixed green salad.

—**LORI LOCKREY** PICKERING, ON

PREP: 20 MIN.
COOK: 4 HOURS + STANDING
MAKES: 6 SERVINGS

- 2 **medium onions, coarsely chopped**
- 2 **tablespoons butter, softened**
- ¼ **teaspoon grated lemon peel**
- 1 **broiler/fryer chicken (4 to 5 pounds)**
- ¼ **cup chicken stock**
- 4 **sprigs fresh parsley**
- 4 **fresh dill sprigs**
- 3 **tablespoons lemon juice**
- 1 **teaspoon salt**
- 1 **teaspoon paprika**
- ½ **teaspoon dried thyme**
- ¼ **teaspoon pepper**

1. Place onions on the bottom of a 6-qt. slow cooker. In a small bowl, mix butter and lemon peel.
2. Tuck wings under the chicken; tie the drumsticks together. With your fingers, carefully loosen skin from the chicken breast; rub butter mixture under the skin. Secure skin to the underside of the breast with toothpicks. Place the chicken over the onions, breast side up. Add stock, parsley and dill.
3. Drizzle lemon juice over the chicken; sprinkle with seasonings. Cook, covered, on low for 4-5 hours (a thermometer inserted into a thigh should read at least 170°).
4. Remove the chicken from the slow cooker; tent it with foil. Let stand for 15 minutes before carving.

SLOW COOKER CHICKEN & DUMPLINGS

Here's a homey dish that people just can't wait to dive into! Yes, you can have chicken and dumplings from the slow cooker. The homemade classic takes a bit of work but is certainly worth it.

—**DANIEL ANDERSON** KENOSHA, WI

PREP: 20 MIN.
COOK: 6 HOURS + STANDING
MAKES: 8 SERVINGS

- 6 **boneless skinless chicken thighs, chopped**
- ½ **teaspoon salt, divided**
- ½ **teaspoon pepper, divided**
- 1 **tablespoon canola oil**
- 3 **celery ribs, chopped**
- 2 **medium carrots, peeled and chopped**
- 1 **large onion, chopped**
- 3 **garlic cloves, minced**
- 2 **tablespoons tomato paste**
- ⅓ **cup all-purpose flour**
- 4 **cups chicken broth, divided**
- 2 **bay leaves**
- 1 **teaspoon dried thyme**

DUMPLINGS
- 2 **cups all-purpose flour**
- 3 **teaspoons baking powder**
- 1 **teaspoon salt**
- ¼ **teaspoon pepper**
- 1 **cup whole milk**
- 4 **tablespoons melted butter**

1. Sprinkle chicken with ¼ teaspoon salt and ¼ teaspoon pepper. Meanwhile, in a large skillet, heat oil over medium-high heat. Add chicken; cook and stir until no longer pink, 6-8 minutes. Transfer to a 6-qt slow cooker.
2. In the same skillet, cook the celery, carrots and onion until tender, about 6-8 minutes. Add garlic, tomato paste and the remaining salt and pepper; cook 1 minute. Stir in flour; cook 1 minute longer. Whisk in 2 cups chicken broth; cook and stir until thickened. Transfer to the slow cooker. Stir in bay leaves, thyme and the remaining chicken broth.

ITALIAN TURKEY MEATBALLS

What's not to love about moist and tender homemade Italian meatballs? Because they're made with lean turkey, they're lower in saturated fat, too!

—**MARY BERG** LAKE ELMO, MN

PREP: 45 MIN. • **COOK:** 4 HOURS
MAKES: 12 SERVINGS

- 3 slices white bread, torn into small pieces
- ½ cup fat-free milk
- 2 pounds lean ground turkey
- ¼ cup grated Parmesan cheese
- ¼ cup minced fresh parsley
- 2 large eggs, lightly beaten
- 3 garlic cloves, minced
- 4 teaspoons Italian seasoning, divided
- 1 teaspoon salt, divided
- 1 teaspoon pepper, divided
- 2 medium onions, chopped
- 1 medium green pepper, chopped
- 4 garlic cloves, minced
- 2 cans (28 ounces each) crushed tomatoes in puree
- 2 cans (6 ounces each) tomato paste
- 1 tablespoon sugar
- 2 bay leaves
  Hot cooked pasta
  Additional minced fresh parsley and grated Parmesan cheese, optional

1. Preheat broiler. Combine bread and milk in a large bowl; let stand until liquid is absorbed. Add the next five ingredients, 2 teaspoons of the Italian seasoning, ½ teaspoon salt and ½ teaspoon pepper; mix lightly but thoroughly. Shape into 1½-in. balls; place on a greased rack of a broiler pan. Broil 5-6 in. from heat until lightly browned, 4-5 minutes.
2. In a 6-qt. slow cooker, mix the next six ingredients and the remaining Italian seasoning, salt and pepper. Add bay leaves and meatballs; gently stir into sauce.
3. Cook, covered, on low until meatballs are cooked through, 4-5 hours. Discard bay leaves. Serve with pasta; if desired, sprinkle with additional parsley and Parmesan cheese.

Freeze option: Omitting additional parsley and Parmesan cheese, freeze the cooled meatball mixture in freezer containers. To use, partially thaw in refrigerator overnight. Microwave, covered, on high in a microwave-safe dish until heated through, stirring gently and adding a little water if necessary. If desired, sprinkle with additional parsley and Parmesan.

SIMPLE CHICKEN TAGINE

Flavored with cinnamon and a touch of sweetness from the apricots, this stew tastes like you spent all day in the kitchen! I like to sprinkle it with toasted almonds or cashews and serve it with hot couscous.

—**ANGELA BUCHANAN** LONGMONT, CO

PREP: 15 MIN. • **COOK:** 6 HOURS
MAKES: 6 SERVINGS

- 2¼ pounds bone-in chicken thighs, skin removed
- 1 large onion, chopped
- 2 medium carrots, sliced
- ¾ cup unsweetened apple juice
- 1 garlic clove, minced
- 1 teaspoon salt
- ½ teaspoon ground cinnamon
- ½ teaspoon pepper
- 1 cup chopped dried apricots
  Hot cooked couscous

1. Place the chicken, onion and carrots in a 3- or 4-qt. slow cooker coated with cooking spray. In a small bowl, combine apple juice, garlic, salt, cinnamon and pepper; pour over the vegetables.
2. Cover and cook on low for 6-8 hours or until the chicken is tender.
3. Remove chicken from slow cooker; shred meat with two forks. Skim fat from cooking juices; stir in apricots. Return the shredded chicken to slow cooker; heat though. Serve with couscous.

Freeze option: Freeze cooled stew in freezer containers. To use, partially thaw in refrigerator overnight. Heat through in a saucepan, stirring occasionally and adding a little water if necessary. Serve with couscous.

TURKEY STUFFED PEPPERS

I created this as a healthier alternative to traditional stuffed peppers. I work 12-hour shifts as a nurse, so I often rely on the slow cooker for feeding my family.

—**MANDY PEMBERTON** DENHAM SPRINGS, LA

PREP: 35 MIN. • **COOK:** 4 HOURS
MAKES: 6 SERVINGS

- 2 medium sweet yellow or orange peppers
- 2 medium sweet red peppers
- 2 medium green peppers
- 1 pound lean ground turkey
- 1 small red onion, finely chopped
- 1 small zucchini, shredded
- 2 cups cooked brown rice
- 1 jar (16 ounces) spaghetti sauce, divided
- 1 tablespoon Creole seasoning
- ¼ teaspoon pepper
- 2 tablespoons shredded Parmesan cheese

1. Cut tops from peppers and remove the seeds. Finely chop enough tops to measure 1 cup for filling.
2. In a large skillet, cook turkey, onion and the reserved chopped peppers over medium heat 6-8 minutes or until the turkey is no longer pink and vegetables are tender, breaking up turkey into crumbles; drain.
3. Stir in the zucchini; cook and stir 2 minutes longer. Add rice, ⅔ cup of the spaghetti sauce, Creole seasoning and pepper.
4. Spread ½ cup of the spaghetti sauce onto the bottom of a greased 6-qt. slow cooker. Fill the peppers with the turkey mixture; place over the sauce. Pour the remaining spaghetti sauce over peppers; sprinkle with cheese. Cook, covered, on low for 4-5 hours or until peppers are tender and filling is heated through.

Test Kitchen Note: The following spice mix may be substituted for 1 teaspoon Creole seasoning: ¼ teaspoon each salt, garlic powder and paprika; and a pinch each of dried thyme, ground cumin and cayenne pepper.

Per 1 stuffed pepper: 290 cal., 10g fat (3g sat. fat), 63mg chol., 818mg sod., 31g carb. (9g sugars, 5g fiber), 19g pro.
Diabetic Exchanges: 3 lean meat, 1½ starch, 1 vegetable.

ITALIAN TURKEY
MEATBALLS

MEXICAN
TURKEY
MEAT LOAF

MEXICAN TURKEY MEAT LOAF

Here's a zesty, flavorful meat loaf you can really sink your teeth into! It's great with black beans, rice, green salad with lime vinaigrette, or any of your favorite Tex-Mex sides.

—**KRISTEN MILLER** GLENDALE, WI

PREP: 25 MIN.
COOK: 3 HOURS + STANDING
MAKES: 1 LOAF (6 SERVINGS)

- 2 slices white bread, torn into small pieces
- ⅓ cup 2% milk
- 1 pound lean ground turkey
- ½ pound fresh chorizo
- 1 medium sweet red pepper, finely chopped
- 1 small onion, finely chopped
- 1 jalapeno pepper, seeded and finely chopped
- 2 large eggs, lightly beaten
- 2 tablespoons minced fresh cilantro
- 2 garlic cloves, minced
- 2 teaspoons chili powder
- 1 teaspoon salt
- 1 teaspoon ground cumin
- ½ teaspoon dried oregano
- ½ teaspoon pepper
- ¼ teaspoon cayenne pepper
- ⅔ cup salsa, divided
  Additional minced fresh cilantro
  Hot cooked Spanish rice

1. Combine bread and milk in a large bowl; let stand until liquid is absorbed. Add next 14 ingredients and ⅓ cup of the salsa; mix lightly but thoroughly.
2. On an 18x7-in. piece of heavy-duty foil, shape the meat mixture into 10x6-in. oval loaf. Lifting with foil, transfer to a 6-qt. oval slow cooker. Press the ends of foil up the sides of the slow cooker.
3. Cook, covered, on low until a thermometer reads 165°, 3-4 hours. Lifting with foil, drain fat into slow cooker before removing meat loaf to a platter; top with the remaining salsa and sprinkle with cilantro. Let stand for 10 minutes before slicing. Serve with rice.

FREEZE IT
GARLIC CHICKEN & BROCCOLI

This simple riff on Chinese chicken proves you can savor the take-out taste you crave while still eating right.

—**CONNIE KRUPP** RACINE, WI

PREP: 15 MIN. • **COOK:** 3 HOURS
MAKES: 8 SERVINGS

- 2 pounds boneless skinless chicken breasts, cut into 1-in. pieces
- 4 cups fresh broccoli florets
- 4 medium carrots, julienned
- 1 can (8 ounces) sliced water chestnuts, drained
- 6 garlic cloves, minced
- 3 cups reduced-sodium chicken broth
- ¼ cup reduced-sodium soy sauce
- 2 tablespoons brown sugar
- 2 tablespoons sesame oil
- 2 tablespoons rice vinegar
- ½ teaspoon salt
- ½ teaspoon pepper
- ⅓ cup cornstarch
- ⅓ cup water
  Hot cooked rice

1. In a 4- or 5-qt. slow cooker, combine the chicken, broccoli, carrots, water chestnuts and garlic. In a large bowl, mix the next seven ingredients; pour over the chicken mixture. Cook, covered, on low until the chicken and broccoli are tender, about 3-4 hours.
2. Remove chicken and vegetables; keep warm. Strain cooking juices into a small saucepan; skim fat. Bring juices to a boil. In a small bowl, mix cornstarch and water until smooth; stir into the cooking juices. Return to a boil; cook and stir for 1-2 minutes or until thickened. Serve with chicken, vegetables and hot cooked rice.
Freeze option: Place the chicken and vegetables in freezer containers; top with sauce. Cool and freeze. To use, partially thaw in refrigerator overnight. Microwave the food, covered, on high in a microwave-safe dish until heated through, stirring it gently and adding a little broth or water if necessary.

GARLIC CHICKEN & BROCCOLI

SAUCY CHICKEN
& TORTELLINI

SLOW COOKER TURKEY BREAST WITH GRAVY

This quick-prep recipe lets you feast on turkey at any time of year. We save the rich broth for gravy and soup.

—JOYCE HOUGH ANNAPOLIS, MD

PREP: 25 MIN.
COOK: 5 HOURS + STANDING
MAKES: 12 SERVINGS

- 2 teaspoons dried parsley flakes
- 1 teaspoon salt
- 1 teaspoon poultry seasoning
- ½ teaspoon paprika
- ½ teaspoon pepper
- 2 medium onions, chopped
- 3 medium carrots, cut into ½-inch slices
- 3 celery ribs, coarsely chopped
- 1 bone-in turkey breast (6 to 7 pounds), skin removed
- ¼ cup all-purpose flour
- ½ cup water

1. Mix the first five ingredients in a small bowl. Place vegetables in a 6- or 7-qt. slow cooker; top with turkey. Rub turkey with the seasoning mixture.
2. Cook the food, covered, on low until a thermometer inserted in the turkey reads at least 170°, 5-6 hours. Remove from slow cooker; let stand, covered, for 15 minutes before slicing.
3. Strain cooking juices into a small saucepan. Mix the flour and water until smooth; stir into the cooking juices. Bring to a boil; cook and stir until thickened, 1-2 minutes. Serve with turkey.

Per serving: 6 ounces cooked turkey with 3 tablespoons gravy: 200 cal., 1g fat (0 sat. fat), 117mg chol., 270mg sod., 2g carb. (0 sugars, 0 fiber), 43g pro.
Diabetic Exchanges: 6 lean meat.

SAUCY CHICKEN & TORTELLINI

This heartwarming dish is something I threw together years ago for my oldest daughter. Whenever she's having a rough day, I put on the slow cooker and prepare this special recipe.

—MARY MORGAN DALLAS, TX

PREP: 10 MIN. • **COOK:** 6¼ HOURS
MAKES: 8 SERVINGS

- 1½ pounds boneless skinless chicken breasts, cut in 1-inch cubes
- ½ pound sliced fresh mushrooms
- 1 large onion, chopped
- 1 medium sweet red pepper, cut in ½-inch pieces
- 1 medium green pepper, cut in ½-inch pieces
- 1 can (2¼ ounces) sliced ripe olives, drained
- 1 jar (24 ounces) marinara sauce
- 1 jar (15 ounces) Alfredo sauce
- 2 packages (9 ounces each) refrigerated cheese tortellini
  Grated Parmesan cheese, optional
  Torn fresh basil, optional

1. In a 5-qt. slow cooker, combine the first seven ingredients. Cook, covered, on low until chicken is tender, 6-8 hours.
2. Stir in Alfredo sauce and tortellini. Cook, covered, until tortellini is tender, 15-20 minutes. If desired, top with Parmesan cheese and basil.
Freeze option: Place chicken and vegetables in freezer containers; top with sauce. Cool and freeze. To use, partially thaw in refrigerator overnight. Microwave, covered, on high in a microwave-safe dish until heated through, stirring gently and adding a little water if necessary.

GREEK DINNER

I got this recipe from my sister, and my family just loves how good it makes the kitchen smell. The amount of garlic might seem a bit high, but you get every bit of the flavor without it overpowering the other ingredients.

—**TERRI CHRISTENSEN** MONTAGUE, MI

PREP: 20 MIN. • **COOK:** 5 HOURS
MAKES: 6 SERVINGS

- 6 **medium Yukon Gold potatoes, quartered**
- 1 **broiler/fryer chicken (3½ pounds), cut up and skin removed**
- 2 **large onions, quartered**
- 1 **whole garlic bulb, separated and peeled**
- 3 **teaspoons dried oregano**
- 1 **teaspoon salt**
- ¾ **teaspoon pepper**
- ½ **cup plus 1 tablespoon water, divided**
- 1 **tablespoon olive oil**
- 4 **teaspoons cornstarch**

1. Place potatoes in a 5-qt. slow cooker. Add chicken, onions and garlic. Combine oregano, salt, pepper and ½ cup water; pour over the chicken and vegetables. Drizzle with oil. Cover and cook on low for 5-6 hours or until chicken juices run clear and the vegetables are tender.
2. Remove chicken and vegetables to a serving platter; keep warm. Strain cooking juices and skim fat; transfer to a small saucepan. Bring liquid to a boil. Combine cornstarch and the remaining water until smooth. Gradually stir into the pan. Bring to a boil; cook and stir for 2 minutes or until thickened. Serve with chicken and vegetables.

TOP TIP

WHAT POTATO?

Waxy potatoes—Yukon golds, new potatoes, red potatoes and fingerlings, to name a few—hold their shape best in the slow cooker. Save russet potatoes and Idaho potatoes for when you want to mash.

FREEZE IT
SAUCY INDIAN-STYLE CHICKEN & VEGETABLES

This easy Indian dish will be loved by all. Feel free to add more or less curry sauce according to your taste.

—**ERICA POLLY** SUN PRAIRIE, WI

PREP: 15 MIN. • **COOK:** 4 HOURS
MAKES: 8 SERVINGS

- 2 **medium sweet potatoes, peeled and cut into 1½-inch pieces**
- 2 **tablespoons water**
- 2 **medium sweet red peppers, cut into 1-inch pieces**
- 3 **cups fresh cauliflowerets**
- 2 **pounds boneless skinless chicken thighs, cubed**
- 2 **jars (15 ounces each) tikka masala curry sauce**
- ¾ **teaspoon salt**

Minced fresh cilantro, optional
Naan flatbreads, warmed

1. Microwave sweet potatoes and water, covered, on high just until potatoes begin to soften, 3-4 minutes.
2. In a 5- or 6-qt. slow cooker, combine vegetables and chicken; add sauce and salt. Cook, covered, on low until meat is tender, 4-5 hours. If desired, top with cilantro; serve with warmed naan.
Freeze option: Omit the cilantro and naan; freeze the cooled chicken and vegetable mixture in freezer containers. To use, partially thaw in the refrigerator overnight. Microwave, covered, on high in a microwave-safe dish until it is heated through, stirring gently and adding a little water if necessary. If desired, add a sprinkle of cilantro. Serve the dish with warmed naan.

SAUCY INDIAN-STYLE CHICKEN & VEGETABLES

"I wanted to find a creative way to use the leftover cranberries from Thanksgiving dinner. This sounds like an unlikely combination, but the results are incredible!"
—**LISA WORKMAN** BOONES MILL, VA

SLOW-COOKED CRANBERRY CHICKEN

SLOW-COOKED CRANBERRY CHICKEN

PREP: 10 MIN. • **COOK:** 5 HOURS
MAKES: 4 SERVINGS

- 4 **bone-in chicken breast halves (10 ounces each), skin removed**
- 1½ **cups fresh or frozen cranberries, chopped**
- ½ **cup packed brown sugar**
- ¼ **cup molasses**
- 2 **tablespoons orange juice**
- 2 **tablespoons cider vinegar**
- 2 **teaspoons prepared mustard**
  Hot cooked rice

1. Place chicken in a 4-qt. slow cooker. In a small bowl, combine cranberries, brown sugar, molasses, orange juice, vinegar and mustard; pour over chicken.
2. Cook, covered, on low for 4-5 hours or until chicken is tender. Remove meat from bone or shred if desired. Serve with cranberry mixture and rice.

SLOW COOKER MUSHROOM CHICKEN & PEAS

Some amazingly fresh mushrooms that I found at our farmers market inspired this recipe. When you start with the best ingredients, you can't go wrong.
—**JENN TIDWELL** FAIR OAKS, CA

PREP: 10 MIN. • **COOK:** 3 HOURS 10 MIN.
MAKES: 4 SERVINGS

- 4 **boneless skinless chicken breast halves (6 ounces each)**
- 1 **envelope onion mushroom soup mix**
- 1 **cup water**
- ½ **pound sliced baby portobello mushrooms**
- 1 **medium onion, chopped**
- 4 **garlic cloves, minced**
- 2 **cups frozen peas, thawed**

1. Place chicken in a 3-qt. slow cooker. Sprinkle with the soup mix, pressing to help the seasonings adhere. Add water, mushrooms, onion and garlic.
2. Cook, covered, on low 3-4 hours or until chicken is tender (a thermometer inserted in chicken should read at least 165°). Stir in peas; cook, covered, 10 minutes longer or until heated through.

Per 1 chicken breast half with ¾ cup vegetable mixture: 292 cal., 5g fat (1g sat. fat), 94mg chol., 566mg sod., 20g carb. (7g sugars, 5g fiber), 41g pro.
Diabetic Exchanges: 5 lean meat, 1 starch, 1 vegetable.

PINEAPPLE CURRY CHICKEN

Curry has a moderate-to-strong delivery, so add it early in the cooking process for good balance with pineapple, coconut and ginger.
—**ROBIN HAAS** CRANSTON, RI

PREP: 25 MIN. • **COOK:** 6 HOURS
MAKES: 6 SERVINGS

- 2 **cans (8 ounces each) unsweetened pineapple chunks, undrained**
- 6 **bone-in chicken breast halves, skin removed (12 ounces each)**
- 1 **can (15 ounces) garbanzo beans, rinsed and drained**
- 1 **large onion, cut into 1-inch pieces**
- 1 **cup julienned carrots**
- 1 **medium sweet red pepper, cut into strips**
- ½ **cup light coconut milk**
- 2 **tablespoons cornstarch**
- 2 **tablespoons sugar**
- 3 **teaspoons curry powder**
- 2 **garlic cloves, minced**
- 2 **teaspoons minced fresh gingerroot**
- 1 **teaspoon salt**
- 1 **teaspoon pepper**
- 1 **teaspoon lime juice**
- ½ **teaspoon crushed red pepper flakes**
  Hot cooked rice
- ⅓ **cup minced fresh basil**
  Toasted flaked coconut, optional

1. Drain pineapple, reserving ¾ cup juice. Place chicken, beans, vegetables and the pineapple in a 6-qt. slow cooker. In a small bowl, combine coconut milk and cornstarch until smooth. Stir in sugar, curry powder, garlic, ginger, salt, pepper, lime juice, pepper flakes and reserved juice; pour over the chicken.
2. Cover and cook on low for 6-8 hours or until the chicken is tender. Serve with rice; sprinkle with basil and, if desired, some coconut.

TOMATO BALSAMIC CHICKEN

I came up with this saucy chicken during a busy holiday season. As new parents, my husband and I appreciate having a go-to meal that's easy, homemade and delicious.
—**ANNE COLVIN** CHICAGO, IL

PREP: 25 MIN. • **COOK:** 6 HOURS
MAKES: 6 SERVINGS

- 2 **medium carrots, chopped**
- ½ **cup thinly sliced shallots**
- 2 **pounds bone-in chicken thighs, skin removed**
- 1 **tablespoon all-purpose flour**
- ½ **cup reduced-sodium chicken broth**
- 1 **can (14½ ounces) petite diced tomatoes, undrained**
- ¼ **cup balsamic vinegar**
- 1 **tablespoon olive oil**
- 2 **garlic cloves, minced**
- 1 **bay leaf**
- ½ **teaspoon Italian seasoning**
- ½ **teaspoon salt**
- ¼ **teaspoon pepper**
  Hot cooked orzo

1. Place carrots and shallots in a 3- or 4-qt. slow cooker; top with chicken. In a bowl, whisk flour and broth until smooth; stir in tomatoes, vinegar, oil, garlic and seasonings. Pour over the chicken. Cook, covered, on low until the chicken and carrots are tender, 6-8 hours.
2. Remove the chicken; cool slightly. Discard bay leaf and, if desired, skim the fat from the carrot mixture.
3. Remove chicken from the bones; shred slightly with two forks. Return the meat to the slow cooker and heat it through. Serve with orzo.
Freeze option: Freeze cooled chicken mixture in freezer containers. To use, partially thaw in refrigerator overnight. Heat through in a saucepan, stirring the food occasionally.
Per serving: ¾ cup chicken mixture: 235 cal., 11g fat (3g sat. fat), 77mg chol., 433mg sod., 12g carb. (7g sugars, 2g fiber), 23g pro.
Diabetic Exchanges: 3 lean meat, 1 vegetable, ½ fat.

AUTUMN APPLE CHICKEN

I'd just been apple picking and wanted to prepare something new with the bounty. Slow-cooking chicken with apples and barbecue sauce filled my whole house with the most delicious smell. We couldn't wait to eat.

—CAITLYN HAUSER BROOKLINE, NH

PREP: 20 MIN. • **COOK:** 3½ HOURS
MAKES: 4 SERVINGS

- 1 tablespoon canola oil
- 4 bone-in chicken thighs (about 1½ pounds), skin removed
- ¼ teaspoon salt
- ¼ teaspoon pepper
- 2 medium Fuji or Gala apples, coarsely chopped
- 1 medium onion, chopped
- 1 garlic clove, minced
- ⅓ cup barbecue sauce
- ¼ cup apple cider or juice
- 1 tablespoon honey

1. In a large skillet, heat oil over medium heat. Brown chicken thighs on both sides; sprinkle with salt and pepper. Transfer to a 3-qt. slow cooker; top with apples.
2. Add onion to the same skillet; cook and stir over medium heat 2-3 minutes or until tender. Add garlic; cook 1 minute longer. Stir in barbecue sauce, apple cider and honey; increase the heat to medium-high. Cook 1 minute, stirring to loosen browned bits from the pan. Pour over the chicken and apples. Cook, covered, on low for 3½-4½ hours or until the chicken is tender.
Freeze option: Freeze cooled chicken mixture in freezer containers. To use, partially thaw in refrigerator overnight. Heat through in a covered saucepan, stirring occasionally.
Per 1 chicken thigh with ½ cup apple mixture: 333 cal., 13g fat (3g sat. fat), 87mg chol., 456mg sod., 29g carb. (22g sugars, 3g fiber), 25g pro.
Diabetic Exchanges: 4 lean meat, 1½ starch, ½ fruit.

SLOW-COOKED CHICKEN & STUFFING

This tasty, no-fuss main dish has a flavorful blend of seasonings and the irresistible duo of tender chicken and moist dressing. It's nice enough for the holidays and easy enough to fix year-round.

—ANGELA MARQUART NEW WASHINGTON, OH

PREP: 25 MIN. • **COOK:** 4½ HOURS
MAKES: 14-16 SERVINGS

- 2½ cups chicken broth
- 1 cup butter, cubed
- ½ cup chopped onion
- ½ cup chopped celery
- 1 can (4 ounces) mushroom stems and pieces, drained
- ¼ cup dried parsley flakes
- 1½ teaspoons rubbed sage
- 1 teaspoon poultry seasoning
- 1 teaspoon salt
- ½ teaspoon pepper
- 12 cups day-old bread cubes (½-inch pieces)
- 2 large eggs
- 1 can (10¾ ounces) condensed cream of chicken soup, undiluted
- 5 to 6 cups cubed cooked chicken

1. In a large saucepan, combine the first 10 ingredients. Simmer for 10 minutes; remove from the heat. Place bread cubes in a large bowl. Combine eggs and soup; stir into the broth mixture until smooth. Pour over the bread and toss well.
2. In a 5-qt. slow cooker, layer half of the stuffing and chicken; repeat layers. Cover and cook on low for 4½-5 hours or until a thermometer inserted in the stuffing reads 160°.

> **TOP TIP**
>
> ### DAY-OLD BREAD CUBES
> - Start with a good-quality firm bread that is beginning to dry out. You can buy day-old bread in the bakery section of the store, or use bread that you bought previously. If you use fresh bread, dry the cubes in the oven after cutting.
> - For 3 cups of dry bread cubes, cut three to four slices of firm bread into ½-inch cubes.
> - Spread in a single layer on a 15x10x1-in. baking pan.
> - Bake at 300° for 10-12 minutes or until dry, stirring twice (bread cubes will continue to dry as they cool).

CHICKEN SOFT TACOS

My family loves these tacos. I've found it's convenient to throw the chicken filling together before I leave for work. At the end of the day, I just have to roll it up in a tortilla with the remaining ingredients and dinner's ready in minutes. The chicken also makes a great topping for salad.

—CHERYL NEWENDORP PELLA, IA

PREP: 30 MIN. • **COOK:** 5 HOURS
MAKES: 5 SERVINGS

- 1 broiler/fryer chicken (3½ pounds), cut up and skin removed
- 1 can (8 ounces) tomato sauce
- 1 can (4 ounces) chopped green chilies
- ⅓ cup chopped onion
- 2 tablespoons chili powder
- 2 tablespoons Worcestershire sauce
- ¼ teaspoon garlic powder
- 10 flour tortillas (8 inches), warmed
- 1¼ cups shredded cheddar cheese
- 1¼ cups salsa
- 1¼ cups shredded lettuce
- 1 large tomato, chopped
- ¾ cup sour cream, optional

1. Place chicken in a 4-qt. slow cooker. Combine tomato sauce, chilies, onion, chili powder, Worcestershire sauce and garlic powder; pour over chicken. Cover and cook on low for 5-6 hours or until the chicken is tender and juices run clear.
2. Remove the chicken. Shred the meat with two forks and return it to the slow cooker; heat through. Spoon ½ cup of the chicken mixture down the center of each tortilla. Top with cheese, salsa, lettuce, tomato and, if desired, sour cream; roll up.

"My family loves lasagna and I love the slow cooker. I wanted to try something a little different from the classic lasagna we usually make. This recipe not only tastes incredible, it's hearty and convenient, too."
—KELLY SILVERS EDMOND, OK

CHICKEN & ARTICHOKE LASAGNA

CHICKEN & ARTICHOKE LASAGNA

PREP: 30 MIN.
COOK: 3 HOURS + STANDING
MAKES: 8 SERVINGS

- 2 cans (14 ounces each) water-packed artichoke hearts, drained and finely chopped
- 1 cup shredded Parmesan cheese, divided
- ¼ cup loosely packed basil leaves, finely chopped
- 3 garlic cloves, minced, divided
- 1 pound ground chicken
- 1 tablespoon canola oil
- 1 cup finely chopped onion
- ¾ teaspoon salt
- ½ teaspoon pepper
- ½ cup white wine
- 1 cup half-and-half cream
- 1 package (8 ounces) cream cheese, softened
- 1 cup shredded Monterey Jack cheese
- 1 large egg
- 1½ cups 2% cottage cheese
- 9 no-cook lasagna noodles
- 2 cups shredded part-skim mozzarella cheese
  Prepared pesto, optional
  Additional basil, optional

1. Fold two 18-in. square pieces of foil into thirds. Crisscross strips and place them on the bottom and up the sides of a 6-qt. slow cooker. Coat strips with cooking spray. Combine artichoke hearts, ½ cup of the Parmesan cheese, basil and 2 garlic cloves.

2. In a large skillet, crumble chicken over medium heat 6-8 minutes or until no longer pink; drain. Set chicken aside. Add oil and onion; cook and stir just until tender, 6-8 minutes. Add salt, pepper and remaining garlic; cook 1 minute longer. Stir in wine. Bring to a boil; cook until liquid is reduced by half, 4-5 minutes. Stir in cream, cream cheese and Monterey Jack cheese. Return the chicken to pan. In a bowl, combine egg, cottage cheese and remaining Parmesan.

3. Spread ¾ cup of the meat mixture into the slow cooker. Layer with 3 noodles (breaking noodles as necessary to fit), ¾ cup meat mixture, ½ cup cottage cheese mixture, 1 cup artichoke mixture and ½ cup mozzarella cheese. Repeat layers twice; top with the remaining mozzarella cheese. Cook, covered, on low until the noodles are tender, 3-4 hours. Remove the slow cooker insert and let stand 30 minutes. If desired, serve with pesto and sprinkle with additional basil.

SLOW COOKER
CHICKEN BOG

SLOW COOKER CHICKEN BOG

Chicken Bog is a South Carolina tradition with a lot of variations (think herbs, spices, fresh veggies), but the standard ingredients remain: sausage, chicken and rice. This slow-cooked rendition is a simple take on the classic.

—**ANNA HANSON** SPANISH FORK, UT

PREP: 20 MIN. • **COOK:** 4 HOURS
MAKES: 8 CUPS

- 1 tablespoon canola oil
- 1 medium onion, chopped
- 8 ounces smoked sausage, halved and sliced ½-inch thick
- 3 garlic cloves, minced
- 5 cups chicken broth, divided
- 2 cups uncooked converted rice
- 1 teaspoon salt
- 1 teaspoon pepper
- 1 rotisserie chicken (about 3 pounds), meat removed and shredded
  Thinly sliced green onions, optional
  Hot sauce

1. In a large skillet, heat oil over medium heat. Add onion and sausage; cook until sausage is lightly browned. Add the garlic and cook 1 minute more; then transfer to a 5-qt. slow cooker.
2. Stir in 4 cups of the broth, the rice, salt and pepper. Cook, covered, on low until rice is tender, 4-5 hours. Stir in the chicken and the remaining broth. Cook, covered, on low until chicken is heated through, about 30 minutes. If desired, sprinkle with green onions. Serve with hot sauce.
Freeze option: Omit green onions and hot sauce; freeze cooled meat mixture, juices and rice in freezer containers. To use, partially thaw in the refrigerator overnight. Microwave, covered, on high until heated through, stirring gently and adding a little broth or water if necessary.

EASY CHICKEN TAMALE PIE

All you need are some simple ingredients from the pantry to put this slow cooker meal together. I love that I can go fishing while it cooks.

—**PETER HALFERTY** CORPUS CHRISTI, TX

PREP: 20 MIN. • **COOK:** 7 HOURS
MAKES: 8 SERVINGS

- 1 pound ground chicken
- 1 teaspoon ground cumin
- 1 teaspoon chili powder
- ½ teaspoon salt
- ¼ teaspoon pepper
- 1 can (15 ounces) black beans, rinsed and drained
- 1 can (14½ ounces) diced tomatoes, undrained
- 1 can (11 ounces) whole kernel corn, drained
- 1 can (10 ounces) enchilada sauce
- 2 green onions, chopped
- ¼ cup minced fresh cilantro
- 1 package (8½ ounces) corn bread/ muffin mix
- 2 large eggs, lightly beaten
- 1 cup shredded Mexican cheese blend
  Optional toppings: sour cream, salsa and minced fresh cilantro

1. In a large skillet, cook chicken over medium heat 6-8 minutes or until no longer pink, breaking into crumbles. Stir in seasonings.
2. Transfer to a 4-qt. slow cooker. Stir in beans, tomatoes, corn, enchilada sauce, green onions and cilantro. Cook, covered, on low for 6-8 hours or until heated through.
3. In a small bowl, combine the muffin mix and eggs; spoon over the chicken mixture. Cook, covered, on low 1-1½ hours longer or until a toothpick inserted in the corn bread layer comes out clean.
4. Sprinkle with cheese; let stand, covered, 5 minutes. If desired, serve with toppings.

EASY CHICKEN TAMALE PIE

BARBECUE CHICKEN COBB SALAD

SLOW-COOKED CHICKEN MARBELLA

Here's a great summertime slow cooker recipe! It's sweet, briny, savory and herbal, and it packs a big punch of garlic. The Mediterranean flavors make me think of dinner on the patio with family or friends.

—**BETH JACOBSON** MILWAUKEE, WI

PREP: 30 MIN. • **COOK:** 4 HOURS
MAKES: 6 SERVINGS

- 1 **cup pitted green olives, divided**
- 1 **cup pitted dried plums, divided**
- 2 **tablespoons dried oregano**
- 2 **tablespoons brown sugar**
- 2 **tablespoons capers, drained**
- 2 **tablespoons olive oil**
- 4 **garlic cloves, minced**
- ½ **teaspoon salt**
- ½ **teaspoon pepper**
- 6 **bone-in chicken thighs (about 2 pounds), skin removed**
- ¼ **cup reduced-sodium chicken broth**
- 1 **tablespoon minced fresh parsley**
- 1 **tablespoon white wine**
- 1 **tablespoon lemon juice**
  Hot cooked couscous

1. Place ½ cup olives, ½ cup dried plums, oregano, brown sugar, capers, oil, garlic, salt and pepper in food processor; then process until smooth. Transfer mixture to a 4-qt. slow cooker. Place chicken in slow cooker. Cook, covered, on low 4-5 hours or until the chicken is tender.
2. Chop the remaining olives and dried plums. Remove the chicken from the slow cooker; keep it warm. Then stir the chicken broth, parsley, wine, lemon juice and the remaining olives and plums into the olive mixture. Serve with chicken and couscous.

BARBECUE CHICKEN COBB SALAD

I turned barbecue chicken into a major salad with romaine and carrots, sweet peppers and avocados. That's how I got my family to eat more veggies!

—**CAMILLE BECKSTRAND** LAYTON, UT

PREP: 30 MIN. • **COOK:** 3 HOURS
MAKES: 6 SERVINGS

- 1 **bottle (18 ounces) barbecue sauce**
- 2 **tablespoons brown sugar**
- ½ **teaspoon garlic powder**
- ¼ **teaspoon paprika**
- 1½ **pounds boneless skinless chicken breasts**
- 12 **cups chopped romaine**
- 3 **plum tomatoes, chopped**
- 2 **small carrots, thinly sliced**
- 1 **medium sweet red or green pepper, chopped**
- 2 **avocados, peeled and chopped**
- 3 **hard-cooked large eggs, chopped**
- 6 **bacon strips, cooked and crumbled**
- 1½ **cups shredded cheddar cheese**
  Salad dressing of your choice

1. In a greased 3-qt. slow cooker, mix barbecue sauce, brown sugar, garlic powder and paprika. Add chicken; turn to coat. Cook, covered, on low for 3-4 hours or until chicken is tender (a thermometer should read at least 165°).
2. Remove chicken and cut into bite-size pieces. In a bowl, toss chicken with 1 cup of the barbecue sauce mixture. Place the romaine on large serving platter; arrange chicken, vegetables, avocado, eggs, bacon and cheese over romaine. Drizzle with dressing.

TOP TIP

PLUMS OR PRUNES?
The traditional name of the dried fruit—prunes—was changed to be more descriptive; outside the U.S., they're still called prunes. Plums come in a variety of colors—green, yellow, purple, red and black. Several varieties are dried to make prunes.

SLOW-COOKED
CHICKEN MARBELLA

Other Entrees

SLOW COOKER MEMPHIS-STYLE RIBS

After eating dinner at the legendary Rendezvous Restaurant, I created a slow-cooked version of dry-rub Memphis ribs. Smoked paprika in the rub mimics the flavor from grilling over hot coals.

—MATTHEW HASS FRANKLIN, WI

PREP: 15 MIN. • **COOK:** 5 HOURS
MAKES: 6 SERVINGS

- ½ cup white vinegar
- ½ cup water
- 2 racks pork baby back ribs (about 5 pounds)
- 3 tablespoons smoked paprika
- 2 tablespoons brown sugar
- 2 teaspoons salt
- 2 teaspoons coarsely ground pepper
- 1 teaspoon garlic powder
- 1 teaspoon onion powder
- 1 teaspoon ground cumin
- 1 teaspoon ground mustard
- 1 teaspoon dried thyme
- 1 teaspoon dried oregano
- 1 teaspoon celery salt
- ¾ teaspoon cayenne pepper

1. Combine vinegar and water; brush over ribs. Pour remaining vinegar mixture into a 6-qt. slow cooker. Mix remaining ingredients; sprinkle ribs with half the seasoning blend and reserve half. Cut into serving-size pieces; transfer to slow cooker.

2. Cook, covered, on low until tender, 5-6 hours. Remove ribs; skim fat from cooking juices. Using a clean brush, brush ribs generously with skimmed cooking juices; sprinkle with reserved seasoning. Serve ribs with remaining juices.

SLOW COOKER
MEMPHIS-STYLE RIBS

ASIAN SLOW
COOKER PORK

4. Coarsely shred pork into bite-size pieces; serve with sauce over rice. Sprinkle with sesame seeds and, if desired, green onions.

Per serving (calculated without rice): 203 cal., 7g fat (2g sat. fat), 56mg chol., 342mg sod., 11g carb. (7g sugars, 1g fiber), 23g pro.

Diabetic Exchanges: 3 lean meat, 1 starch.

CHERRY BALSAMIC PORK LOIN

After having a wonderful cherry topping for Brie from a local market, I knew I had to create one for pork. If you're crazy about cherries, add even more.

—**SUSAN STETZEL** GAINESVILLE, NY

PREP: 20 MIN.
COOK: 3 HOURS + STANDING
MAKES: 8 SERVINGS (1⅓ CUPS SAUCE)

- 1 **boneless pork loin roast (3 to 4 pounds)**
- 1 **teaspoon salt**
- ½ **teaspoon pepper**
- 1 **tablespoon canola oil**
- ¾ **cup cherry preserves**
- ½ **cup dried cherries**
- ⅓ **cup balsamic vinegar**
- ¼ **cup packed brown sugar**

1. Sprinkle roast with salt and pepper. In a large skillet, heat oil over medium-high heat. Brown roast on all sides.

2. Transfer to a 6-qt. slow cooker. In a small bowl, mix preserves, cherries, vinegar and brown sugar until blended; pour over roast. Cook, covered, on low for 3-4 hours or until tender (a thermometer inserted in pork should read at least 145°).

3. Remove roast from slow cooker; tent with foil. Let stand 15 minutes before slicing. Skim fat from cooking juices. Serve pork with sauce.

ASIAN SLOW COOKER PORK

Slow-cooked dishes are a favorite in our home, and this pork roast with honey, soy and spices is perfect for chilly evenings. The aroma fills the house with a scent that calls out, "Welcome home!"

—**SHEREE SHOWN** JUNCTION CITY, OR

PREP: 25 MIN. • **COOK:** 4½ HOURS
MAKES: 12 SERVINGS

- 2 **large onions, thinly sliced**
- 3 **garlic cloves, minced**
- ½ **teaspoon salt**
- ½ **teaspoon pepper**
- 1 **boneless pork loin roast (3 pounds)**
- 1 **tablespoon canola oil**
- 3 **bay leaves**
- ¼ **cup hot water**
- ¼ **cup honey**
- ¼ **cup reduced-sodium soy sauce**
- 2 **tablespoons rice vinegar**
- 1 **teaspoon ground ginger**
- ½ **teaspoon ground cloves**
- 3 **tablespoons cornstarch**
- ¼ **cup cold water**
  Hot cooked rice
- 2 **tablespoons sesame seeds, toasted**
  Sliced green onions, optional

1. Place onions in a 5-qt. slow cooker. Mix garlic, salt and pepper. Cut roast in half; rub with garlic mixture. In a large skillet, brown pork in oil on all sides. Transfer to slow cooker; add bay leaves.

2. In a small bowl, mix hot water and honey; stir in soy sauce, vinegar and spices. Pour over pork. Cook, covered, on low for 4-5 hours or until the meat is tender.

3. Remove the pork from slow cooker; keep warm. Discard the bay leaves. For sauce, mix cornstarch and cold water until smooth; gradually stir into the slow cooker. Cover and cook on high for 30 minutes or until thickened, stirring twice.

"People have told me this is better than the gravy their Sicilian grandmothers used to make. But don't tell the old generation that!"
—**EMORY DOTY** JASPER, GA

SICILIAN MEAT SAUCE

SICILIAN MEAT SAUCE

PREP: 30 MIN. • **COOK:** 6 HOURS
MAKES: 12 SERVINGS

- 3 tablespoons olive oil, divided
- 3 pounds bone-in country-style pork ribs
- 1 medium onion, chopped
- 3 to 5 garlic cloves, minced
- 2 cans (28 ounces each) crushed or diced tomatoes, drained
- 1 can (14½ ounces) Italian diced tomatoes, drained
- 3 bay leaves
- 2 tablespoons chopped fresh parsley
- 2 tablespoons chopped capers, drained
- ½ teaspoon dried basil
- ½ teaspoon dried rosemary, crushed
- ½ teaspoon dried thyme
- ½ teaspoon crushed red pepper flakes
- ½ teaspoon salt
- ½ teaspoon sugar
- 1 cup beef broth
- ½ cup dry red wine or additional beef broth
  Hot cooked pasta
  Grated Parmesan cheese, optional

1. In a Dutch oven, heat 2 tablespoons olive oil over medium-high heat. Brown pork ribs in batches; transfer to a 6-qt. slow cooker.

2. Add the remaining oil to the Dutch oven; saute onion for 2 minutes. Add garlic; cook 1 minute more. Add next 10 ingredients. Pour in broth and red wine; bring to a light boil. Transfer to slow cooker. Cook, covered, until pork is tender, about 6 hours.

3. Discard bay leaves. Remove meat from slow cooker; shred or pull apart, discarding bones. Return meat to sauce. Serve over pasta; if desired, sprinkle with Parmesan cheese.

PORK TACOS WITH MANGO SALSA

PORK TACOS WITH MANGO SALSA

I've made quite a few tacos in my day, but you can't beat the tender filling made in a slow cooker. These are by far the best pork tacos we've had—and we've tried plenty. Make the mango salsa from scratch if you have time! Yum.
—**AMBER MASSEY** ARGYLE, TX

PREP: 25 MIN. • **COOK:** 6 HOURS
MAKES: 12 SERVINGS

- 2 tablespoons lime juice
- 2 tablespoons white vinegar
- 3 tablespoons chili powder
- 2 teaspoons ground cumin
- 1½ teaspoons salt
- ½ teaspoon pepper
- 3 cups cubed fresh pineapple
- 1 small red onion, coarsely chopped
- 2 chipotle peppers in adobo sauce
- 1 bottle (12 ounces) dark Mexican beer
- 3 pounds pork tenderloin, cut into 1-inch cubes
- ¼ cup chopped fresh cilantro
- 1 jar (16 ounces) mango salsa
  Corn tortillas (6 inches), warmed

OPTIONAL TOPPINGS
  Cubed fresh pineapple
  Cubed avocado
  Queso fresco

1. Puree the first nine ingredients in a blender; stir in beer. In a 5- or 6-qt. slow cooker, combine the pork and pineapple mixture. Cook, covered, on low until pork is very tender, 6-8 hours. Stir to break up pork.

2. Stir cilantro into salsa. Using a slotted spoon, serve pork mixture in tortillas; add salsa and toppings as desired.

Freeze option: Freeze cooled meat mixture and cooking juices in freezer containers. To use, partially thaw in refrigerator overnight. Heat through in a saucepan, stirring occasionally.

Per ⅔ cup pork mixture with 2 tablespoons salsa: 178 cal., 4g fat (1g sat. fat), 64mg chol., 656mg sod., 9g carb. (5g sugars, 2g fiber), 23g pro. **Diabetic Exchanges:** 3 lean meat, ½ starch.

SAUCY RANCH
PORK & POTATOES

SAUCY RANCH
PORK & POTATOES

A while back, my sister shared a tasty ranch pork roast recipe. I tweaked it so I could use what was already in my pantry, and this dish was born.
—KENDRA ADAMSON LAYTON, UT

PREP: 20 MIN. • **COOK:** 4 HOURS
MAKES: 6 SERVINGS

- 2 **pounds red potatoes (about 6 medium), cut into ¾-inch cubes**
- ¼ **cup water**
- 6 **boneless pork loin chops (6 ounces each)**
- 2 **cans (10¾ ounces each) condensed cream of chicken soup, undiluted**
- 1 **cup 2% milk**
- 1 **envelope ranch salad dressing mix**
  Minced fresh parsley, optional

1. Place potatoes and water in a large microwave-safe dish. Microwave, covered, on high for 3-5 minutes or until potatoes are almost tender; drain.
2. Transfer potatoes and pork chops to a 4- or 5-qt. slow cooker. Mix condensed soup, milk and salad dressing mix; pour over pork chops. Cook, covered, on low for 4-5 hours or until pork and potatoes are tender (a thermometer inserted in pork should read at least 145°). If desired, sprinkle with parsley.

TOP TIP

LOW AND HIGH
Slow cookers vary, so refer to the instruction manual first. But in general, the slow cooker is about 200° at "low" and 300° at "high."

FREEZE IT

BRAZILIAN PORK &
BLACK BEAN STEW

During high school, I spent a year in Brazil and fell in love with the culture and food. One of my favorite dishes was feijoada, a chili/stew served over white rice. I introduced this easy recipe to my family, and it has become one of our favorite comfort foods.
—ANDREA ROMANCZYK MAGNA, UT

PREP: 15 MIN. + SOAKING
COOK: 7 HOURS
MAKES: 8 SERVINGS

- 1½ **cups dried black beans**
- 1 **pound smoked kielbasa or Polish sausage, sliced**
- 1 **pound boneless country-style pork ribs**
- 1 **package (12 ounces) fully cooked Spanish chorizo links, sliced**
- 1 **smoked ham hock**
- 1 **large onion, chopped**
- 3 **garlic cloves, minced**
- 2 **bay leaves**
- ¾ **teaspoon salt**
- ½ **teaspoon pepper**
- 5 **cups water**
  Hot cooked rice

1. Rinse and sort beans; soak according to package directions. Drain and rinse, discarding soaking liquid.
2. In a 6-qt. slow cooker, combine beans with the next nine ingredients. Add water; cook, covered, on low until meat and beans are tender, 7-9 hours.
3. Remove pork ribs and ham hock. When cool enough to handle, remove meat from bones; discard the bones and bay leaves. Shred meat with two forks; return to slow cooker. Serve with hot cooked rice.
Freeze option: Freeze cooled stew in freezer containers. To use, partially thaw in refrigerator overnight. Heat through in a saucepan, stirring occasionally and adding a little water if necessary.

PORK, BEAN & RICE BURRITOS

3. Spoon a scant ⅓ cup shredded pork across center of each tortilla; top with a scant ⅓ cup each beans and rice. Fold bottom and sides of tortilla over filling and roll up. Serve with toppings as desired.

Freeze option: Cool filling ingredients before making burritos. Individually wrap burritos in paper towels and foil; freeze in a resealable plastic freezer bag. To use, remove foil; place paper towel-wrapped burrito on a microwave-safe plate. Microwave on high for 3-4 minutes or until heated through, turning once. Let stand 20 seconds. Serve with toppings of your choice.

EAT SMART

APRICOT PORK ROAST

Serve this delightful roast with rice or mashed potatoes and veggies. We like the leftovers served on buns the next day.
—**PATRICIA DEFOSSE** WILMINGTON, DE

PREP: 15 MIN. • **COOK:** 6 HOURS
MAKES: 6 SERVINGS

- 1 **boneless pork loin roast (2 to 3 pounds)**
- 1 **jar (12 ounces) apricot preserves**
- 1 **cup vegetable broth**
- 2 **tablespoons cornstarch**
- ¼ **cup cold water**

1. Place roast in a 3-qt. slow cooker. In a small bowl, combine preserves and broth; pour over roast. Cover and cook on low for 6-8 hours or until tender. Remove meat to a serving platter; keep warm.

2. Skim fat from cooking juices; transfer to a small saucepan. Bring liquid to a boil. Combine cornstarch and water until smooth. Gradually stir into pan. Bring to a boil; cook and stir for 2 minutes or until thickened. Serve with pork.

Per 4-ounce serving: 337 cal., 7g fat (3g sat. fat), 75mg chol., 223mg sod., 39g carb. (21g sugars, 0 fiber), 30g pro.
Diabetic Exchanges: 4 lean meat, 2 starch.

FREEZE IT

PORK, BEAN & RICE BURRITOS

The combination of spices is key to this slow-cooked pork—my family's favorite burrito filling. The aroma that fills the air as the pork slowly simmers is like a Mexican restaurant. It's a perfect recipe for tailgate parties.
—**VALONDA SEWARD** COARSEGOLD, CA

PREP: 25 MIN.
COOK: 6 HOURS.
MAKES: 10 SERVINGS

SPICE RUB
- 2½ **teaspoons garlic powder**
- 2 **teaspoons onion powder**
- 1¼ **teaspoons salt**
- 1 **teaspoon white pepper**
- 1 **teaspoon pepper**
- ½ **teaspoon ground cumin**
- ½ **teaspoon dried oregano**
- ½ **teaspoon cayenne pepper**

BURRITOS
- 1 **boneless pork shoulder butt roast (3 pounds)**
- 1 **cup water**
- 2 **tablespoons beef bouillon granules**
- 10 **flour tortillas (10 inches)**
- 3 **cups canned pinto beans, rinsed and drained**
- 3 **cups cooked Spanish rice**
  Optional toppings: salsa, chopped tomato, shredded lettuce, sour cream and guacamole

1. Mix spice rub ingredients; rub over pork. Transfer to a 6-qt. slow cooker. In a small bowl, mix water and beef granules; pour around roast. Cook, covered, on low 6-8 hours or until meat is tender.

2. Remove roast; cool slightly. Reserve ½ cup cooking juices; discard remaining juices. Shred pork with two forks. Return pork and reserved juices to slow cooker; heat through.

CREAMY BRATWURST STEW

I adapted a baked stew recipe from the newspaper to create a simple slow-cooked version. Rich, hearty and creamy, this is the best comfort food for cold winter nights.

—**SUSAN HOLMES** GERMANTOWN, WI

PREP: 20 MIN. • **COOK:** 6½ HOURS
MAKES: 8 SERVINGS

- 1¾ pounds potatoes (about 4 medium), peeled and cubed
- 2 medium carrots, chopped
- 2 celery ribs, chopped
- 1 medium onion, chopped
- 1 medium green pepper, chopped
- 2 pounds uncooked bratwurst links
- ½ cup chicken broth
- 1 teaspoon salt
- 1 teaspoon dried basil
- ½ teaspoon pepper
- 2 cups half-and-half cream
- 1 tablespoon cornstarch
- 3 tablespoons cold water

1. Place the first five ingredients in a 5-qt. slow cooker; toss to combine. Top with bratwurst. Mix broth and seasonings; pour over top.
2. Cook, covered, on low until sausage is cooked through and vegetables are tender, 6-7 hours. Remove sausages from slow cooker; cut into 1-in. slices. Add to potato mixture; stir in cream.
3. Mix cornstarch, water until smooth; stir into stew. Cook, covered, on high until thickened, about 30 minutes.

CREAMY BRATWURST STEW

CHINESE-STYLE RIBS

When I was working two jobs, slow-cooking was my way of life. Sometimes I had more than one slow cooker going at a time to help me feed my family home-cooked meals. It's nice to walk in after a hard day's work and have dinner ready. These ribs are quick, easy and delicious.

—**PAULA MARCHESI** LENHARTSVILLE, PA

PREP: 20 MIN. • **COOK:** 6 HOURS
MAKES: 6 SERVINGS

- 3 pounds boneless country-style pork ribs
- 6 green onions, cut into 1-inch pieces
- 1 can (8 ounces) sliced water chestnuts, drained
- ¾ cup hoisin sauce
- 3 tablespoons soy sauce
- 2 tablespoons sherry or chicken stock
- 5 garlic cloves, minced
- 1 tablespoon minced fresh gingerroot
- 1 tablespoon light corn syrup
- 1 tablespoon orange marmalade
- 1 teaspoon pumpkin pie spice
- ½ teaspoon crushed red pepper flakes
- 2 tablespoons cornstarch
- 2 tablespoons water
  Hot cooked rice
  Additional sliced green onions, optional

1. Place pork, green onions and water chestnuts in a 5-qt slow cooker. Mix hoisin sauce, soy sauce, sherry, garlic, gingerroot, corn syrup, marmalade, pie spice and pepper flakes in a bowl. Pour over pork. Cook, covered, on low until meat is tender, 6-8 hours.
2. Remove to a serving platter; keep warm. Skim fat from cooking juices; transfer to a small saucepan. Bring to a boil. Mix cornstarch and water until smooth. Gradually stir into saucepan. Bring to a boil; cook and stir until thickened, about 2 minutes. Serve with ribs, rice and, if desired, additional green onions.

SLOW-SIMMERED
MEAT RAGU

SLOW-SIMMERED MEAT RAGU

After a day simmering in the slow cooker, this ragu is not your typical spaghetti sauce. It's so hearty, it's almost like a stew.
—**LAURIE LACLAIR** NORTH RICHLAND HILLS, TX

PREP: 30 MIN. • **COOK:** 6 HOURS
MAKES: 10 SERVINGS

- 1 **jar (24 ounces) tomato basil pasta sauce**
- 1 **can (14½ ounces) Italian diced tomatoes, undrained**
- 2 **jars (6 ounces each) sliced mushrooms, drained**
- 1 **can (8 ounces) tomato sauce**
- 1 **jar (3½ ounces) prepared pesto**
- 1½ **pounds chicken tenderloins**
- 1 **medium sweet red pepper, chopped**
- ½ **cup chopped pepperoni**
- ½ **cup pitted ripe olives, halved**
- 1 **teaspoon dried oregano**
- ½ **teaspoon hot pepper sauce**
- 1 **pound Italian sausage links, cut into 1-inch pieces**
- 1 **medium onion, chopped**
  Hot cooked angel hair pasta

1. In a 5- or 6-qt. slow cooker, combine the first 11 ingredients. Heat a large skillet over medium heat. Add sausage and onion; cook and stir until sausage is no longer pink and onion is tender. Drain. Add to slow cooker.
2. Cook, covered, on low for 6-8 hours or until the chicken is tender. Serve with pasta.
Freeze option: Do not cook or add pasta. Freeze cooled sauce in freezer containers. To use, partially thaw in refrigerator overnight. Cook pasta according to package directions. Place the meat mixture in a large saucepan; heat through, stirring occasionally and adding a little water if necessary. Proceed as directed.

GRANDMA EDNA'S CAJUN PORK

My grandma used to make this every year as part of our Christmas dinner. These days, I make it for my own family at the holidays. We love to carry on the delicious tradition of Grandma's Cajun Pork.
—**TONYA CLINE** GREENVILLE, OH

PREP: 35 MIN. • **COOK:** 6 HOURS
MAKES: 12 SERVINGS (2¼ CUPS SAUCE)

- 1 **small onion**
- 1 **celery rib**
- 1 **small green pepper**
- 3 **tablespoons butter**
- 3 **garlic cloves, minced**
- 2 **teaspoons dried thyme**
- 1 **teaspoon paprika**
- ½ **teaspoon each salt, white pepper and pepper**
- ½ **teaspoon ground mustard**
- ½ **teaspoon hot pepper sauce**
- 1 **boneless pork loin roast (4 pounds)**
- 2 **tablespoons cornstarch**
- 2 **tablespoons cold water**

1. Finely chop vegetables. In a large skillet, saute vegetables in butter until tender. Add garlic; cook 1 minute longer. Stir in seasonings and pepper sauce.
2. Cut several slits in roast to within ½ in. of bottom. Place in a 5-qt. slow cooker. Spoon onion mixture between slits and over the top of meat. Cover and cook on low for 6-8 hours or until pork is tender.
3. Transfer roast to a serving platter; keep warm. Pour cooking juices into a small saucepan. Combine cornstarch and water until smooth; stir into the pan. Bring to a boil; cook and stir for 2 minutes or until thickened. Serve with roast.
Per serving: 225 cal., 10g fat (4g sat. fat), 83mg chol., 167mg sod., 3g carb. (0 sugars, 1g fiber), 29g pro.
Diabetic Exchanges: 4 lean meat, ½ fat.

EASY SLOW-COOKED PORK TENDERLOIN

I find that simple dinners are the best comfort foods that my family really desires. Simple, good ingredients are the key to my success in the kitchen. Three ingredients poured over the pork are all you need for the most mouth-watering dish you've ever tasted!

—**GRACE NELTNER** LAKESIDE PARK, KY

PREP: 5 MIN.
COOK: 1¾ HOURS + STANDING
MAKES: 6 SERVINGS

- ¼ cup olive oil
- 2 tablespoons soy sauce
- 1 tablespoon Montreal steak seasoning
- 2 pork tenderloins (1 pound each)
  Mashed potatoes or cooked wild rice

In a 5-qt. slow cooker, mix oil, soy sauce and steak seasoning. Add pork; turn to coat. Cook, covered, on low until a thermometer inserted in pork reads 145°, 1¾ to 2¼ hours. Let stand for 10 minutes before slicing. Serve with mashed potatoes.

COLA BARBECUE RIBS

Enjoy the smoky goodness of a summer barbecue all year long, no matter the weather, by preparing these moist and tender ribs in your slow cooker.

—**KAREN SHUCK** EDGAR, NE

PREP: 10 MIN. • **COOK:** 9 HOURS
MAKES: 4 SERVINGS

- ¼ cup packed brown sugar
- 2 garlic cloves, minced
- 1 teaspoon salt
- ½ teaspoon pepper
- 3 tablespoons liquid smoke, optional
- 4 pounds pork spareribs, cut into serving-size pieces
- 1 medium onion, sliced
- ½ cup cola
- 1½ cups barbecue sauce

1. In a small bowl, combine the brown sugar, garlic, salt, pepper and, if desired, liquid smoke; rub over ribs.
2. Layer ribs and onion in a greased 5- or 6-qt. slow cooker; pour cola over ribs. Cover and cook on low for 8-10 hours or until ribs are tender. Drain liquid. Pour sauce over ribs and cook 1 hour longer.

FRUITED PORK CHOPS

Here's one of my favorite slow cooker recipes. I often prepare these tender pineapple pork chops for guests. I like to serve them with brown rice.

—**CINDY RAGAN** NORTH HUNTINGDON, PA

PREP: 10 MIN. • **COOK:** 6¼ HOURS
MAKES: 6 SERVINGS

- 3 tablespoons all-purpose flour
- 1½ teaspoons dried oregano
- ¾ teaspoon salt
- ¼ teaspoon garlic powder
- ¼ teaspoon pepper
- 6 boneless pork loin chops (5 ounces each)
- 1 tablespoon olive oil
- 1 can (20 ounces) unsweetened pineapple chunks
- ¾ cup unsweetened pineapple juice
- ¼ cup water
- 2 tablespoons brown sugar
- 2 tablespoons dried minced onion
- 2 tablespoons tomato paste
- ¼ cup raisins

1. In a large resealable plastic bag, combine flour, oregano, salt, garlic powder and pepper; add pork chops, one at a time, and shake to coat. In a nonstick skillet, brown the chops in oil on both sides. Transfer to a 5-qt. slow cooker.
2. Drain pineapple, reserving juice; set pineapple aside. In a bowl, combine the ¾ cup unsweetened pineapple juice with the reserved pineapple juice from the can. Stir in the water, brown sugar, onion and tomato paste; pour over chops. Sprinkle with raisins.
3. Cover and cook on low for 6-8 hours or until meat is tender. Stir in reserved pineapple. Cover and cook 15 minutes longer or until heated through.
Per serving: 366 cal., 12g fat (4g sat. fat), 79mg chol., 353mg sod., 31g carb. (0 sugars, 2g fiber), 32g pro.
Diabetic Exchanges: 4 lean meat, 2 fruit.

EASY SLOW-COOKED PORK TENDERLOIN

ASIAN RIBS

PINEAPPLE-GLAZED PORK TENDERLOIN

My husband doesn't think a meal is a meal without meat. I prefer something lighter, so this recipe satisfies us both. You can also roast this in the oven if you're short on time.

—TRACY DALIN GOODING, ID

PREP: 10 MIN. • **COOK:** 3¼ HOURS
MAKES: 6 SERVINGS

- 3 pork tenderloins (about ¾ pound each), cut in half crosswise
- ½ teaspoon salt
- ½ teaspoon pepper
- 1 jar (12 ounces) pineapple preserves
- ½ cup frozen pineapple juice concentrate, thawed
- 2 garlic cloves, minced
- 1 tablespoon Dijon mustard
- 1 teaspoon dried rosemary, crushed
- 2 tablespoons cornstarch
- 1 tablespoon cold water

1. Sprinkle pork with salt and pepper; place in a 3- to 4-qt. slow cooker. Whisk together the next five ingredients; pour over pork. Cook, covered, on low until a thermometer reads 145° and the meat is tender, 2-3 hours.

2. Remove from heat; let stand at least 5 minutes before slicing. Whisk together cornstarch and water; add to cooking juices. Cook until thickened, about 15 minutes. Serve with pork.

TOP TIP

CONVERTING SLOW COOKING TO ROASTING

Most slow cooker recipes can be made in a Dutch oven instead (and vice versa). The cook time in the oven will be less than half the time in a slow cooker set to high. Remember that slow-cooked recipes retain more liquid than oven cooking, so add liquid if necessary, or place a sheet of foil over the Dutch oven before setting the lid in place.

ASIAN RIBS

My husband adores this dish, and I love how good it makes the house smell! The mild, tangy, salty-sweet sauce with fresh ginger and garlic is delicious with rice or noodles.

—JULIE KO ROGERS, AR

PREP: 15 MIN.
COOK: 6 HOURS
MAKES: 6 SERVINGS
(ABOUT 4 CUPS SAUCE)

- 6 pounds pork baby back ribs, cut into serving-size pieces
- 1⅓ cups packed brown sugar
- 1 cup reduced-sodium soy sauce
- ¼ cup rice vinegar
- ¼ cup sesame oil
- ¼ cup minced fresh gingerroot
- 6 garlic cloves, minced
- 1 teaspoon crushed red pepper flakes
- ¼ cup cornstarch
- ¼ cup cold water
  Thinly sliced green onions and sesame seeds, optional

1. Place ribs in a 6-qt. slow cooker. In a small bowl, combine brown sugar, soy sauce, vinegar, oil, ginger, garlic and pepper flakes; pour over ribs. Cover and cook on low for 6-7 hours or until meat is tender.

2. Remove meat to a serving platter; keep warm. Skim fat from the cooking juices; transfer to a small saucepan. Bring to a boil.

3. Combine cornstarch and water until smooth. Gradually stir into the pan. Bring to a boil; cook and stir for 2 minutes or until thickened. Serve with ribs. Garnish with onions and sesame seeds if desired.

PINEAPPLE-GLAZED PORK TENDERLOIN

DENVER OMELET
FRITTATA

DENVER OMELET FRITTATA

Here's the perfect brunch dish to serve company after church or another early outing. Pepper, onion and ham go into this classic breakfast preparation, made simple thanks to the slow cooker.

—CONNIE EATON PITTSBURGH, PA

PREP: 25 MIN. • **COOK:** 3 HOURS
MAKES: 6 SERVINGS

- 1 cup water
- 1 tablespoon olive oil
- 1 medium Yukon Gold potato, peeled and sliced
- 1 small onion, thinly sliced
- 12 large eggs
- 1 teaspoon hot pepper sauce
- ½ teaspoon salt
- ¼ teaspoon pepper
- ½ pound deli ham, chopped
- ½ cup chopped sweet green pepper
- 1 cup shredded cheddar cheese, divided

1. Layer two 24-in. pieces of aluminum foil; starting with a long side, fold foil to create a 1-in.-wide strip. Shape the strip into a coil to make a rack for the bottom of a 6-qt. oval slow cooker. Add water to the slow cooker; set the foil rack in water.
2. In a large skillet, heat oil over medium-high heat. Add potato and onion; cook and stir 4-6 minutes or until potato is lightly browned. Transfer to a greased 1½-qt. baking dish (dish must fit in slow cooker).
3. In a large bowl, whisk eggs, pepper sauce, salt and pepper; stir in ham, green pepper and ½ cup cheese. Pour over potato mixture. Top with the remaining cheese. Place dish on foil rack.
4. Cook, covered, on low for 3-4 hours or until eggs are set and a knife inserted in the center comes out clean.

PORK CHOPS WITH SCALLOPED POTATOES

Here's a homey meal that feels Sunday-special. My sister gave me this recipe as a casserole baked in the oven, but I've also fixed it in the slow cooker and on the stovetop.

—ELIZABETH JOHNSTON GLENDALE, AZ

PREP: 30 MIN. • **COOK:** 8 HOURS
MAKES: 6 SERVINGS

- 4 medium potatoes, peeled and thinly sliced
- 6 bone-in pork loin chops (7 ounces each)
- 1 tablespoon canola oil
- 2 large onions, sliced and separated into rings
- 2 teaspoons butter
- 3 tablespoons all-purpose flour
- ¼ teaspoon salt
- ¼ teaspoon pepper
- 1 can (14½ ounces) reduced-sodium chicken broth
- 1 cup fat-free milk

1. Place potatoes in a 5- or 6-qt. slow cooker coated with cooking spray. In a large nonstick skillet, brown pork chops in oil on both sides in batches.
2. Place chops over potatoes. Saute onions in drippings until tender; place over chops. Melt butter in skillet. Combine flour, salt, pepper and broth until smooth. Stir into the pan. Add milk. Bring to a boil; cook and stir for 2 minutes or until thickened.
3. Pour sauce over onions. Cover and cook on low for 8-10 hours or until pork is tender. Skim fat and thicken cooking juices if desired.

ITALIAN PORK CHOPS

Tomato sauce seasoned with oregano, basil and garlic gives tender chops a zesty Italian flavor. This is one of the few ways I will eat pork chops.

—VICKIE LOWE LITITZ, PA

PREP: 20 MIN. • **COOK:** 6 HOURS
MAKES: 4 SERVINGS

- 4 bone-in pork loin chops (1 inch thick)
- ½ pound fresh mushrooms, sliced
- 1 medium onion, chopped
- 1 garlic clove, minced
- 2 cans (8 ounces each) tomato sauce
- 1 tablespoon lemon juice
- ½ teaspoon salt
- ½ teaspoon each dried oregano, basil and parsley flakes
- ¼ cup cornstarch
- ¼ cup cold water
  Green pepper rings, optional

1. In a nonstick skillet, brown the pork chops in oil on both sides. In a 3-qt. slow cooker, combine the mushrooms, onion and garlic. Top with the pork chops.
2. In a bowl, combine tomato sauce, lemon juice, salt, oregano, basil and parsley. Pour over pork. Cover and cook on low for 6-8 hours or until meat is tender. Remove pork and keep warm. Transfer the mushroom mixture to a saucepan.
3. In a small bowl, combine the cornstarch and water until smooth; add to saucepan. Bring to a boil; cook and stir for 2 minutes or until thickened. Serve over pork chops.
4. Garnish with green pepper rings if desired.

TOMATO-TOPPED
ITALIAN PORK CHOPS

PULLED PORK TATERS

This recipe is as manly as it gets—part meat, part potatoes, completely delicious.

—**SHANNON HARRIS** TYLER, TX

PREP: 15 MIN. • **COOK:** 6 HOURS
MAKES: 6 SERVINGS

- 1 **boneless pork loin roast (2 to 3 pounds)**
- 1 **medium onion, chopped**
- 1 **cup ketchup**
- 1 **cup root beer**
- ¼ **cup cider vinegar**
- 2 **tablespoons Worcestershire sauce**
- 1 **tablespoon Louisiana-style hot sauce**
- 2 **teaspoons salt**
- 2 **teaspoons pepper**
- 1 **teaspoon ground mustard**
- 6 **large potatoes**
- 1 **tablespoon cornstarch**
- 1 **tablespoon cold water**
- 6 **tablespoons butter**
- 1½ **cups shredded cheddar cheese**
- 6 **tablespoons sour cream**

1. Place roast in a 5-qt. slow cooker. Top with onion. Combine ketchup, root beer, vinegar, Worcestershire, hot sauce, salt, pepper and mustard; pour over top. Cover and cook on low for 6 to 8 hours or until the meat is tender.

2. Meanwhile, scrub and pierce the potatoes. Bake at 400° for 50-55 minutes or until tender.

3. Remove pork from the slow cooker; shred meat with two forks. Skim fat from the cooking juices; transfer to a large saucepan. Bring liquid to a boil. Combine cornstarch and water until smooth; gradually stir into the pan. Bring to a boil; cook and stir for 2 minutes or until thickened. Return the meat to cooking juices; heat through.

4. With a sharp knife, cut an "X" in each potato; fluff with a fork. Top each with butter and pork mixture; sprinkle with cheese. Top with sour cream.

EAT SMART

TOMATO-TOPPED ITALIAN PORK CHOPS

With a slow cooker and this surefire recipe, you're only seven ingredients away from a delicious meal.

—**KRYSTLE CHASSE** RADIUM HOT SPRINGS, BC

PREP: 25 MIN. **COOK:** 8 HOURS
MAKES: 6 SERVINGS

- 6 **bone-in pork loin chops (7 ounces each)**
- 1 **tablespoon canola oil**
- 1 **small onion, chopped**
- ½ **cup chopped carrot**
- 1 **can (14½ ounces) diced tomatoes, drained**
- ¼ **cup reduced-fat balsamic vinaigrette**
- 2 **teaspoons dried oregano**

1. In a large skillet, brown chops in oil on both sides in batches. Transfer to a 4- or 5-qt. slow cooker coated with cooking spray. Saute onion and carrot in drippings until tender. Stir in tomatoes, vinaigrette and oregano; pour over chops.

2. Cover and cook on low for 8-10 hours or until meat is tender.

Per 1 pork chop: 267 cal., 12g fat (3g sat. fat), 86mg chol., 234mg sod., 7g carb. (4g sugars, 2g fiber), 31g pro.
Diabetic Exchanges: 4 lean meat, 1 vegetable, 1 fat.

TENDER PORK CHOPS

My family has enjoyed these simple pork chops for years. The meat is so tender and juicy that it falls right off the bone!

—**PATRICIA DICK** ANDERSON, IN

PREP: 20 MIN. • **COOK:** 6 HOURS
MAKES: 6 SERVINGS

- ½ **cup all-purpose flour**
- 1½ **teaspoons ground mustard**
- 1 **teaspoon seasoned salt**
- ½ **teaspoon garlic powder**
- 6 **bone-in pork loin chops (8 ounces each)**
- 2 **tablespoons canola oil**
- 1 **can (10½ ounces) condensed chicken with rice soup, undiluted**

1. In a large resealable plastic bag, combine flour, mustard, seasoned salt and garlic powder. Add pork chops, one at a time, and shake to coat.

2. In a large skillet, brown the chops in oil on both sides. Place in a 3-qt. slow cooker. Pour soup over the pork. Cover and cook on low for 6-7 hours or until the meat is tender.

CARNE GUISADA

CARNE GUISADA

After moving temporarily out of state, my boyfriend and I really missed the spicy flavors of our Texas home. We made this recipe often. It goes really well with homemade flour tortillas. We love it over brown rice, too.

—KELLY EVANS DENTON, TX

PREP: 25 MIN. • **COOK:** 7 HOURS
MAKES: 12 SERVINGS (ABOUT 2 QUARTS)

- 1 bottle (12 ounces) beer
- ¼ cup all-purpose flour
- 2 tablespoons tomato paste
- 1 jalapeno pepper, seeded and chopped
- 4 teaspoons Worcestershire sauce
- 1 bay leaf
- 2 to 3 teaspoons crushed red pepper flakes
- 2 teaspoons chili powder
- 1½ teaspoons ground cumin
- ½ teaspoon salt
- ½ teaspoon paprika
- 2 garlic cloves, minced
- ½ teaspoon red wine vinegar
  Dash liquid smoke, optional

- 1 boneless pork shoulder butt roast (3 pounds), cut into 2-inch pieces
- 2 large unpeeled red potatoes, chopped
- 1 medium onion, chopped
  Whole wheat tortillas or hot cooked brown rice, lime wedges and chopped fresh cilantro, optional

1. In a 4- or 5-qt. slow cooker, mix the first 13 ingredients and, if desired, liquid smoke. Stir in pork, potatoes and onion. Cook, covered, on low until pork is tender, 7-9 hours.
2. Discard bay leaf; skim fat from the cooking juices. Shred pork slightly with two forks. Serve with remaining ingredients as desired.
Test Kitchen Note: Wear disposable gloves whenever cutting hot peppers; the oils can burn the skin. Avoid touching your face.
Per ⅔ cup: 261 cal., 12g fat (4g sat. fat), 67mg chol., 200mg sod., 16g carb. (3g sugars, 2g fiber), 21g pro.
Diabetic Exchanges: 3 medium-fat meat, 1 starch.

GLAZED ROSEMARY PORK ROAST

For a change of pace, I serve this pork roast at holiday gatherings in place of the traditional turkey or ham. A glaze infused with rosemary, thyme and sage makes the flavor of this roast unbeatable.

—JOYCE MANIER BEECH GROVE, IN

PREP: 20 MIN. • **COOK:** 4 HOURS
MAKES: 8 SERVINGS

- 1 boneless pork loin roast (3 pounds)
- 1 tablespoon butter
- 1 teaspoon olive oil
- 1 large onion, sliced
- 1 tablespoon brown sugar
- 1 tablespoon minced fresh rosemary
- 1 teaspoon dried thyme
- 1 teaspoon rubbed sage
- 1 teaspoon grated orange peel
- ½ teaspoon pepper
- ¼ teaspoon salt
- ⅔ cup apricot jam
- ½ cup orange juice
- 1 bay leaf

1. In a large skillet, brown roast in butter and oil on all sides. Transfer to a 4- or 5-qt. slow cooker. Add onion to pan; cook and stir until tender. Stir in brown sugar, herbs, orange peel, pepper and salt. Spread over pork. Combine jam and orange juice; pour over top. Add bay leaf.
2. Cover and cook on low for 4 hours or until a thermometer reads 160°. Discard bay leaf.
Per 5 ounces cooked pork: 314 cal., 10g fat (4g sat. fat), 88mg chol., 145mg sod., 22g carb. (13g sugars, 1g fiber), 33g pro.

MAKE AN HERB CHART

"Instead of reaching for the salt shaker, I turn to an herb chart taped inside my cabinet door. It lists the herbs and meats that go well together. I rub the herbs over the meat before cooking. They add flavor while lowering sodium."

—SHERRON C. BRYANT, AL

SLOW COOKER
SWEET-AND-
SOUR PORK

SLOW COOKER SAUSAGE & WAFFLE BAKE

PREP: 20 MIN. • **COOK:** 5 HOURS
MAKES: 12 SERVINGS

- 2 **pounds bulk spicy breakfast pork sausage**
- 1 **tablespoon rubbed sage**
- ½ **teaspoon fennel seed**
- 1 **package (12.3 ounces) frozen waffles, cut into bite-sized pieces**
- 8 **large eggs**
- 1¼ **cups half-and-half cream**
- ¼ **cup maple syrup**
- ¼ **teaspoon salt**
- ¼ **teaspoon pepper**
- 2 **cups shredded cheddar cheese Additional maple syrup**

1. Fold two 18-in.-long pieces of foil into two 18x4-in. strips. Line the perimeter of a 5-qt. slow cooker with foil strips; spray with cooking spray.
2. In a large skillet, cook and crumble sausage over medium heat; drain. Add sage and fennel.
3. Place waffles in the slow cooker; top with sausage. In a bowl, mix eggs, cream, syrup and seasonings. Pour over sausage and waffles. Top with cheese. Cook, covered, on low until set, 5-6 hours. Remove insert and let stand, uncovered, for 15 minutes. Serve with additional maple syrup.

TOP TIP

RUB YOUR OWN SAGE
Most dried sage in the spice section of the grocery store is "rubbed" sage, even if it's not labeled that way. You can make your own by drying whole sage leaves from your garden, then crushing them into a powder in a mortar and pestle, or with your fingers.

FREEZE IT

SLOW COOKER SWEET-AND-SOUR PORK

Chinese food is a big temptation for us, so I lightened up a favorite takeout dish.
—**ELYSE ELLIS** LAYTON, UT

PREP: 15 MIN. • **COOK:** 6¼ HOURS
MAKES: 4 SERVINGS

- ½ **cup sugar**
- ½ **cup packed brown sugar**
- ½ **cup chicken broth**
- ⅓ **cup white vinegar**
- 3 **tablespoons lemon juice**
- 3 **tablespoons reduced-sodium soy sauce**
- 3 **tablespoons tomato paste**
- ½ **teaspoon garlic powder**
- ¼ **teaspoon ground ginger**
- ¼ **teaspoon pepper**
- 1½ **pounds boneless pork loin chops, cut into 1-inch cubes**
- 1 **large onion, cut into 1-inch pieces**
- 1 **large green pepper, cut into 1-inch pieces**
- 1 **can (8 ounces) pineapple chunks, drained**

ADDITIONAL INGREDIENTS
- 3 **tablespoons cornstarch**
- ⅓ **cup chicken broth**
  Hot cooked rice

1. In a 3- or 4-qt. slow cooker, mix the first 10 ingredients. Stir in pork, onion, green pepper and pineapple. Cook, covered, on low 6-8 hours or until the pork is tender.
2. In a small bowl, mix cornstarch and broth until smooth; gradually stir into cooking juices. Cook, covered, on low 15-20 minutes longer or until sauce is thickened. Serve with rice.

Freeze option: In a large resealable plastic freezer bag, combine the first 10 ingredients. Add pork, onion, green pepper and pineapple; seal bag, turn to coat, then freeze. To use, place filled freezer bag in refrigerator 48 hours or until contents are completely thawed. Cook as directed.

"Here's an easy dish guaranteed to create excitement at the breakfast table! Nothing is missing from this sweet and savory combination. It's so wrong, it's right!"
—**COURTNEY LENTZ** BOSTON, MA

SLOW COOKER
SAUSAGE &
WAFFLE BAKE

BUTTERMILK-MUSHROOM
PORK CHOPS

BUTTERMILK-MUSHROOM PORK CHOPS

I went through several variations before creating the pork chops my family considers perfect! I wanted something rich, delicious and tasty that was still relatively healthy. I suggest serving it with salad or grilled asparagus.

—KRISTIN STONE LITTLE ELM, TX

PREP: 25 MIN. • **COOK:** 3½ HOURS
MAKES: 6 SERVINGS

- ¼ cup all-purpose flour
- 1 teaspoon salt, divided
- ½ teaspoon pepper
- 6 boneless pork loin chops (6 to 8 ounces each)
- 2 tablespoons canola oil
- 1 tablespoon butter
- 1 pound medium fresh mushrooms, quartered
- ½ cup white wine or chicken broth
- 1 tablespoon minced fresh basil
- 1 can (10¾ ounces) condensed cream of mushroom soup, undiluted
- 1 cup buttermilk
  Hot cooked egg noodles
  Additional basil

1. In a shallow bowl, mix the flour, ½ teaspoon salt and the pepper. Add pork chops, one at a time, and toss to coat; shake off excess.
2. In a large skillet, brown the pork chops in oil in batches. Transfer meat and drippings to a 4-qt. slow cooker.
3. In the same skillet, heat butter over medium heat. Add mushrooms; cook and stir until tender, 6-8 minutes. Add wine, stirring to loosen browned bits from pan. Pour mushroom mixture over pork chops; sprinkle with basil.
4. Cook, covered, on low until meat is tender, 3-4 hours. Whisk together soup, buttermilk and remaining salt; pour over pork chops. Cook, covered, 30 minutes longer. Stir before serving. Serve with noodles; sprinkle with additional basil.
Test Kitchen Note: Warmed buttermilk will appear curdled.

EAT SMART

CHICKPEA & POTATO CURRY

I make chana masala, the classic Indian dish, in my slow cooker. Browning the onion, ginger and garlic first really makes the sauce amazing.

—ANJANA DEVASAHAYAM SAN ANTONIO, TX

PREP: 25 MIN.
COOK: 6 HOURS
MAKES: 6 SERVINGS

- 1 tablespoon canola oil
- 1 medium onion, chopped
- 2 garlic cloves, minced
- 2 teaspoons minced fresh gingerroot
- 2 teaspoons ground coriander
- 1 teaspoon garam masala
- 1 teaspoon chili powder
- ½ teaspoon salt
- ½ teaspoon ground cumin
- ¼ teaspoon ground turmeric
- 1 can (15 ounces) crushed tomatoes
- 2 cans (15 ounces each) chickpeas, rinsed and drained
- 1 large baking potato, peeled and cut into ¾-inch cubes
- 2½ cups vegetable stock
- 1 tablespoon lime juice
  Chopped fresh cilantro
  Hot cooked rice
  Sliced red onion, optional
  Lime wedges, optional

1. In a large skillet, heat oil over medium-high heat; saute onion until tender, 2-4 minutes. Add garlic, ginger and dry seasonings; cook and stir 1 minute. Stir in tomatoes; transfer to a 3- or 4-qt. slow cooker.
2. Stir in chickpeas, potato and stock. Cook, covered, on low until the potato is tender and the flavors are blended, 6-8 hours.
3. Stir in lime juice; sprinkle with cilantro. Serve with rice and, if desired, red onion and lime wedges.
Per 1¼ cups chickpea mixture: 240 cal., 6g fat (0 sat. fat), 0 chol., 767mg sod., 42g carb. (8g sugars, 9g fiber), 8g pro.

CHICKPEA & POTATO CURRY

Soups, Sides & Sandwiches

VEGETARIAN PEA SOUP

I adapted this recipe from several I found online. When I was a vegetarian for health reasons, it was a favorite. Even my husband, who loves meat, asked for seconds!

—**CORRIE GAMACHE** PALMYRA, VA

PREP: 15 MIN. • **COOK:** 7 HOURS
MAKES: 8 SERVINGS (2 QUARTS)

- 1 package (16 ounces) dried green split peas, rinsed
- 1 medium leek (white portion only), chopped
- 3 celery ribs, chopped
- 1 medium potato, peeled and chopped
- 2 medium carrots, chopped
- 1 garlic clove, minced
- ¼ cup minced fresh parsley
- 4 cans (14½ ounces each) vegetable broth
- 1½ teaspoons ground mustard
- ½ teaspoon pepper
- ½ teaspoon dried oregano
- 1 bay leaf

In a 5-qt. slow cooker, combine all ingredients. Cover and cook on low for 7-8 hours or until peas are tender. Discard bay leaf.

TEX-MEX CHILI

I dreamed up this hearty chili with a Tex-Mex twist years ago. It's still everyone's favorite and the go-to recipe in our family cookbook.

—**MARTHA HOOK** TYLER, TX

PREP: 20 MIN. • **COOK:** 4 HOURS
MAKES: 9 SERVINGS

- 1½ pounds ground beef
- 1 medium onion, chopped
- 5 garlic cloves, minced
- 1 can (14½ ounces) diced tomatoes, undrained
- 1 cup water
- 1 cup V8 juice
- ¼ cup brewed coffee
- 2 envelopes chili seasoning
- 1 can (16 ounces) refried beans
- 1 can (15 ounces) Ranch Style beans (pinto beans in seasoned tomato sauce)
- 2 tablespoons ground cumin
- 2 tablespoons chili powder
- ¼ teaspoon lemon juice

1. In a large skillet, cook beef and onion over medium heat until meat is no longer pink. Add garlic; cook 1 minute longer. Drain. Stir in the tomatoes, water, juice, coffee and chili seasoning.
2. Transfer to a 4-qt. slow cooker. Stir in remaining ingredients. Cover and cook on low for 4-5 hours to allow flavors to blend.

CHEESY HASH BROWN POTATOES

I adapted this recipe for my slow cooker so I could bring along my favorite potatoes to a potluck picnic. Little shortcuts like canned soup and frozen hash browns mean the dish is easy to assemble.

—**BECKY WESEMAN** BECKER, MN

PREP: 5 MIN. • **COOK:** 4 HOURS
MAKES: 8 SERVINGS

- 2 cans (10¾ ounces each) condensed cheddar cheese soup, undiluted
- 1⅓ cups buttermilk
- 2 tablespoons butter, melted
- ½ teaspoon seasoned salt
- ¼ teaspoon garlic powder
- ¼ teaspoon pepper
- 1 package (32 ounces) frozen cubed hash brown potatoes
- ¼ cup grated parmesan cheese
- 1 teaspoon paprika

In a 3-qt. slow cooker, combine the first six ingredients; stir in hash browns. Sprinkle with cheese and paprika. Cook, covered, on low 4 to 4½ hours or until potatoes are tender.

CHIPOTLE PULLED CHICKEN

I love chicken that has a chipotle kick to it. This is a terrific meal when I'm looking for something extra tasty.

—**TAMRA PARKER** MANLIUS, NY

PREP: 15 MIN. • **COOK:** 3 HOURS
MAKES: 12 SERVINGS

- 2 **cups ketchup**
- 1 **small onion, finely chopped**
- ¼ **cup Worcestershire sauce**
- 3 **tablespoons reduced-sodium soy sauce**
- 2 **tablespoons brown sugar**
- 2 **tablespoons cider vinegar**
- 3 **garlic cloves, minced**
- 1 **tablespoon molasses**
- 2 **teaspoons dried oregano**
- 2 **teaspoons minced chipotle pepper in adobo sauce plus 1 teaspoon sauce**
- 1 **teaspoon ground cumin**
- 1 **teaspoon smoked paprika**
- ¼ **teaspoon salt**
- ¼ **teaspoon crushed red pepper flakes**
- 2½ **pounds boneless skinless chicken breasts**
- 12 **sesame seed hamburger buns, split and toasted**

1. In a 3-qt. slow cooker, combine the first 14 ingredients; add chicken. Cook, covered, on low 3-4 hours or until chicken is tender (a thermometer should read at least 165°).
2. Remove chicken from slow cooker. Shred with two forks; return to slow cooker. Using tongs, place chicken mixture on bun bottoms. Replace tops.
Freeze option: Freeze cooled meat mixture and sauce in freezer containers. To use, partially thaw in the refrigerator overnight. Heat through in a saucepan, stirring occasionally.

SALMON SWEET POTATO SOUP

SALMON SWEET POTATO SOUP

I created this recipe as a healthier alternative to whitefish chowder, which is a favorite in the area where I grew up. The salmon and sweet potatoes boost the nutrition, and the slow cooker makes it more convenient. It's especially comforting on a cold fall or winter day!

—**MATTHEW HASS** FRANKLIN, WI

PREP: 20 MIN. • **COOK:** 5½ HOURS
MAKES: 8 SERVINGS (3 QUARTS)

- 1 **tablespoon olive oil**
- 1 **medium onion, chopped**
- 1 **medium carrot, chopped**
- 1 **celery rib, chopped**
- 3 **garlic cloves, minced**
- 2 **medium sweet potatoes, peeled and cut into ½-inch cubes**
- 1½ **cups frozen corn, thawed**
- 6 **cups reduced-sodium chicken broth**
- 1 **teaspoon celery salt**
- 1 **teaspoon dill weed**
- ½ **teaspoon salt**
- ¾ **teaspoon pepper**
- 1½ **pounds salmon fillets, skin removed and cut into ¾-inch pieces**
- 1 **can (12 ounces) fat-free evaporated milk**
- 2 **tablespoons minced fresh parsley**

1. In a large skillet, heat oil over medium heat. Add onion, carrot and celery; cook and stir until tender, 4-5 minutes. Add garlic; cook 1 minute longer. Transfer to a 5-qt. slow cooker. Add the next seven ingredients. Cook, covered, on low until sweet potatoes are tender, 5-6 hours.
2. Stir in salmon, milk and parsley. Cook, covered, until fish just begins to flake easily with a fork, 30-40 minutes longer.
Per 1½ cups: 279 cal., 10g fat (2g sat. fat), 45mg chol., 834mg sod., 26g carb. (13g sugars, 3g fiber), 22g pro.
Diabetic Exchanges: 3 lean meat, 1½ starch, ½ fat.

GARLIC-DILL
SODA BREAD

GARLIC-DILL SODA BREAD

It's amazing how bread can be made in a slow cooker, and that is why this recipe is so awesome—who knew it could be so simple! Let the inviting aroma of dill and cheese fill your kitchen.

—**MELISSA HANSEN** MILWAUKEE, WI

PREP: 15 MIN. • **COOK:** 1½ HOURS
MAKES: 1 LOAF (12 WEDGES)

- 4 **cups all-purpose flour**
- 2 **tablespoons dried parsley flakes**
- 1 **tablespoon dried minced onion**
- 2 **teaspoons garlic powder**
- 1½ **teaspoons dill weed**
- 1 **teaspoon salt**
- 1 **teaspoon baking soda**
- 1 **teaspoon ground mustard**
- 1¾ **cups buttermilk**
- 1 **cup shredded sharp cheddar cheese**

1. In a large bowl, whisk the first eight ingredients. Add buttermilk and cheese; stir just until moistened. Turn onto a lightly floured surface; knead gently 6-8 times or just until dough comes together. Shape dough into a 6-in. round loaf. Using a sharp knife, score surface with 1-in. deep cuts in a crisscross pattern. Place in a greased 5-qt. slow cooker.

2. Cook, covered, on high for 1½ to 2 hours or until a thermometer reads 190°-200°.

3. Preheat broiler. Remove bread; place on a baking sheet. Broil 6-8 in. from heat for 2-3 minutes or until golden brown. Remove to a wire rack to cool completely.

THAI CHICKEN NOODLE SOUP

THAI CHICKEN NOODLE SOUP

This soup is a semi-homemade version that coaxes all of the flavor out of a rotisserie chicken. All the prep work for this can be done the day before so you can toss it into the slow cooker with ease.

—**BETH JACOBSON** MILWAUKEE, WI

PREP: 20 MIN. • **COOK:** 6 HOURS
MAKES: 8 SERVINGS

- 1 **large onion, halved**
- 1 **piece fresh ginger (3 to 4 inches), halved lengthwise**
- 1 **tablespoon canola oil**
- 1 **rotisserie chicken**
- 1 **cinnamon stick (3 inches)**
- 5 **whole cloves**
- 3 **whole star anise**
- 1 **teaspoon coriander seeds**
- 1 **teaspoon fennel seed**
- 3 **quarts reduced-sodium chicken broth**
- 1 **package (8.8 ounces) rice noodles**
- 2 **tablespoons brown sugar**
- 2 **tablespoons fish sauce**
- 1 **tablespoon lime juice**
  Optional ingredients: bean sprouts, fresh basil leaves, fresh cilantro leaves, thinly sliced green onions, chili garlic sauce, fish sauce and lime wedges

1. Preheat broiler. Place onion and ginger in a foil-lined 15x10x1-in. baking pan; drizzle with oil. Broil 3-4 in. from heat for 8-10 minutes or until well browned. Meanwhile, remove chicken from bones; reserve carcass and shred meat. Place carcass, onion, ginger, spices and broth in a 6-qt slow cooker. Cook on low for 6-8 hours.

2. Cook noodles according to package instructions. Strain soup and keep warm; discard carcass, vegetables and spices. Stir in brown sugar, fish sauce and lime juice. Place noodles and chicken in soup bowls. Ladle broth into soup bowls. Add toppings of your choice.

CUBAN
PULLED PORK
SANDWICHES

BEEF & POTATO SOUP

Slow-cooker easy, this lightened-up soup is a tradition after church services at our house.

—SHEILA HOLDERMAN BERTHOLD, ND

PREP: 30 MIN. • **COOK:** 6½ HOURS
MAKES: 10 SERVINGS (3 QUARTS)

- 1½ pounds lean ground beef (90% lean)
- ¾ cup chopped onion
- ½ cup all-purpose flour
- 2 cans (14½ ounces each) reduced-sodium chicken broth, divided
- 5 medium potatoes, peeled and cubed
- 5 medium carrots, chopped
- 3 celery ribs, chopped
- 3 teaspoons dried basil
- 2 teaspoons dried parsley flakes
- 1 teaspoon garlic powder
- ½ teaspoon pepper
- 12 ounces reduced-fat process cheese (Velveeta), cubed
- 1½ cups 2% milk
- ½ cup reduced-fat sour cream

1. In a large skillet, cook beef and onion over medium heat until meat is no longer pink; drain. Combine flour and 1 can broth until smooth. Add to beef mixture. Bring to a boil; cook and stir for 2 minutes or until thickened.
2. Transfer to a 5-qt. slow cooker. Stir in the potatoes, carrots, celery, seasonings and remaining broth. Cover and cook on low for 6-8 hours or until vegetables are tender.
3. Stir in cheese and milk. Cover and cook 30 minutes longer or until cheese is melted. Just before serving, stir in sour cream.

CUBAN PULLED PORK SANDWICHES

I lived in Florida for a while and loved the pork they would make, so I went about making it for myself! The flavorful meat makes amazing Cuban sandwiches, but you also can use it in traditional pulled pork sandwiches or even tacos.

—LACIE GRIFFIN AUSTIN, TX

PREP: 30 MIN. • **COOK:** 8 HOURS
MAKES: 16 SERVINGS

- 1 cup orange juice
- ½ cup lime juice
- 12 garlic cloves, minced
- 2 tablespoons spiced rum, optional
- 2 tablespoons ground coriander
- 2 teaspoons salt
- 2 teaspoons white pepper
- 2 teaspoons pepper
- 1 teaspoon cayenne pepper
- 5 to 6 pounds boneless pork shoulder roast, cut into four pieces
- 1 tablespoon olive oil

SANDWICHES
- 2 loaves (1 pound each) French bread
  Yellow mustard, optional
- 16 dill pickle slices
- 1½ pounds thinly sliced deli ham
- 1½ pounds Swiss cheese, sliced

1. In a 6- or 7-qt. slow cooker, combine first nine ingredients. Add pork; cook, covered, on low until tender, 8-10 hours. Remove roast; shred with two forks. In a large skillet, heat oil over medium-high heat. Cook meat in batches until lightly browned and crisp in spots.
2. Cut each loaf of bread in half lengthwise. If desired, spread mustard over cut sides of bread. Layer bottom halves of bread with pickles, pork, ham and cheese. Replace tops. Cut each loaf into eight slices.

BROWNING GROUND MEATS IN A SKILLET
When browning ground meats, press down on the meat with a potato masher while cooking to break the meat apart and get it to cook better.

PUMPKIN APPLE SOUP

BEEF & THREE-BEAN CHILI

Here is a wonderful chili that will make your kitchen smell so good as it cooks. We love eating it with homemade bread or corn bread.

—**NANCY WHITFORD** EDWARDS, NY

PREP: 20 MIN. • **COOK:** 5 HOURS
MAKES: 9 SERVINGS

- 1½ pounds beef stew meat, cut into 1-inch pieces
- 2 teaspoons chili powder
- 2 tablespoons canola oil
- 2 small onions, chopped
- 1 can (16 ounces) kidney beans, rinsed and drained
- 1 can (15 ounces) white kidney or cannellini beans, rinsed and drained
- 1 can (15 ounces) black beans, rinsed and drained
- 2 cans (14½ ounces each) diced tomatoes, undrained
- 1 cup beef broth
- 1 can (6 ounces) tomato paste
- 2 jalapeno peppers, seeded and chopped
- 1 tablespoon brown sugar
- 2 garlic cloves, minced
- ½ teaspoon salt
- ½ teaspoon pepper
- ¼ teaspoon ground cumin
  Sour cream, optional

1. Sprinkle beef with chili powder. In a large skillet, heat oil over medium heat. Brown beef and onion in batches.
2. Meanwhile, in a 5-qt. slow cooker coated with cooking spray, combine beans, tomatoes, broth, tomato paste, jalapenos, brown sugar, garlic, salt, pepper and cumin. Stir in beef, onion and drippings.
3. Cook, covered, on low for 5-6 hours or until meat is tender. If desired, serve with sour cream.
Test Kitchen Note: Wear disposable gloves when cutting hot peppers; the oils can burn skin. Avoid touching your face.

PUMPKIN APPLE SOUP

I often make a butternut squash soup on the stove in the fall. This year, I had pumpkins from a local farm and only time for the slow cooker. The apples set the soup off perfectly! If using fresh pumpkin, be sure to puree it well to avoid stringy soup.

—**REBECCA PHILLIPS** FAYETTEVILLE, NC

PREP: 15 MIN. • **COOK:** 6½ HOURS
MAKES: 8 SERVINGS (2 QUARTS)

- 1 can (15 ounces) solid-pack pumpkin
- 2 tart apples, peeled and cut into ½-inch pieces
- 1 medium onion, coarsely chopped
- 3 garlic cloves, minced
- 1 teaspoon dried thyme
- 2 bay leaves
- ¼ teaspoon Louisiana-style hot sauce
- 1 carton (32 ounces) chicken broth
- ½ teaspoon salt
- ¼ teaspoon pepper
- 14 ounces smoked sausage, coarsely chopped
- ½ cup half-and-half cream
- 2 tablespoons brown sugar
  Sliced apple, optional

1. In a 5-qt. slow cooker, combine the first seven ingredients. Stir in broth, salt and pepper. Cook, covered, on low until flavors are blended, 6-8 hours.
2. Add sausage, cream and brown sugar to the slow cooker. Cook until heated through, 30-35 minutes. Discard bay leaves. If desired, serve with sliced apple.

**SLOW COOKER
PUMPKIN
YEAST BREAD**

SLOW COOKER
PUMPKIN YEAST BREAD

Savor the rich flavors of fall with this homey loaf you can bake up in the slow cooker. Butterscotch adds a sweet surprise.

—ERICA POLLY SUN PRAIRIE, WI

PREP: 20 MIN.
COOK: 2½ HOURS + COOLING
MAKES: 1 LOAF (12 SLICES)

- ⅓ **cup packed brown sugar**
- 1 **package (¼ ounce) quick-rise yeast**
- 2 **teaspoons pumpkin pie spice**
- ¾ **teaspoon salt**
- 3½ **to 4 cups all-purpose flour**
- ¾ **cup 2% milk**
- 2 **tablespoons butter, cubed**
- ¾ **cup canned pumpkin**
- 1 **large egg, lightly beaten**
- ⅓ **cup raisins**
- ⅓ **cup chopped pecans, toasted**
- ⅓ **cup butterscotch chips, optional**

1. In a large bowl, mix brown sugar, yeast, pie spice, salt and 1½ cups flour. In a small saucepan, heat milk and butter to 120°-130°; stir into dry ingredients. Stir in pumpkin, egg and enough remaining flour to form a soft dough (dough will be sticky).

2. Turn dough onto a floured surface; knead until smooth and elastic, about 6-8 minutes. During the last few minutes of kneading add raisins, pecans and, if desired, chips. Shape into a 6-in. round loaf; transfer to a greased piece of double thickness heavy-duty foil (about 12 in. square). Lifting with foil, place in a 6-qt. slow cooker. Press foil against bottom and sides of slow cooker.

3. Cook, covered, on high 2½ to 3 hours or until a thermometer reads 190°-200°. Remove to a wire rack. Cool completely before slicing.

CELEBRATION
BRUSSELS SPROUTS

This recipe hits all the flavor points and makes a fantastic Thanksgiving or Christmas side. Plus, you have to love a dish that requires minimal effort and doesn't take up oven space. You can always omit the bacon if you need a vegetarian option.

—LAUREN KNOELKE MILWAUKEE, WI

PREP: 20 MIN. • **COOK:** 2 HOURS
MAKES: 10 SERVINGS

- 2 **pounds fresh Brussels sprouts, sliced**
- 2 **large apples (Fuji or Braeburn), chopped**
- ⅓ **cup dried cranberries**
- 8 **bacon strips, cooked and crumbled, divided**
- ⅓ **cup cider vinegar**
- ¼ **cup maple syrup**
- 2 **tablespoons olive oil**
- 1 **teaspoon salt**
- ½ **teaspoon fresh ground pepper**
- ¾ **cup chopped hazelnuts or pecans, toasted**

1. In a large bowl, combine Brussels sprouts, apples, cranberries and ¼ cup bacon. In a small bowl, whisk vinegar, syrup, oil, salt and pepper; pour over Brussels sprouts mixture, tossing to coat. Transfer to a 5-qt. slow cooker. Cook, covered, on low for 2-4 hours or until sprouts reach desired tenderness, stirring once.

2. To serve, sprinkle with hazelnuts and remaining bacon.

TOP TIP

3 WAYS TO TOAST NUTS:

1. Heat a dry skillet, pour in nuts, spread in a single layer. Stir. Cook 3 to 5 minutes.

2. Preheat oven to 350°. Place nuts in a single layer in shallow baking pan. Bake 10 minutes, stirring halfway through.

3. Place nuts in a microwave-safe dish. Microwave, uncovered, on high for 2-3 minutes or until lightly toasted, stirring twice.

CELEBRATION
BRUSSELS SPROUTS

EASY
POTSTICKER
SOUP

EASY POTSTICKER SOUP

Because I have soup often, I'm always coming up with something new. I saw potstickers in the freezer and decided to feature them in Asian soup. The results were delicious. Rice vinegar adds just the right tang. Stir in chopped cabbage or bok choy if you like.

—DARLENE BRENDEN SALEM, OR

PREP: 15 MIN. • **COOK:** 5¼ HOURS
MAKES: 6 SERVINGS

- ½ **pound Chinese or napa cabbage, thinly sliced**
- 2 **celery ribs, thinly sliced**
- 2 **medium carrots, cut into matchsticks**
- ⅓ **cup thinly sliced green onions**
- 2 to 3 **tablespoons soy sauce**
- 2 **tablespoons rice vinegar**
- 3 **garlic cloves, minced**
- 2 **teaspoons minced fresh gingerroot or ½ teaspoon ground ginger**
- ½ **teaspoon sesame oil**
- 6 **cups reduced-sodium chicken broth**
- 1 **package (16 ounces) frozen chicken potstickers**

In a 4-qt. slow cooker, combine the first nine ingredients. Stir in broth. Cook, covered, on low until vegetables are tender, 5-6 hours. Add potstickers; cook, covered, on high until heated through, 15-20 minutes.

BEEF BARLEY SOUP

My husband doesn't usually consider a bowl of soup dinner, but when I serve this hearty soup with hot corn bread on the side, it gets a thumbs-up from him!

—GINNY PERKINS COLUMBIANA, OH

PREP: 15 MIN. • **COOK:** 9 HOURS
MAKES: 8 SERVINGS (2½ QUARTS)

- 1½ **pounds beef stew meat**
- 1 **tablespoon canola oil**
- 1 **can (14½ ounces) diced tomatoes**
- 1 **cup chopped onion**
- 1 **cup diced celery**
- 1 **cup sliced fresh carrots**
- ½ **cup chopped green pepper**
- 4 **cups beef broth**
- 2 **cups water**
- 1 **cup spaghetti sauce**
- ⅔ **cup medium pearl barley**
- 1 **tablespoon dried parsley flakes**
- 2 **teaspoons salt**
- 1½ **teaspoons dried basil**
- ¾ **teaspoon pepper**

1. In a large skillet, brown meat in oil over medium heat; drain.
2. Meanwhile, in a 5-qt. slow cooker, combine the vegetables, broth, water, spaghetti sauce, barley and seasonings.
3. Stir in beef. Cover and cook on low for 9-10 hours or until meat is tender. Skim fat.

CHEESY CAULIFLOWER SOUP

If you prefer chunky soup, skip the blender step in this recipe and stir the cheese and cream into the slow cooker, then heat on high until the cheese is melted.

—SHERYL PUNTER WOODSTOCK, ON

PREP: 25 MIN. • **COOK:** 5½ HOURS
MAKES: 9 SERVINGS (2¼ QUARTS)

- 1 **large head cauliflower, broken into florets**
- 2 **celery ribs**
- 2 **large carrots**
- 1 **large green pepper**
- 1 **small sweet red pepper**
- 1 **medium red onion**
- 4 **cups chicken broth**
- ½ **teaspoon Worcestershire sauce**
- ¼ **teaspoon salt**
- ⅛ **teaspoon pepper**
- 2 **cups shredded cheddar cheese**
- 2 **cups half-and-half cream**

1. Place cauliflower in a 4-qt. slow cooker. Chop the celery, carrots, peppers and onion; add to slow cooker. Stir in the broth, Worcestershire sauce, salt and pepper. Cover and cook on low for 5-6 hours or until vegetables are tender.
2. In a blender, process soup in batches until smooth. Return all to slow cooker; stir in cheese and cream. Cover and cook on high for 30 minutes or until cheese is melted.

BARBECUE BRATS & PEPPERS

I live in brat country, and this barbecue-style recipe feeds a crowd. The sauce gives it a welcome change from the same old grilled brat.

—MARIA ZRUCKY KRONENWETTER, WI

PREP: 15 MIN. • **COOK:** 6 HOURS
MAKES: 10 SERVINGS

- 2 **bottles (12 ounces each) beer or nonalcoholic beer**
- 1 **bottle (18 ounces) barbecue sauce**
- ½ **cup ketchup**
- 1 **large sweet onion, halved and sliced**
- 1 **large sweet yellow pepper, cut into strips**
- 1 **large sweet orange pepper, cut into strips**
- 1 **jalapeno pepper, thinly sliced**
- 1 **serrano pepper, thinly sliced**
- 10 **uncooked bratwurst links**
- 10 **brat or hot dog buns, split**

1. Place the first eight ingredients in a 5-qt. slow cooker; stir to combine. In a large skillet, brown bratwurst on all sides over medium-high heat; transfer to slow cooker.
2. Cook, covered, on low for 6-8 hours or until sausages are cooked through and vegetables are tender. Using tongs, serve bratwurst and pepper mixture on buns.
Test Kitchen Note: Wear disposable gloves when cutting hot peppers; the oils can burn skin. Avoid touching your face.

HEARTY SAUSAGE SOUP

In a large skillet, brown kielbasa in batches. Transfer to a 6-qt. slow cooker. Stir in remaining ingredients. Cook, covered, on low for 6-8 hours or until vegetables are tender. Skim fat.

ASIAN BBQ PORK BUNS

PREP: 25 MIN. • **COOK:** 6 HOURS
MAKES: 8 SERVINGS

- 1 boneless pork shoulder butt roast (3 pounds)
- 1¾ teaspoons salt, divided
- 1¼ teaspoons coarsely ground pepper, divided
- 1 tablespoon canola oil
- ½ cup water
- 1 bottle (12 ounces) regular chili sauce (such as Heinz)
- ½ cup hoisin sauce
- 3 tablespoons rice vinegar
- 1 tablespoon minced fresh gingerroot
- 4 cups coleslaw mix
- ¼ cup Asian toasted sesame salad dressing
- 8 split sesame seed hamburger buns, toasted

1. Sprinkle pork roast with 1½ teaspoons salt and 1 teaspoon pepper. In a large skillet, heat oil over medium-high heat. Add pork; brown on all sides. Transfer pork and drippings to a greased 4-qt. slow cooker. Add water; cook, covered, on low until pork is tender, 5-6 hours. Remove pork; discard cooking juices.
2. When pork is cool enough to handle, shred meat with two forks. Return to slow cooker. Stir together chili sauce, hoisin sauce, vinegar and ginger. Pour over pork; toss to coat. Cook until heated through, about 1 hour.
3. Meanwhile, toss coleslaw mix with dressing and remaining salt and pepper. Serve shredded pork topped with coleslaw on toasted buns.

HEARTY SAUSAGE SOUP

My family loves a big bowl of soup like this one that brims with sausage and veggies. We enjoy having it with hot rolls on Christmas Day.
—**BARBARA TILGHMAN** BEL AIR, MD

PREP: 30 MIN. • **COOK:** 6 HOURS
MAKES: 14 SERVINGS (3½ QUARTS)

- 2 pounds smoked kielbasa or Polish sausage, sliced
- 4 cups coarsely chopped cabbage
- 2 cans (15½ ounces each) great northern beans, rinsed and drained
- 6 medium carrots, thinly sliced
- 3 medium potatoes, cubed
- 2 celery ribs, thinly sliced
- 1 small onion, chopped
- 2 cups water
- 1 can (14½ ounces) Italian diced tomatoes, undrained
- 1 can (14½ ounces) chicken broth
- 1 teaspoon dried basil
- ½ teaspoon salt
- ½ teaspoon dried savory
- ¼ teaspoon garlic powder
- ¼ teaspoon pepper

"Here's a quick way to get a delicious and comforting dinner on the table that pleases everyone on busy evenings. Sometimes I add a little reduced-sodium soy sauce to the barbecue sauce. If your family loves Asian food like mine does, they will fall for these pork buns."
—**TERESA RALSTON** NEW ALBANY, OH

ASIAN BBQ PORK BUNS

**CROCK-POT
CAJUN CORN**

CROCK-POT CAJUN CORN

My husband loves corn on the cob. Making it like this is so tasty, and there is no standing over a hot stove on a summer day waiting for the water to boil! You can use any blend of seasoning that you like. We like a little spice, so the Cajun seasoning works well for us. I find when I use it I don't need any additional salt.
—**AUDRA RORICK** SCOTT CITY, KS

PREP: 15 MIN. • **COOK:** 4 HOURS
MAKES: 4 SERVINGS

- 4 **tablespoons butter, softened**
- 2 **teaspoons Cajun seasoning,
  or more to taste**
- 4 **medium ears sweet corn,
  husks removed**
- ¾ **cup water**

1. Combine butter and Cajun seasoning until well blended. Place each ear of corn on a double thickness of heavy-duty foil. Spread butter mixture over each ear. Wrap foil tightly around corn.
2. Place ears in a 6-qt. slow cooker; add water. Cook, covered, on high until corn is tender, 4-6 hours.
Mexican Street Corn: Subsitute mayonnaise and chili powder for butter and Cajun seasoning. Cook as directed; serve with queso fresco and lime wedges.
Garlic Parmesan Corn: Substitute 1 clove minced garlic for Cajun seasoning; sprinkle corn with Parmesan cheese. Cook as directed.

TOP TIP

"I make a big batch of homemade mashed potatoes and freeze individual servings in muffin cups. Once they're frozen, I pop them out and store them in resealable plastic freezer bags. During the week, I pull out as many servings as I need and heat them in the microwave."

—**GRETCHEN B.** SURPRISE, AZ

MEDITERRANEAN
SLOW COOKER
MASHED POTATOES

MEDITERRANEAN SLOW COOKER MASHED POTATOES

I love to use my slow cooker when family comes over. When I make my special turkey meat loaf, this is a no-fuss side dish that tastes amazing!
—**KRISTEN HEIGL** STATEN ISLAND, NY

PREP: 20 MIN. • **COOK:** 2 HOURS
MAKES: 10 SERVINGS

- 4 **pounds red potatoes, cubed**
- 1 **cup (8 ounces) sour cream**
- ½ **cup butter, softened**
- 3 **garlic cloves, minced**
- 2 **tablespoons snipped fresh dill**
- ¾ **teaspoon salt**
- ½ **teaspoon pepper**
- 1 **cup crumbled
  feta cheese**

Place potatoes in a 6-qt. stockpot; add water to cover. Bring to a boil. Reduce heat; cook, uncovered, 10-15 minutes or until tender. Drain and coarsely mash. Combine next six ingredients in a greased 5-qt. slow cooker; stir in the mashed potatoes and feta until well combined. Cook, covered, on low until heated through, 2-3 hours.

FAVORITE ITALIAN
BEEF SANDWICHES

SPICY VEGGIE & LENTIL SOUP

I enjoy this recipe for the simple fact that it's meatless, easy on the pocket and simply delicious! You can substitute any vegetable you like— it's all a matter of preference. Serve bread or a salad on the side.

—GERALDINE HENNESSEY GLENDALE, NY

PREP: 15 MIN.
COOK: 6½ HOURS
MAKES: 8 SERVINGS (2 QUARTS)

- 2 cups halved fresh green beans
- 2 cups fresh cauliflowerets
- 1 cup dried lentils, rinsed and drained
- 1 cup fresh baby carrots, halved diagonally
- 1 medium onion, chopped
- 1 jalapeno pepper, seeded and finely chopped
- 2 garlic cloves, minced
- 4 cups beef or vegetable stock
- 2 bay leaves
- 2 teaspoons smoked paprika
- 1 teaspoon dried oregano
- 1 teaspoon salt
- ¼ teaspoon pepper
- 1 can (14½ ounces) diced tomatoes with spicy red pepper, undrained

FAVORITE ITALIAN BEEF SANDWICHES

I'm a paramedic and firefighter, and slow-cooked recipes like this one suit my unpredictable schedule. My husband, children and the hungry bunch at the firehouse love these robust sandwiches that have a little zip.

—KRIS SWIHART PERRYSBURG, OH

PREP: 20 MIN. • **COOK:** 8 HOURS
MAKES: 10-12 SERVINGS

- 1 jar (11½ ounces) pepperoncini
- 1 boneless beef chuck roast (3½ to 4 pounds)
- ¼ cup water
- 1¾ teaspoons dried basil
- 1½ teaspoons garlic powder
- 1½ teaspoons dried oregano
- 1¼ teaspoons salt
- ¼ teaspoon pepper
- 1 large onion, sliced and quartered
- 10 to 12 hard rolls, split

1. Drain the pepperoncini, reserving liquid. Remove and discard stems of peppers; set peppers aside. Cut roast into large chunks; place a third of the meat in a 5-qt. slow cooker. Add water.
2. In a small bowl, combine the seasonings; sprinkle half over beef. Layer with half of the remaining meat, then the onion and pepperoncini. Pour pepperoncini liquid over the top. Add remaining meat to slow cooker; sprinkle with remaining seasonings.
3. Cover and cook on low for 8-9 hours or until meat is tender. Shred beef with two forks. Using a slotted spoon, serve beef and peppers on rolls.

Test Kitchen Note: Look for pepperoncini (pickled peppers) in the pickle and olive section of your grocery store.

1. In a 4-qt. slow cooker, combine the first 13 ingredients. Cook, covered, on low until vegetables and lentils are tender, 6-8 hours.
2. Discard the bay leaves. Stir in diced tomatoes; cook, covered, 30 minutes longer.

Test Kitchen Note: Wear disposable gloves when cutting hot peppers; the oils can burn skin. Avoid touching your face.

Per 1 cup: 146 cal., 1g fat (0 sat. fat), 0 chol., 693mg sod., 27g carb. (7g sugars, 5g fiber), 10g pro.

Diabetic Exchanges: 1½ starch, 1 lean meat.

SPICY VEGGIE
& LENTIL SOUP

Snacks & Sweets

SLOW COOKER
TEQUILA
POACHED PEARS

SLOW COOKER TEQUILA POACHED PEARS

Bring out this creative sweet when you want to impress dinner guests. Tequila certainly makes it a unique dessert, but it is deliciously refreshing with lovely fresh pears and mint.

—NANCY HEISHMAN LAS VEGAS, NV

PREP: 20 MIN. • **COOK:** 4 HOURS
MAKES: 8 SERVINGS

- 2 **cups water**
- 1 **can (11.3 ounces) pear nectar**
- 1 **cup tequila**
- ½ **cup sugar**
- 2 **tablespoons lime juice**
- 2 **teaspoons grated lime peel**
- 1 **cinnamon stick (3 inches)**
- ¼ **teaspoon ground nutmeg**
- 8 **whole Anjou pears, peeled**
  Sweetened whipped cream
  Fresh mint leaves

1. In a large saucepan, combine the first eight ingredients. Bring to a boil over medium-high heat; boil 2 minutes, stirring constantly.

2. Place pears in a 4- or 5-qt. slow cooker; add liquid. Cook, covered, on low until tender, 4-5 hours. Remove cinnamon stick and discard. Pour 3 cups cooking liquid in a small saucepan. Bring to a boil; cook, uncovered, until liquid is reduced to 1 cup, about 20 minutes.

3. Halve pears lengthwise and core them. Serve with sauce, whipped cream and mint leaves.

SLOW COOKER
CINNAMON ROLL

SLOW COOKER CINNAMON ROLL

Come home to the heavenly aroma of fresh-baked cinnamon rolls! This better-for-you version tastes just as decadent as a regular cinnamon roll, but it sneaks in some whole grains.
—NICK IVERSON MILWAUKEE, WI

PREP: 15 MIN. + RISING • **COOK:** 4 HOURS
MAKES: 12 SERVINGS

- 1 package (¼ ounce) active dry yeast
- ¾ cup warm water (110° to 115°)
- ½ cup quick-cooking oats
- ½ cup whole wheat flour
- ¼ cup packed brown sugar
- 2 tablespoons butter, melted
- 1 large egg
- 1 teaspoon salt
- 1¾ to 2¼ cups all-purpose flour

FILLING
- 3 tablespoons butter, softened
- ⅓ cup granulated sugar
- 2 teaspoons ground cinnamon

ICING
- 1 cup confectioners' sugar
- 2 tablespoons half-and-half cream
- 4 teaspoons butter, softened

1. Dissolve the yeast in warm water. Add next six ingredients plus 1 cup all-purpose flour. Beat on medium speed until smooth. Stir in enough remaining flour to form a soft dough (dough will be sticky).
2. Turn onto a lightly floured surface; knead until smooth and elastic, about 6-8 minutes. Roll into an 18x12-in. rectangle. For filling, spread dough with butter, combine sugar and cinnamon; sprinkle over dough within ½ in. of edges.
3. Roll up jelly-roll style, starting with a long side; pinch seam to seal. Cut crosswise in half to form two rolls. Place rolls side by side; pinch top ends together to seal. Using a sharp knife, cut rolls lengthwise in half; loosely twist strips around each other. Pinch bottom ends together to seal. Shape into a coil; place on parchment paper. Transfer to a 6-qt. slow cooker. Let rise until doubled, about 1 hour.
4. Cook, covered, on low until bread is lightly browned, 4-5 hours. Remove from slow cooker and cool slightly. Beat icing ingredients until smooth. Spread over warm roll.

BUTTER CHICKEN MEATBALLS

My husband and I love meatballs, and we love the Indian dish of butter chicken. Before an appetizer party, we had the idea to combine these two favorites, and the results got rave reviews! Want them as a main dish? Just serve with basmati rice.
—SHANNON DOBOS CALGARY, AB

PREP: 30 MIN.
COOK: 3 HOURS
MAKES: ABOUT 3 DOZEN

- 1½ pounds ground chicken or turkey
- 1 large egg, lightly beaten
- ½ cup soft bread crumbs
- 1 teaspoon garam masala
- ½ teaspoon tandoori masala seasoning
- ½ teaspoon salt
- ¼ teaspoon cayenne pepper
- 3 tablespoons minced fresh cilantro, divided
- 1 jar (14.1 ounces) butter chicken sauce

1. Combine the first seven ingredients plus 2 tablespoons cilantro; mix lightly but thoroughly. With wet hands, shape into 1-in. balls. Place meatballs in a 3-qt. slow cooker coated with cooking spray.
2. Pour butter sauce over meatballs. Cook, covered, on low until meatballs are cooked through, 3-4 hours. Top with remaining cilantro.
Test Kitchen Note: Look for butter chicken sauce in the Indian foods section. Look for garam masala in the spice aisle.
To make soft bread crumbs: Tear bread into pieces and place in a food processor or blender. Cover and pulse until crumbs form. One slice of bread yields ½ to ¾ cup crumbs.

HEALTHY GREEK BEAN DIP

Folks will love to eat their veggies when this zesty crowd-pleasing dip is nearby. It's a fresh alternative to hummus, comes together in no time, can be made ahead and even stores in the freezer!

—KELLY SILVERS EDMOND, OK

PREP: 15 MIN. • **COOK:** 2 HOURS
MAKES: 3 CUPS

- 2 **cans (15 ounces each) cannellini beans, rinsed and drained**
- ¼ **cup water**
- ¼ **cup finely chopped roasted sweet red peppers**
- 2 **tablespoons finely chopped red onion**
- 2 **tablespoons olive oil**
- 2 **tablespoons lemon juice**
- 1 **tablespoon snipped fresh dill**
- 2 **garlic cloves, minced**
- ¼ **teaspoon salt**
- ¼ **teaspoon pepper**
- 1 **small cucumber, peeled, seeded and finely chopped**
- ½ **cup fat-free plain Greek yogurt**
   Additional snipped fresh dill
   Baked pita chips or assorted fresh vegetables

Process beans and water in a food processor until smooth. Transfer to a greased 1½-qt. slow cooker. Add the next eight ingredients. Cook, covered, on low until heated through, 2-3 hours. Stir in cucumber and yogurt; cool slightly. Sprinkle with additional dill. Serve warm or cold with chips or assorted fresh vegetables.

Freeze option: Omitting cucumber, yogurt and additional dill, freeze cooled dip in freezer containers. To use, thaw in refrigerator overnight. To serve dip warm, heat through in a saucepan, stirring occasionally. Or serve cold. Stir the cucumber and yogurt into finished dip; sprinkle with additional dill. Serve with chips or vegetables.

Per ¼ cup: 86 cal., 3g fat (0 sat. fat), 0 chol., 260mg sod., 11g carb. (1g sugars, 3g fiber), 4g pro.
Diabetic Exchanges: 1 starch, ½ fat.

ASIAN WRAPS

PREP: 30 MIN. • **COOK:** 3½ HOURS
MAKES: 1 DOZEN

- 2 **pounds boneless skinless chicken breast halves**
- ¼ **cup reduced-sodium soy sauce**
- ¼ **cup ketchup**
- ¼ **cup honey**
- 2 **tablespoons minced fresh gingerroot**
- 2 **tablespoons sesame oil**
- 1 **small onion, finely chopped**
- 2 **tablespoons cornstarch**
- 2 **tablespoons water**
- 12 **round rice papers (8 inches)**
- 3 **cups broccoli coleslaw mix**
- ¾ **cup crispy chow mein noodles**

1. Place chicken in a 3-qt. slow cooker. In a small bowl, whisk soy sauce, ketchup, honey, ginger and oil; stir in onion. Pour over the chicken. Cook, covered, on low 3-4 hours or until chicken is tender. Remove chicken; shred with two forks and refrigerate until assembly.

2. In a small bowl, mix cornstarch and water until smooth; gradually stir into honey mixture. Cook, covered, on high 20-30 minutes or until sauce is thickened. Toss chicken with ¾ cup sauce; reserve remaining sauce for serving.

3. Fill a large shallow dish partway with water. Dip a rice paper wrapper into water just until pliable, about 45 seconds (do not soften completely); allow excess water to drip off.

4. Place wrapper on a flat surface. Layer ¼ cup coleslaw, ⅓ cup chicken mixture and 1 tablespoon noodles across bottom third of wrapper. Fold in both sides of wrapper; fold bottom over filling, then roll up tightly. Place on a serving plate, seam side down. Repeat with remaining ingredients. Serve with reserved sauce.

Per 1 wrap: 195 cal., 5g fat (1g sat. fat), 42mg chol., 337mg sod., 21g carb. (8g sugars, 1g fiber), 17g pro.
Diabetic Exchanges: 2 lean meat, 1½ starch, ½ fat.

HEALTHY GREEK BEAN DIP

"Loaded with flavor, my Asian Wraps take a healthy approach to a takeout classic. Instead of ordering Chinese, give these savory bites a try!"

—MELISSA HANSEN MILWAUKEE, WI

ASIAN WRAPS

SLOW COOKER
MARINATED
MUSHROOMS

CRANBERRY HOT WINGS

SLOW COOKER MARINATED MUSHROOMS

Here's a terrific healthy addition to any buffet spread. Mushrooms and pearl onions seasoned with herbs, balsamic vinegar and red wine are terrific as an appetizer or alongside a beef roast.
—**COURTNEY WILSON** FRESNO, CA

PREP: 15 MIN. • **COOK:** 6 HOURS
MAKES: 20 SERVINGS

- 2 **pounds medium fresh mushrooms**
- 1 **package (14.4 ounces) frozen pearl onions, thawed**
- 4 **garlic cloves, minced**
- 2 **cups reduced-sodium beef broth**
- ½ **cup dry red wine**
- 3 **tablespoons balsamic vinegar**
- 3 **tablespoons olive oil**
- 1 **teaspoon salt**
- 1 **teaspoon dried basil**
- ½ **teaspoon dried thyme**
- ½ **teaspoon pepper**
- ¼ **teaspoon crushed red pepper flakes**

Place mushrooms, onions and garlic in a 5- or 6-qt. slow cooker. In a small bowl, whisk remaining ingredients; pour over mushrooms. Cook, covered, on low until mushrooms are tender, 6-8 hours.

Freeze option: Freeze the cooled mushrooms and juices in freezer containers. To use, partially thaw in refrigerator overnight. Microwave, covered, on high in a microwave-safe dish until heated through, stirring gently and adding a little broth or water if necessary.

TOP TIP

MAKE IT A BUFFET

For an appetizer buffet that serves as a meal, offer five or six different appetizers (including some substantial selections) and plan on eight to nine pieces per guest. Rely on a few slow-cooked bites. Not only can you use the slow cooker to keep the appetizers warm, but you'll also save yourself time in the kitchen.

CRANBERRY HOT WINGS

Cranberry wings remind me of all the wonderful celebrations and parties we've had through the years. My daughter's friends can't get enough of them.
—**NOREEN MCCORMICK DANEK** CROMWELL, CT

PREP: 45 MIN. • **COOK:** 3 HOURS
MAKES: ABOUT 4 DOZEN

- 1 **can (14 ounces) jellied cranberry sauce**
- ½ **cup orange juice**
- ¼ **cup hot pepper sauce**
- 2 **tablespoons soy sauce**
- 2 **tablespoons honey**
- 1 **tablespoon packed brown sugar**
- 1 **tablespoon Dijon mustard**
- 2 **teaspoons garlic powder**
- 1 **teaspoon dried minced onion**
- 1 **garlic clove, minced**
- 5 **pounds chicken wings (about 24 wings)**
- 1 **teaspoon salt**
- 4 **teaspoons cornstarch**
- 2 **tablespoons cold water**

1. Whisk together first 10 ingredients. For chicken, use a sharp knife to cut through two wing joints; discard wing tips. Place wings in a 6-qt. slow cooker; sprinkle with salt. Pour cranberry mixture over top. Cook, covered, on low until tender, 3-4 hours.

2. To serve, remove the chicken wings to a 15x10x1-in. pan; arrange in a single layer. Preheat broiler.

3. Transfer cooking juices to a skillet; skim fat. Bring juices to a boil; cook until mixture is reduced by half, 15-20 minutes, stirring occasionally. Mix the cornstarch and water until smooth; stir into juices. Return to a boil, stirring constantly; cook and stir until thickened, 1-2 minutes.

4. Meanwhile, broil wings 3-4 in. from heat until lightly browned, 2-3 minutes. Brush with glaze before serving. Serve with remaining glaze.

SLOW COOKER
MIXED FRUIT &
PISTACHIO CAKE

SLOW COOKER MIXED FRUIT & PISTACHIO CAKE

This cake is easy to make on a lazy day and a guaranteed-delicious dessert for several days, if you can make it last that long. It's wonderful for the fall and even the holidays.

—**NANCY HEISHMAN** LAS VEGAS, NV

PREP: 20 MIN.
COOK: 2 HOURS + COOLING
MAKES: 8 SERVINGS

- 1½ cups all-purpose flour
- 1½ teaspoons ground cinnamon
- ½ teaspoon baking soda
- ½ teaspoon baking powder
- ½ teaspoon ground allspice
- ¼ teaspoon salt
- 1 can (8 ounces) jellied cranberry sauce
- ⅓ cup packed brown sugar
- ⅓ cup buttermilk
- ¼ cup butter, melted
- 2 teaspoons grated orange peel
- ½ teaspoon orange extract
- 1 large egg
- 1 cup mixed dried fruit bits
- 1 cup pistachios
  Sweetened whipped cream, optional

1. Whisk together first six ingredients. In another bowl, combine the next seven ingredients. Add cranberry mixture to flour mixture; stir until smooth. Add dried fruit and pistachios.

2. Pour batter into a greased 1½-qt. baking dish; place in a 6-qt. slow cooker. Lay a 14x12-in. piece of parchment paper over top of slow cooker under the lid. Cook, covered, on high until a toothpick inserted in center comes out clean, about 2½ hours. Remove dish from slow cooker to a wire rack. Cool 30 minutes before inverting onto a serving platter.

3. Cut cake into wedges with a serrated knife; if desired, serve with sweetened whipped cream.

CHAMPIONSHIP BEAN DIP

CHAMPIONSHIP BEAN DIP

My friends and neighbors expect me to bring this irresistible dip to every gathering. When I arrive they ask, "You brought your bean dip, didn't you?" If there are leftovers, we use them to make bean and cheese burritos the next day.

—**WENDI WAVRIN LAW** OMAHA, NE

PREP: 10 MIN. • **COOK:** 2 HOURS
MAKES: 4½ CUPS

- 1 can (16 ounces) refried beans
- 1 cup picante sauce
- 1 cup shredded Monterey Jack cheese
- 1 cup shredded cheddar cheese
- ¾ cup sour cream
- 3 ounces cream cheese, softened
- 1 tablespoon chili powder
- ¼ teaspoon ground cumin
  Tortilla chips and salsa

In a large bowl, combine the first eight ingredients; transfer to a 1½-qt. slow cooker. Cover and cook on high for 2 hours or until heated through, stirring once or twice. Serve with tortilla chips and salsa.

TOP TIP

HAVE IT YOUR WAY
Don't be afraid to add your own twist to Championship Bean Dip. Replace half of the beans with cooked taco meat or grilled chicken you've shredded. Add a few drops of hot pepper sauce or leave out the cumin. Work in a little bit of color by stirring in finely chopped chives, fresh cilantro or tomatoes.

CINNAMON
SPICED APPLES

1. In a 3-qt. slow cooker, combine the first six ingredients. Cook, covered, on low 40 minutes.

2. Stir in ham; cook 20 minutes longer or until heated through. Serve warm with vegetables or chips.

EAT SMART

SLOW COOKER LAVA CAKE

Because I love chocolate, this decadent slow-cooked cake has long been a family favorite. This cake can be served warm or cold. It's your call!

—ELIZABETH FARRELL HAMILTON, MT

PREP: 15 MIN.
COOK: 2 HOURS + STANDING
MAKES: 8 SERVINGS

- 1 cup all-purpose flour
- 1 cup packed brown sugar, divided
- 5 tablespoons baking cocoa, divided
- 2 teaspoons baking powder
- ¼ teaspoon salt
- ½ cup fat-free milk
- 2 tablespoons canola oil
- ½ teaspoon vanilla extract
- ⅛ teaspoon ground cinnamon
- 1¼ cups hot water

1. In a large bowl, whisk flour, ½ cup brown sugar, 3 tablespoons cocoa, baking powder and salt. In another bowl, whisk milk, oil and vanilla until blended. Add to flour mixture; stir just until moistened.

2. Spread into a 3-qt. slow cooker coated with cooking spray. In a small bowl, mix cinnamon and the remaining brown sugar and cocoa; stir in hot water. Pour over batter (do not stir).

3. Cook, covered, on high 2 to 2½ hours or until a toothpick inserted in cake portion comes out clean. Turn off slow cooker; let stand 15 minutes before serving.

Per serving: 207 cal., 4g fat (0 sat. fat), 0 chol., 191mg sod., 41g carb. (28g sugars, 1g fiber), 3g pro.

CINNAMON SPICED APPLES

If you're feeling festive, scoop some vanilla ice cream over a bowl of my cinnamon spiced apples. They're homey, aromatic and just plain heavenly.

—AMIE POWELL KNOXVILLE, TN

PREP: 15 MIN. • **COOK:** 3 HOURS
MAKES: 6 CUPS

- ⅓ cup sugar
- ¼ cup packed brown sugar
- 1 tablespoon cornstarch
- 3 teaspoons ground cinnamon
- ⅛ teaspoon ground nutmeg
- 6 large Granny Smith apples, peeled and cut into eighths
- ¼ cup butter, cubed

In a small bowl, mix first five ingredients. Place apples in a greased 5-qt. slow cooker; add sugar mixture and toss to coat. Top with butter. Cook, covered, on low 3-4 hours or until apples are tender, stirring once.

CHIPOTLE HAM & CHEESE DIP

If you like throwing dinner parties for friends, you just can't beat a convenient slow cooker appetizer like this one. Who wants to be stuck in the kitchen? Just set the slow cooker on low and enjoy visiting with your guests.

—LISA RENSHAW KANSAS CITY, MO

PREP: 15 MIN. • **COOK:** 1 HOUR
MAKES: 7 CUPS

- 2 packages (8 ounces each) cream cheese, cubed
- 2 cups (8 ounces) shredded Gouda cheese
- 1 can (12 ounces) evaporated milk
- 1 cup (4 ounces) shredded cheddar cheese
- 2 tablespoons chopped chipotle pepper in adobo sauce
- 1 teaspoon ground cumin
- 2 cups diced fully cooked ham
  Fresh vegetables or tortilla chips

JALAPENO POPPER & SAUSAGE DIP

My workplace had an appetizer contest, and I won it with my jalapeno and cheese dip. Every time I take it anywhere, folks empty the slow cooker.

—BEV SLABIK DILWORTH, MN

PREP: 15 MIN. • **COOK:** 3 HOURS
MAKES: 24 SERVINGS (¼ CUP EACH)

- 1 pound bulk spicy pork sausage
- 2 packages (8 ounces each) cream cheese, cubed
- 4 cups shredded Parmesan cheese (about 12 ounces)
- 1 cup (8 ounces) sour cream
- 1 can (4 ounces) chopped green chilies, undrained
- 1 can (4 ounces) diced jalapeno peppers, undrained
  Assorted fresh vegetables

1. In a large skillet, cook sausage over medium heat 6-8 minutes or until no longer pink, breaking into crumbles. Using a slotted spoon, transfer sausage to a 3-qt. slow cooker.
2. Stir in cream cheese, Parmesan cheese, sour cream, chilies and peppers. Cook, covered, on low 3 to 3½ hours or until heated through. Stir before serving. Serve with vegetables.

TOP TIP

ENDLESS OPTIONS
Spicy pork sausage gives this cheesy dip a kick, but feel free to use ground beef or turkey or even cooked Italian sausage. Consider serving the thick dip with taco, corn or pita chips, or offer it alongside slices of toasted French bread baguette slices.

ONE-BITE TAMALES

I have always loved Mexican foods, but when I went to a potluck and tasted these, I had to ask for the recipe. The bite-size tamales come together so much easier than the traditional type. Keep them in the slow cooker during the party so they stay warm the whole time. You'll find great Southwestern flavor in every bite!

—DOLORES JAYCOX GRETNA, LA

PREP: 40 MIN. • **COOK:** 3 HOURS 20 MIN.
MAKES: ABOUT 5½ DOZEN

- 1¼ cups cornmeal
- ½ cup all-purpose flour
- 5¾ cups V8 juice, divided
- 4 teaspoons chili powder, divided
- 4 teaspoons ground cumin, divided
- 2 teaspoons salt, divided
- 1 teaspoon garlic powder
- ½ to 1 teaspoon cayenne pepper
- 1 pound bulk spicy pork sausage
  Corn chip scoops

1. Preheat oven to 350°. Mix cornmeal, flour, ¾ cup V8 juice, 2 teaspoons chili powder, 2 teaspoons cumin, 1 teaspoon salt, garlic powder and cayenne. Add sausage; mix lightly but thoroughly. Shape into 1-in. balls.
2. Place meatballs on a greased rack in a 15x10-in. pan. Bake until cooked through, 20-25 minutes.
3. Meanwhile, in a 4-qt. slow cooker, mix remaining V8 juice, chili powder, cumin and salt. Gently stir in meatballs. Cook, covered, on low until heated through, 3-4 hours. Serve with tortilla chip scoops.

ONE-BITE
TAMALES

SLOW COOKER
KEY LIME FONDUE

NO-GUILT BEEFY NACHOS

It's true! You can nosh on nachos and feel good about it! This meaty topping has less fat and sodium than typical nacho beef because you use lean meat and make your own seasoning. The versatile dish is great for a party and takes advantage of slow cooking. It even keeps well in the freezer for last-minute snacking. What more could a busy family cook ask for?

—CAROL BETZ GRAND RAPIDS, MI

PREP: 15 MIN. • **COOK:** 4 HOURS
MAKES: 20 SERVINGS (2½ QUARTS)

- 2 **pounds lean ground beef (90% lean)**
- 1 **can Ranch Style beans (pinto beans in seasoned tomato sauce), undrained**
- 2 **tablespoons chili powder**
- 1 **tablespoon brown sugar**
- 2 **teaspoons ground cumin**
- 2 **teaspoons ground coriander**
- 1 **teaspoon dried oregano**
- 1 **teaspoon cayenne pepper**
- 1 **tablespoon cider vinegar**
- ¾ **teaspoon salt**
  Baked tortilla chips
  Shredded cheddar cheese, lettuce, sour cream and guacamole, optional

Combine first eight ingredients in a 4-qt. slow cooker. Cook, covered, on low until meat is crumbly, 4-6 hours. Stir in vinegar and salt. Serve with tortilla chips and, if desired, toppings.

Freeze option: Freeze cooled meat mixture in freezer containers. To use, partially thaw in refrigerator overnight. Heat through in a saucepan, stirring occasionally and adding a little water if necessary. Serve with chips and toppings if desired.

Per ½ cup beef mixture: 99 cal., 4g fat (2g sat. fat), 28mg chol., 232mg sod., 5g carb. (1g sugars, 1g fiber), 10g pro.

SLOW COOKER KEY LIME FONDUE

Love fondue but want something other than the milk chocolate variety? Dip into my key lime fondue! I like to use graham crackers, fresh fruit and cubed pound cake for dippers.

—ELISABETH LARSEN PLEASANT GROVE, UT

PREP: 5 MIN. • **COOK:** 50 MIN.
MAKES: 3 CUPS

- 1 **can (14 ounces) sweetened condensed milk**
- 12 **ounces white baking chocolate, finely chopped**
- ½ **cup Key lime or regular lime juice**
- 1 **tablespoon grated lime peel**
  Graham crackers, macaroon cookies, fresh strawberries and sliced ripe bananas

1. In a 1½-qt. slow cooker, combine milk, white chocolate and lime juice.
2. Cook, covered, on low 50-60 minutes or until chocolate is melted. Stir in lime peel. Serve with graham crackers, cookies and fruit.

NO-GUILT
BEEFY
NACHOS

"Spoil yourself or those you love with these delightful portable custards. Here's a cute take on the Mexican dessert classic. Tuck a jar into your lunch box for a sweet treat."

—MEGUMI GARCIA MILWAUKEE, WI

SLOW COOKER
FLAN IN A JAR

SLOW COOKER FLAN IN A JAR

PREP: 25 MIN.
COOK: 2 HOURS + COOLING
MAKES: 6 SERVINGS

- ½ cup sugar
- 1 tablespoon plus 3 cups hot water (110°-115°)
- 6 canning jars (4 ounces each) with lids and bands
- 1 cup coconut or whole milk
- ⅓ cup whole milk
- ⅓ cup sweetened condensed milk
- 2 large eggs plus 1 large egg yolk, lightly beaten
  Pinch salt
- 1 teaspoon vanilla extract
- 1 teaspoon dark rum, optional

1. In a small heavy saucepan, spread sugar; cook, without stirring, over medium-low heat until it begins to melt. Gently drag melted sugar to center of pan so sugar melts evenly. Cook, stirring constantly, until melted sugar turns a deep amber color, about 2 minutes. Immediately remove from heat and carefully stir in 1 tablespoon hot water. Quickly pour into jars.

2. In a small saucepan, heat coconut milk and whole milk until bubbles form around sides of pan; remove from heat. In a large bowl, whisk condensed milk, eggs, egg yolk and salt until blended but not foamy. Slowly stir in hot milk; stir in vanilla and, if desired, rum. Strain through a fine sieve. Pour the egg mixture into prepared jars. Center lids on jars; screw on bands until fingertip tight.

3. Add remaining hot water to a 6-qt. slow cooker; place jars in slow cooker. Cook, covered, on high 2 hours or until centers are set. Cool 10 minutes on a wire rack. Remove jars to a 13x9-in. baking pan filled halfway with ice water; cool 10 minutes. Refrigerate until cold, about 1 hour. Run a knife around sides of jars; invert flans onto dessert plates.

CHEESE-TRIO ARTICHOKE & SPINACH SPREAD

No appetizer lineup is complete without at least one amazing spread, and this is it! Creamy, cheesy and chock-full of veggies, it will quickly become your new go-to party contribution.

—**DIANE SPEARE** KISSIMMEE, FL

PREP: 20 MIN. • **COOK:** 2 HOURS
MAKES: 4 CUPS

- 1 cup chopped fresh mushrooms
- 1 tablespoon butter
- 2 garlic cloves, minced
- 1½ cups mayonnaise
- 1 package (8 ounces) cream cheese, softened
- 1 cup plus 2 tablespoons grated Parmesan cheese, divided
- 1 cup (4 ounces) shredded part-skim mozzarella cheese, divided
- 1 can (14 ounces) water-packed artichoke hearts, rinsed, drained and chopped
- 1 package (10 ounces) frozen chopped spinach, thawed and squeezed dry
- ¼ cup chopped sweet red pepper
  Toasted French bread baguette slices

1. In a large skillet, saute mushrooms in butter until tender. Add garlic; cook 1 minute longer.

2. In a large bowl, combine the mayonnaise, cream cheese, 1 cup Parmesan cheese and ¾ cup mozzarella cheese. Add the mushroom mixture, artichokes, spinach and red pepper.

3. Transfer to a 3-qt slow cooker. Sprinkle with remaining cheeses. Cover and cook on low for 2-3 hours or until heated through. Serve with toasted baguette slices.

PINEAPPLE-ORANGE SPICED TEA

The sweet aroma of this tea wafting from a slow cooker warms the dreariest day. My daughter served it for a holiday open house, and coffee drinkers were instantly converted. I bring it to the office to spice up our break-room beverage selections.

—**CAROLE J. DRENNAN** ABILENE, TX

PREP: 15 MIN. • **COOK:** 2 HOURS
MAKES: 12 SERVINGS (1 CUP EACH)

- 2 quarts boiling water
- 16 individual tea bags
- 2 cinnamon sticks (3 inches)
- 1 piece fresh gingerroot (½ inch), peeled and thinly sliced
- 4 whole cloves
- 1 cup sugar
- 1 can (12 ounces) frozen orange juice concentrate, thawed
- 1 can (12 ounces) frozen pineapple juice concentrate, thawed
- 1 cup pomegranate or cranberry juice
- ½ cup lemon juice
  Orange slices, optional

1. In a 5- or 6-qt. slow cooker, combine boiling water and tea bags. Cover and let stand 5 minutes.

2. Meanwhile, place cinnamon sticks, ginger and cloves on a double thickness of cheesecloth. Gather corners of cloth to enclose seasonings; tie securely with string. Discard tea bags. Stir in the remaining ingredients; add spice bag. Cook, covered, on low until heated through, 2-3 hours. Discard spice bag. Stir before serving. If desired, serve with orange slices.

ASPARAGUS
HAM DINNER,
PAGE 132

Stovetop Suppers

In a hurry to put dinner on the table? Who isn't? From soccer moms to empty nesters, everyone has **the need for speed** when it comes to dinner. See this section of family-friendly stovetop recipes when you need **meal-in-one specialties** that come together fast!

Beef & Ground Beef

BROCCOLI BEEF STIR-FRY

My family often requests this tasty combination of tender beef and nutritious vegetables. It's especially satisfying in the summer when I use my garden-grown broccoli and onions.
—**RUTH STAHL** SHEPHERD, MT

START TO FINISH: 25 MIN.
MAKES: 4 SERVINGS

- 3 tablespoons cornstarch, divided
- 2 tablespoons plus ½ cup water, divided
- ½ teaspoon garlic powder
- 1 pound boneless beef top round steak, cut into thin 3-inch strips
- 2 tablespoons vegetable oil, divided
- 4 cups fresh broccoli florets
- 1 small onion, cut into wedges
- ⅓ cup soy sauce
- 2 tablespoons brown sugar
- 1 teaspoon ground ginger
  Hot cooked rice

1. In a large resealable bag, combine 2 tablespoons cornstarch, 2 tablespoons water and garlic powder; add beef. Seal bag and turn to coat.
2. In a large skillet or wok over medium-high heat, stir-fry beef in 1 tablespoon oil until beef is no longer pink; remove and keep warm.
3. Stir-fry broccoli and onion in remaining oil for 4-5 minutes. Return beef to pan.
4. In a small bowl, combine the soy sauce, brown sugar, ginger, remaining cornstarch and water until smooth; add to the pan. Cook and stir for 2 minutes or until thickened. Serve with rice.

STEAKS WITH MUSHROOMS

I cut the small steaks off a good roast, then individually wrap and freeze them so I can take out only the number of them I need.
—**JEANETTE CAKOUROS** BRUNSWICK, ME

START TO FINISH: 25 MIN.
MAKES: 2 SERVINGS

- 2 boneless beef sirloin steaks (5 ounces each)
- ½ teaspoon salt
- ¼ teaspoon pepper
- 2 tablespoons butter
- 1 cup sliced fresh mushrooms

1. Rub both sides of steaks with salt and pepper. In a large skillet, cook steaks in butter until meat reaches desired doneness (for medium-rare, a thermometer should read 145°; for medium, 160°; for well-done, 170°). Remove and keep warm.
2. In the same skillet, saute mushrooms until tender. Serve with steaks.

EAT SMART

FETA STEAK TACOS

These tacos have the perfect combo of Mexican and Mediterranean flavors. They're a big hit with my family.
—**DEBBIE REID** CLEARWATER, FL

START TO FINISH: 30 MIN.
MAKES: 8 SERVINGS

- 1 beef flat iron steak or top sirloin steak (1¼ pounds), cut into thin strips
- ¼ cup Greek vinaigrette
- ½ cup fat-free plain Greek yogurt
- 2 teaspoons lime juice
- 1 tablespoon oil from sun-dried tomatoes
- 1 small green pepper, cut into thin strips
- 1 small onion, cut into thin strips
- ¼ cup chopped oil-packed sun-dried tomatoes
- ¼ cup sliced Greek olives
- 8 whole wheat tortillas (8 inches), warmed
- ¼ cup crumbled garlic and herb feta cheese
  Lime wedges

1. In a large bowl, toss beef with vinaigrette; let stand 15 minutes. In a small bowl, mix yogurt and lime juice.
2. In a large skillet, heat oil from sun-dried tomatoes over medium-high heat. Add pepper and onion; cook and stir for 3-4 minutes or until crisp-tender. Remove to a small bowl; stir in sun-dried tomatoes and olives.
3. Place same skillet over medium-high heat. Add beef; cook and stir for 2-3 minutes or until meat is no longer pink. Remove from pan.
4. Serve steak and pepper mixture in tortillas; top with cheese. Serve with yogurt mixture and lime wedges.
Per 1 taco with 1 tablespoon yogurt mixture: 317 cal., 15g fat (4g sat. fat), 48mg chol., 372mg sod., 25g carb. (2g sugars, 3g fiber), 20g pro.
Diabetic Exchanges: 3 lean meat, 2 fat, 1½ starch.

FETA STEAK
TACOS

SHORT RIB
POUTINE

BEEF STROGANOFF

Creamy and comforting, you'll crave this hearty beef Stroganoff no matter the weather.

—**PATTY RODY** PUYALLUP, WA

START TO FINISH: 30 MIN.
MAKES: 5 SERVINGS

- 5 tablespoons all-purpose flour, divided
- ½ teaspoon salt
- 1 pound beef top sirloin steak, cut into thin strips
- 4 tablespoons butter, divided
- 1 cup sliced fresh mushrooms
- ½ cup chopped sweet onion
- 1 garlic clove, minced
- 1 tablespoon tomato paste
- 1¼ cups beef broth
- 1 cup (8 ounces) sour cream
- 2 tablespoons sherry or beef broth
  Hot cooked egg noodles or brown rice

1. In a large resealable plastic bag, combine 2 tablespoons flour and ½ teaspoon salt. Add beef, a few pieces at a time, and shake to coat. In a large skillet over medium-high heat, brown beef in 2 tablespoons butter. Add mushrooms and onion; cook and stir until vegetables are tender. Add garlic; cook for 1 minute longer. Remove and keep warm.

2. In the same skillet, melt remaining butter. Stir in the tomato paste and remaining flour until smooth. Gradually add broth; bring to a boil. Cook and stir for 2 minutes or until thickened.

3. Carefully return beef mixture to the pan. Add sour cream and sherry; heat through (do not boil). Serve with noodles or rice.

TOP TIP

PERK IT UP

I add an envelope of ranch salad dressing/dip mix to the sour cream before stirring it into the rice or noodles. I also sprinkle in a few teaspoons of dill weed."

—**KIM PIAZZA** DILLINGHAM, AK

SHORT RIB POUTINE

This dish combines the hearty, spicy flavors of my beloved slow cooker short ribs with my all-time favorite comfort food: fries and gravy. With a little prep in the morning, it's just about ready when I come home from work (plus, the kitchen smells amazing). If you are sensitive to spice, reduce the amount of Sriracha chili sauce.

—**ERIN DEWITT** LONG BEACH, CA

PREP: 45 MIN. • **COOK:** 6 HOURS
MAKES: 4 SERVINGS

- 1 pound well-trimmed boneless beef short ribs
- 3 tablespoons all-purpose flour
- ½ teaspoon pepper
- 2 tablespoons olive oil
- 1 medium onion, coarsely chopped
- 4 garlic cloves, minced
- 1½ cups beef stock, divided
- ¼ cup Sriracha Asian hot chili sauce
- 3 tablespoons ketchup
- 2 tablespoons Worcestershire sauce
- 1 tablespoon packed brown sugar
- 3 cups frozen french-fried potatoes (about 11 ounces)
- 1 cup cheese curds or 4 ounces white cheddar cheese, broken into small chunks

1. Toss short ribs with flour and pepper, shaking off excess; reserve remaining flour mixture. In a large skillet, heat oil over medium-high heat; brown ribs on all sides. Transfer to a 3-qt. slow cooker, reserving drippings.

2. In the same skillet, saute onion in drippings over medium heat until tender, 2-3 minutes. Add garlic; cook and stir 1 minute. Stir in 1 cup stock; bring to a boil, stirring to loosen browned bits.

3. In a small bowl, whisk reserved flour mixture, chili sauce, ketchup, Worcestershire sauce, brown sugar and remaining stock until smooth; stir into onion mixture. Pour over ribs.

4. Cook, covered, on low until ribs are tender, 6-8 hours. Remove ribs; shred with two forks and keep warm. Skim fat from onion mixture; puree using an immersion blender. (Or, cool slightly and puree in a blender; return to slow cooker to heat through.)

5. Cook potatoes according to package directions. Serve beef over potatoes; top with gravy and cheese.

COUNTRY-FRIED STEAKS

My mother was raised in the South, and this down-home recipe reminds me of her. It calls for cube steak instead of round steak, so there's no need to pound the meat. I just dip and coat the beef, then cook it in my cast-iron skillet.

—**BONNIE MALLOY** NORWOOD, PA

START TO FINISH: 30 MIN.
MAKES: 4 SERVINGS

- 5 tablespoons all-purpose flour, divided
- ¼ cup cornmeal
- ½ teaspoon salt
- ¼ teaspoon pepper
- 4 beef cube steaks (4 ounces each)
- 1 large egg white
- 1 teaspoon water
- 2 tablespoons canola oil, divided

GRAVY

- 1 tablespoon butter
- 2 tablespoons all-purpose flour
- 1½ cups 2% milk
- 1 teaspoon beef bouillon granules
- ½ teaspoon dried marjoram
- ¼ teaspoon dried thyme
- ⅛ teaspoon pepper

1. Combine 3 tablespoons flour, cornmeal, salt and pepper; set aside. Coat steaks with remaining flour. Beat egg white and water. Dip the steaks in the egg mixture, then dredge in the cornmeal mixture.

2. In a large skillet, cook two steaks in 1 tablespoon oil over medium-high heat for 5-7 minutes on each side or until crisp, lightly browned and cooked to desired doneness. Remove steaks and keep warm. Repeat with the remaining oil and steaks.

3. Meanwhile, for gravy, melt butter in a small saucepan; stir in flour until smooth. Gradually add milk. Bring to a boil over medium heat; cook and stir for 2 minutes or until thickened. Reduce heat to medium-low. Add the bouillon, marjoram, thyme and pepper; simmer, uncovered, for 4-5 minutes, stirring occasionally. Serve with steaks.

PORCUPINE MEATBALLS

These well-seasoned meatballs in a rich tomato sauce are one of my mom's best main dishes. I used to love this meal when I was growing up. I made it at home for my children, and now my daughters make it for their families.

—**DARLIS WILFER** WEST BEND, WI

PREP: 20 MIN. • **COOK:** 1 HOUR
MAKES: 4-6 SERVINGS

- ½ cup uncooked long grain rice
- ½ cup water
- ⅓ cup chopped onion
- 1 teaspoon salt
- ½ teaspoon celery salt
- ⅛ teaspoon pepper
- ⅛ teaspoon garlic powder
- 1 pound ground beef
- 2 tablespoons canola oil
- 1 can (15 ounces) tomato sauce
- 1 cup water
- 2 tablespoons brown sugar
- 2 teaspoons Worcestershire sauce

In a bowl, combine the first seven ingredients. Add beef and mix well. Shape into 1½-in. balls. In a large skillet, brown meatballs in oil; drain. Combine tomato sauce, water, brown sugar and Worcestershire sauce; pour over meatballs. Reduce heat; cover and simmer for 1 hour.

CATALINA TACO SALAD

The teen campers at the youth camp my husband directs love this quick and easy taco salad. Our daughter has requested it two years in a row for her birthday dinner.

—**KAY CURTIS** GUTHRIE, OK

START TO FINISH: 25 MIN.
MAKES: 12 SERVINGS

- 1½ pounds lean ground beef (90% lean)
- 3 cups shredded cheddar cheese
- 1 can (15 ounces) pinto beans, rinsed and drained
- 2 medium tomatoes, seeded and chopped
- 1 large onion, chopped
- 1 bunch romaine, torn
- 1 package (12 ounces) corn chips
- 1 bottle (24 ounces) Catalina salad dressing

1. In a large skillet, cook beef over medium heat until no longer pink; drain. Transfer to a large serving bowl.
2. Add the cheese, beans, tomatoes, onion, romaine and corn chips. Drizzle with dressing; gently toss to coat.

PEPPER STEAK WITH POTATOES

I added sliced red potatoes to one of my favorite recipes for Asian-style pepper steak. Now this hearty supper satisfies everyone at home, including hungry guys with big appetites.

—**KRISTINE MARRA** CLIFTON PARK, NY

START TO FINISH: 30 MIN.
MAKES: 6 SERVINGS

- 1½ pounds red potatoes (about 5 medium), sliced
- ½ cup water
- 1 cup beef broth
- 4 teaspoons cornstarch
- ⅛ teaspoon pepper
- 2 tablespoons olive oil, divided
- 1 pound beef top sirloin steak, thinly sliced
- 1 garlic clove, minced
- 1 medium green pepper, julienned
- 1 small onion, chopped

1. Place potatoes and water in a large microwave-safe dish. Microwave, covered, on high for 5-7 minutes or until tender.
2. Meanwhile, in a small bowl, mix broth, cornstarch and pepper until smooth. In a large skillet, heat 1 tablespoon oil over medium-high heat. Add beef; cook and stir for 2-3 minutes or until no longer pink. Add garlic; cook 1 minute longer. Remove from pan.
3. In the same pan, heat remaining oil. Add green pepper and onion; cook and stir until vegetables are crisp-tender. Stir cornstarch mixture and add to pan. Bring to a boil; cook and stir for 1-2 minutes or until sauce is thickened. Add potatoes and beef to pan; heat through.

Test Kitchen Note: This recipe was tested in a 1,100-watt microwave.
Per cup: 277 cal., 10g fat (2g sat. fat), 55mg chol., 179mg sod., 27g carb. (0 sugars, 3g fiber), 23g pro.
Diabetic Exchanges: 2 meat, 2 vegetable, 1 starch.

ROOTIN'-TOOTIN' CINCINNATI CHILI

Yes, there's root beer in this spicy chili, and it adds a nice touch of sweetness. Serve over spaghetti and let everyone add their own favorite toppings.

—**HOLLY GOMEZ** SEABROOK, NH

PREP: 25 MIN. • **COOK:** 30 MIN.
MAKES: 4 SERVINGS

- 1 pound ground beef
- 1 small onion, chopped
- 1 small green pepper, chopped
- 1 garlic clove, minced
- 1 can (14½ ounces) fire-roasted diced tomatoes, undrained
- 1 cup root beer
- 2 tablespoons chili powder
- 2 tablespoons tomato paste
- 2 tablespoons minced chipotle peppers in adobo sauce
- 1 tablespoon ground cumin
- 1 beef bouillon cube
  Hot cooked spaghetti
  Optional toppings: crushed tortilla chips, chopped green onions and shredded cheddar and Parmesan cheeses

1. In a large saucepan, cook the beef, onion and green pepper over medium heat until meat is no longer pink. Add garlic; cook 1 minute longer. Drain. Add the tomatoes, root beer, chili powder, tomato paste, chipotle peppers, cumin and bouillon. Bring to a boil.
2. Reduce heat; cover and simmer for 20-30 minutes to allow flavors to blend. Serve with spaghetti. Garnish with chips, green onions and cheeses if desired.

READER RAVE

"This chili has quite a kick. If you like, you can tame it down with some cream cheese or mild cheddar. It was loved by all."

—**LINDA CONNOR** TASTEOFHOME.COM

**PEPPER STEAK
WITH POTATOES**

BEEF TERIYAKI
NOODLES

BEEF TERIYAKI NOODLES

At our house, we love to combine fresh ingredients with convenience products. This version starts with beef, mushrooms and stir-fry veggies since we always have them on hand, but feel free make the dish your own. Use what's in the pantry to bring out your inner chef!

—RICHARD ROBINSON PARK FOREST, IL

START TO FINISH: 20 MIN.
MAKES: 4 SERVINGS

- 1 **envelope (4.6 ounces) lo mein noodles and teriyaki sauce mix**
- 1 **pound beef flat iron steak or top sirloin steak, cut into bite-size pieces**
- ¼ **teaspoon salt**
- ¼ **teaspoon pepper**
- 2 **tablespoons canola oil, divided**
- 2 **cups frozen pepper and onion stir-fry blend**
- 1 **cup sliced fresh mushrooms**

1. Prepare noodle mix according to package directions.
2. Meanwhile, sprinkle beef with salt and pepper. In a large skillet, heat 1 tablespoon oil over medium-high heat. Add beef; stir-fry for 6-8 minutes or until no longer pink. Remove from pan; discard drippings.
3. Stir-fry the vegetable blend and mushrooms in remaining oil 3-4 minutes or until vegetables are tender.
4. Return beef to pan. Stir in noodle mixture; heat through.

TOP TIP

FREEZE YOUR VEGETABLES

Freezing peppers and onions is a great way to enjoy garden produce when summer days are long gone. A medium green pepper, chopped, will yield about 1 cup. A large green pepper, chopped, will generally yield 1⅓ to 1½ cups. A medium onion, chopped, will equal about ½ cup; a large onion will yield about 1 cup. Store both green peppers and onions in heavy-duty resealable plastic freezer bags. Green peppers can be frozen for up to six months, and onions can be frozen for up to a year.

CUBAN GROUND BEEF HASH

Called *picadillo* in Spanish, this distinctive hash is terrific served over white rice or even inside plain omelets for a hearty breakfast.

—ADRIANNA STILL CRUZ WESTON, FL

START TO FINISH: 30 MIN.
MAKES: 6 SERVINGS

- 1½ **pounds ground beef**
- 1 **medium green pepper, chopped**
- 1 **medium onion, chopped**
- 1 **can (14½ ounces) diced tomatoes, undrained**
- 3 **tablespoons tomato paste**
- ⅓ **cup raisins**
- ⅓ **cup sliced pimiento-stuffed olives**
- 1 **tablespoon cider vinegar**
- 3 **garlic cloves, minced**
- 2 **teaspoons ground cumin**
- ½ **teaspoon salt**
- ½ **teaspoon pepper**
- ½ **cup frozen peas**
  Hot cooked rice

1. In a large skillet, cook the beef, green pepper and onion over medium heat until meat is no longer pink; drain. Stir in the tomatoes, tomato paste, raisins, olives, vinegar, garlic, cumin, salt and pepper.
2. Bring to a boil. Reduce heat; cover and simmer for 5 minutes. Add peas; cover and cook for 5 minutes longer or until heated through. Serve with rice.

STEAKS WITH POBLANO RELISH

Spice up mealtime with these juicy beef tenderloin steaks topped with a zippy Southwest-style poblano pepper and garlic relish.

—BILLIE MOSS WALNUT CREEK, CA

PREP: 10 MIN. + STANDING
COOK: 10 MIN.
MAKES: 2 SERVINGS

- ½ **poblano or Anaheim pepper, stem and seeds removed**
- 1 **unpeeled garlic clove**
- 1 **teaspoon minced fresh cilantro**
- ½ **teaspoon ground cumin, divided**
- ⅛ **teaspoon plus ¼ teaspoon chili powder, divided**
- 2 **beef tenderloin steaks (4 ounces each)**
- 1 **teaspoon olive oil**
  Dash salt and pepper

1. Broil pepper and garlic clove 4 in. from heat until skin on pepper blisters, about 10-12 minutes. Immediately place pepper and garlic in a bowl; cover and let stand for 15-20 minutes.
2. Peel pepper and garlic, discarding skins; finely chop and place in a small bowl. Stir in cilantro, ¼ teaspoon cumin and ⅛ teaspoon chili powder; set aside.
3. Rub steaks with oil. Combine salt, pepper and remaining cumin and chili powder; rub over steaks. In a nonstick skillet, cook steaks over medium-high heat for 5-7 minutes on each side or until meat reaches desired doneness (for medium-rare, a thermometer should read 145°; for medium, 160°; for well-done, 170°). Let stand for 5 minutes. Serve with poblano relish.
Test Kitchen Note: Wear disposable gloves when cutting hot peppers; the oils can burn skin. Avoid touching your face.
Per 1 steak with 2 tablespoons relish: 208 cal., 11g fat (3g sat. fat), 71mg chol., 133mg sod., 3g carb. (1g sugars, 1g fiber), 24g pro.
Diabetic Exchanges: 3 lean meat, ½ fat.

BEEF & SPINACH GYROS

EAT SMART

VEGGIE FLANK STEAK STIR-FRY

START TO FINISH: 30 MIN.
MAKES: 6 SERVINGS

- 1 can (14½ ounces) reduced-sodium beef broth
- 2 tablespoons reduced-sodium soy sauce
- 3 tablespoons cornstarch
- 2 tablespoons canola oil, divided
- 1 beef flank steak (1 pound), cut into thin strips
- 1 medium green pepper, cut into thin strips
- 1 medium sweet red pepper, cut into thin strips
- 2 medium zucchini, cut into thin strips
- 1 small onion, cut into thin strips
- 3 garlic cloves, minced
- 1 cup fresh snow peas
- 1 cup sliced fresh mushrooms
- 1 can (8 ounces) sliced water chestnuts, drained
  Hot cooked rice

1. Mix broth and soy sauce with cornstarch until smooth. Set aside.

2. In a large skillet, heat 1 tablespoon oil over medium-high heat. Add beef; stir-fry until no longer pink, 2-3 minutes. Remove from pan.

3. In same skillet, heat remaining oil. Stir-fry peppers about 2 minutes. Add zucchini, onion and garlic; cook and stir for 2 minutes longer. Add snow peas, mushrooms and water chestnuts. Stir-fry until crisp-tender, about 2 minutes more.

4. Stir cornstarch mixture and add to pan. Bring to a boil; cook and stir until sauce is thickened, 1-2 minutes. Return beef to skillet; heat through. Serve with hot cooked rice.

Per 1½ cups stir-fry: 229 cal., 11g fat (3g sat. fat), 37mg chol., 381mg sod., 16g carb. (5g sugars, 3g fiber), 18g pro.
Diabetic Exchanges: 2 lean meat, 1 vegetable, ½ starch.

BEEF & SPINACH GYROS

A gyro typically is made of meat, often lamb, roasted on a spit and served sandwich-style in folded pita bread. It's topped with tomato, onion and a Greek-style yogurt. Tradition takes a slight twist with the use of ground beef, spinach and ripe olives in this simple version. *Opa!*
—**MARY JOHNSON** COLOMA, WI

START TO FINISH: 25 MIN.
MAKES: 6 SERVINGS

- 1 pound lean ground beef (90% lean)
- 1 package (10 ounces) frozen chopped spinach, thawed and squeezed dry
- 6 green onions, chopped
- 1 can (2¼ ounces) sliced ripe olives, drained
- 2 teaspoons lemon-pepper seasoning, divided
- 1 large tomato, chopped
- 1 cup (8 ounces) fat-free plain yogurt
- ½ cup reduced-fat mayonnaise
- 6 pita breads (6 inches), halved
- 12 lettuce leaves
- 1 cup (4 ounces) crumbled feta cheese

1. In a large skillet, cook beef over medium heat until no longer pink. Add the spinach, onions, olives and 1 teaspoon lemon pepper; heat through. Stir in tomato; set aside.

2. In a small bowl, combine the yogurt, mayonnaise and remaining lemon pepper. Line pita halves with lettuce; fill with beef mixture and feta cheese. Serve with yogurt sauce.

"I like to fix a colorful stir-fry with savory strips of flank steak and plenty of veggies. We serve this dish over rice for a satisfying supper that's on the table in about a half-hour."
—**GAYLE LEWIS** YUCAIPA, CA

VEGGIE FLANK STEAK STIR-FRY

TOASTED
REUBENS

TOASTED REUBENS

New Yorkers say my Reubens taste like those served in the famous delis there. For a milder flavor, you can omit the horseradish.

—PATRICIA KILE ELIZABETHTOWN, PA

START TO FINISH: 20 MIN.
MAKES: 4 SERVINGS

- 4 teaspoons prepared mustard
- 8 slices rye bread
- 4 slices Swiss cheese
- 1 pound thinly sliced deli corned beef
- 1 can (8 ounces) sauerkraut, rinsed and well drained
- ½ cup mayonnaise
- 3 tablespoons ketchup
- 2 tablespoons sweet pickle relish
- 1 tablespoon prepared horseradish
- 2 tablespoons butter

1. Spread mustard over four slices of bread. Layer with cheese, corned beef and sauerkraut. In a small bowl, mix mayonnaise, ketchup, relish and horseradish; spread over remaining bread. Place over sauerkraut. Spread outsides of sandwiches with butter.
2. In a large skillet, toast sandwiches over medium heat for 3-4 minutes on each side or until golden brown and the cheese is melted.

ITALIAN BEEF STEW

Looking for a heartwarming meal-in-one on a chilly autumn evening? Try my hearty stew. Cubed steak makes it quick and economical.

—MARGARET PESCHKE HADLEY, NY

PREP: 20 MIN. • **COOK:** 1 HOUR
MAKES: 2 SERVINGS

- ¾ pound beef cubed steak, chopped
- 1 cup water
- 1 can (8 ounces) tomato sauce
- 1 small potato, peeled and cubed
- ½ cup sliced fresh carrot
- ½ small onion, cut into thin wedges
- ½ small sweet red pepper, chopped
- 1 tablespoon onion soup mix
- ½ teaspoon Italian seasoning
- ¼ teaspoon garlic powder
- ½ cup frozen peas

1. In a large saucepan coated with cooking spray, brown meat over medium heat for 5 minutes. Stir in the water, tomato sauce, potato, carrot, onion, red pepper, soup mix, Italian seasoning and garlic powder. Bring to a boil. Reduce heat; simmer, uncovered, for 45 minutes.
2. Stir in peas; simmer for 5-10 minutes longer or until vegetables are tender.

FAVORITE HAMBURGER STEW

I got this recipe from a woman at my church when I needed a way to use up a bounty of home-canned tomatoes. My husband loves it, and I like that it's easy to warm up for a carefree dinner in the winter months.
—**MARCIA CLAY** TRUMAN, MN

PREP: 20 MIN. • **COOK:** 65 MIN.
MAKES: 5 BATCHES (15 CUPS TOTAL)

- 2 pounds ground beef
- 2 medium onions, chopped
- 4 cans (14½ ounces each) stewed tomatoes, undrained
- 8 medium carrots, thinly sliced
- 4 celery ribs, thinly sliced
- 2 medium potatoes, peeled and cubed
- 2 cups water
- ½ cup uncooked long grain rice
- 1 to 2 tablespoons salt
- 1 to 2 teaspoons pepper

ADDITIONAL INGREDIENT (FOR EACH BATCH OF STEW)
- 1 cup water

1. In a Dutch oven, cook beef and onions over medium heat until meat is no longer pink; drain. Add the tomatoes, carrots, celery, potatoes, water, rice, salt and pepper; bring to a boil. Reduce heat; cover and simmer for 30 minutes or until vegetables and rice are tender.
2. Uncover; simmer for 20-30 minutes longer or until thickened.
Freeze option: Freeze in 3-cup portions for up to 3 months. To use frozen stew, thaw it in the refrigerator for 24 hours. Transfer to a saucepan; add water. Cook until hot and bubbly.

BEEF FAJITA SALAD

This easy salad features colorful peppers, beans, tomato and tender strips of beef. The beef marinates for only 10 minutes, but it gets great flavor from the lime juice, cilantro and chili powder.
—**ARDEENA HARRIS** ROANOKE, AL

START TO FINISH: 30 MIN.
MAKES: 4 SERVINGS

- ¼ cup lime juice
- 2 tablespoons minced fresh cilantro
- 1 garlic clove, minced
- 1 teaspoon chili powder
- ¾ pound beef top sirloin steak, cut into thin strips
- 1 medium green pepper, julienned
- 1 medium sweet red pepper, julienned
- 1 medium onion, sliced and halved
- 1 teaspoon olive oil
- 1 can (16 ounces) kidney beans, rinsed and drained
- 4 cups torn mixed salad greens
- 1 medium tomato, chopped
- 4 tablespoons fat-free sour cream
- 2 tablespoons salsa

1. In a large resealable plastic bag, combine the lime juice, cilantro, garlic and chili powder; add beef. Seal bag and turn to coat; refrigerate for 10 minutes, turning once.
2. Meanwhile, in a nonstick skillet, cook the peppers and onion in oil over medium-high heat for 5 minutes or until tender. Remove and keep warm. Add beef with marinade to the skillet; cook and stir for 4-5 minutes or until meat is tender and mixture comes to a boil. Add beans and pepper mixture; heat through.
3. Divide the salad greens and tomato among four bowls; top each with 1¼ cups beef mixture, 1 tablespoon sour cream and 1½ teaspoons salsa.

BARBECUED BEEF SANDWICHES

The great thing about this recipe—especially for non-cabbage lovers—is that you can't taste the cabbage in the meat. Yet, at the same time, the vegetable adds a nice heartiness and moistness to the sandwiches.
—**DENISE MARSHALL** BAGLEY, WI

PREP: 15 MIN. • **COOK:** 2½ HOURS
MAKES: 10 SERVINGS

- 2 pounds beef stew meat
- 2 cups water
- 4 cups shredded cabbage
- ½ cup barbecue sauce
- ½ cup ketchup
- ⅓ cup Worcestershire sauce
- 1 tablespoon prepared horseradish
- 1 tablespoon prepared mustard
- 10 hamburger or other sandwich buns, split

1. In a Dutch oven, combine the beef and water. Bring to a boil. Reduce heat; cover and simmer for 1½ hours or until tender. Drain cooking liquid, reserving ¾ cup.
2. Cool beef slightly; shred and return to the Dutch oven. Add the cabbage, barbecue sauce, ketchup, Worcestershire sauce, horseradish, mustard and the reserved cooking liquid. Cover and simmer for 1 hour. Serve warm in buns.

THAI SPINACH
BEEF SALAD

MOM'S SWEDISH MEATBALLS

Mom fixed these meatballs for all sorts of family dinners, potluck suppers and PTA meetings. After smelling the aromas of browning meat and caramelized onions, everyone will be ready to eat.

—MARYBETH MANK MESQUITE, TX

PREP: 30 MIN.
COOK: 40 MIN.
MAKES: 6 SERVINGS

- ¾ cup seasoned bread crumbs
- 1 medium onion, chopped
- 2 large eggs, lightly beaten
- ⅓ cup minced fresh parsley
- 1 teaspoon coarsely ground pepper
- ¾ teaspoon salt
- 2 pounds ground beef

GRAVY
- ½ cup all-purpose flour
- 2¾ cups 2% milk
- 2 cans (10½ ounces each condensed beef consomme, undiluted
- 1 tablespoon Worcestershire sauce
- 1 teaspoon coarsely ground pepper
- ¾ teaspoon salt

NOODLES
- 1 package (16 ounces) egg noodles
- ¼ cup butter, cubed
- ¼ cup minced fresh parsley

1. In a large bowl, combine the first six ingredients. Add beef; mix lightly but thoroughly. Shape into 1½-in. meatballs (about 36). In a large skillet over medium heat, brown meatballs in batches. Using a slotted spoon, remove to paper towels to drain, reserving drippings in pan.
2. For gravy, stir flour into drippings; cook over medium-high heat until light brown (do not burn). Gradually whisk in milk until smooth. Stir in the consomme, Worcestershire sauce, pepper and salt. Bring to a boil over medium-high heat; cook and stir for 2 minutes or until thickened.
3. Reduce heat to medium-low; return meatballs to pan. Cook, uncovered, 15-20 minutes longer or until meatballs are cooked through, stirring occasionally.
4. Meanwhile, cook noodles according to package directions. Drain; toss with butter. Serve with meatball mixture; sprinkle with parsley.

EAT SMART

THAI SPINACH BEEF SALAD

Try this main-dish salad and you'll certainly be satisfied. It's crunchy, meaty and a little bit spicy. Best of all, you can eat a big portion because it's good for you.

—JANET DINGLER CEDARTOWN, GA

START TO FINISH: 20 MIN.
MAKES: 4 SERVINGS

- ¼ cup lime juice
- 2 tablespoons brown sugar
- 2 tablespoons reduced-sodium soy sauce
- 1 teaspoon dried basil
- 1 teaspoon minced fresh mint or ½ teaspoon dried mint
- 1 teaspoon minced fresh gingerroot
- 1 pound beef top sirloin steak, cut into ¼-inch-thick strips
- 1 jalapeno pepper, seeded and chopped
- 1 garlic clove, minced
- 5 ounces fresh baby spinach (about 6 cups)
- 1 large sweet red pepper, julienned
- ½ medium cucumber, julienned

1. For dressing, mix first six ingredients until blended. Place a large nonstick skillet coated with cooking spray over medium-high heat. Add the beef and jalapeno; cook and stir until beef is no longer pink, 1-3 minutes. Add garlic; cook and stir for 1 minute. Remove from heat.
2. Place the spinach, red pepper and cucumber in a large bowl. Add beef; toss with dressing. Serve immediately.
Test Kitchen Note: Wear disposable gloves when cutting hot peppers; the oils can burn skin. Avoid touching your face.
Per 2 cups: 207 cal., 5g fat (2g sat. fat), 46mg chol., 383mg sod., 14g carb. (10g sugars, 2g fiber), 27g pro.
Diabetic Exchanges: 3 lean meat, 2 vegetable.

MOM'S SWEDISH
MEATBALLS

"Marinara sauce and tender meat are real comfort food, especially when served with mashed potatoes, rice or pasta."
—**DONNA-MARIE RYAN** TOPSFIELD, MA

BEEF BRISKET
MARINARA

BEEF BRISKET MARINARA

FAJITA BURGER WRAPS

PREP: 10 MIN. • **COOK:** 3¾ HOURS
MAKES: 10 SERVINGS

- 1 **fresh beef brisket (4 pounds)**
- ½ **teaspoon salt**
- ¼ **teaspoon pepper**
- 2 **tablespoons olive oil**
- 2 **celery ribs, finely chopped**
- 1 **medium carrot, finely chopped**
- ½ **cup dry red wine or beef broth**
- 1 **jar (24 ounces) marinara sauce**

1. Sprinkle brisket with salt and pepper. In a Dutch oven, heat oil over medium heat. Brown brisket on both sides. Remove from pan.
2. Add celery and carrot to same pan; cook and stir for 2-3 minutes or until crisp-tender. Add wine; cook, stirring to loosen browned bits from pan. Stir in marinara sauce.
3. Return brisket to pan; bring to a boil. Reduce heat; simmer, covered, 3½-4 hours or until meat is tender.
4. Remove brisket from pan. Skim fat from sauce. Cut brisket diagonally across the grain into thin slices; serve with sauce.
Per 5 ounces cooked beef with ½ cup sauce: 295 cal., 11g fat (3g sat. fat), 77mg chol., 307mg sod., 9g carb. (6g sugars, 1g fiber), 38g pro.
Diabetic Exchanges: 5 lean meat, ½ starch, ½ fat.

PIEROGI BEEF SKILLET

From-scratch pierogies are a real treat, but who has time to make them? This meal-in-one combines frozen pierogies with mixed veggies and quick-cooking ground beef.
—TASTE OF HOME TEST KITCHEN

START TO FINISH: 30 MIN.
MAKES: 4 SERVINGS

- 1 **pound ground beef**
- ½ **cup chopped onion**
- ¼ **cup all-purpose flour**
- 1 **can (14½ ounces) beef broth**
- 1 **package (16 ounces) frozen cheese and potato pierogies, thawed**
- 2 **cups frozen mixed vegetables, thawed and drained**
- ½ **teaspoon salt**

- ½ **teaspoon pepper**
- ½ **teaspoon Italian seasoning**
- ½ **cup shredded cheddar cheese**

1. In a large skillet, cook beef and onion over medium heat until meat is no longer pink; drain, reserving 3 tablespoons of drippings.
2. Sprinkle flour over beef and drippings; stir until blended. Gradually add beef broth. Bring to a boil; cook and stir for 2 minutes or until thickened.
3. Stir in the pierogies, vegetables and seasonings. Cook, uncovered, for 4-5 minutes or until heated through. Sprinkle with cheese.

FAJITA BURGER WRAPS

This combo gives you a tender burger, crisp veggies and a crunchy shell, plus fajita flavor. Kids love it!
—ANTONIO SMITH CANAL WINCHESTER, OH

START TO FINISH: 30 MIN.
MAKES: 4 SERVINGS

- 1 **pound lean ground beef (90% lean)**
- 2 **tablespoons fajita seasoning mix**
- 2 **teaspoons canola oil**
- 1 **medium green pepper, cut into thin strips**
- 1 **medium red sweet pepper, cut into thin strips**
- 1 **medium onion, halved and sliced**
- 4 **flour tortillas (10 inches)**
- ¾ **cup shredded cheddar cheese**

1. In a large bowl, combine beef and seasoning mix, mixing lightly but thoroughly. Shape into four ½-in.-thick patties.
2. In a large skillet, heat oil over medium heat. Add burgers; cook 4 minutes on each side. Remove from pan. In same skillet, add peppers and onion; cook and stir for 5-7 minutes or until lightly browned and tender.
3. On the center of each tortilla, place ½ cup pepper mixture, one burger and 3 tablespoons cheese. Fold sides of tortilla over burger; fold top and bottom to close, forming a square.
4. Wipe skillet clean. Place wraps in skillet, seam side down. Cook on medium heat for 1-2 minutes on each side or until golden brown and a thermometer inserted in beef reads 160°.

BAVARIAN POT ROAST

I've lived on a farm all my life, and this is one of my favorite meals. My family and the rural community we live in have a strong German background, so this Bavarian roast is a special treat!

—**RENEE SATTERSTROM** FREEPORT, IL

PREP: 20 MIN. • **COOK:** 2 HOURS 35 MIN.
MAKES: 12-15 SERVINGS

- 2 **tablespoons vegetable oil**
- 1 **beef chuck pot roast (about 5 pounds)**
- 1 **tablespoon ground cinnamon**
- 1 **tablespoon vinegar**
- 2 **teaspoons ground ginger**
- 1 to 1½ **teaspoons salt**
- 1½ **cups apple juice**
- 1 **cup water**
- 1 **can (8 ounces) tomato sauce**
- 1 **medium onion, chopped**
- 1 **bay leaf**
- 8 to 12 **ounces fresh whole mushrooms**

1. In a large Dutch oven, heat oil over high and brown meat on all sides. Combine all remaining ingredients except mushrooms; pour over meat. Cover and reduce heat to simmer. Cook for 2½-3 hours or until meat is tender. Transfer meat to a platter; keep warm. Add mushrooms to cooking juices; simmer for 5 minutes. With a slotted spoon, remove mushrooms and spoon over roast.

2. Meanwhile, reduce cooking juices to desired thickness by cooking over high heat. Spoon a portion of the gravy over roast and pass the rest.

ASIAN BURGERS

The East-meets-West flavor of these burgers have made them a family favorite for over 20 years. They're equally delicious cooked on the grill.

—**CHARLOTTE GILTNER** MESA, AZ

START TO FINISH: 30 MIN.
MAKES: 8 SERVINGS

- 2 **tablespoons soy sauce**
- 1 **tablespoon sesame oil**
- 1 **can (8 ounces) sliced water chestnuts, drained and chopped**
- 1 **cup bean sprouts**
- ½ **cup finely chopped fresh mushrooms**
- 1 **celery rib, finely chopped**
- 4 **green onions, finely chopped**
- 1 **teaspoon pepper**
- ½ **teaspoon salt**
- 2 **pounds ground beef**
- 4 **teaspoons canola oil**
- ½ **cup mayonnaise**
- 1 **tablespoon prepared wasabi**
- 8 **sesame seed hamburger buns, split**
- 3 **cups shredded Chinese or napa cabbage**

1. In a large bowl, combine the first nine ingredients. Crumble beef over mixture and mix well. Shape into eight patties.

2. In two large skillets, cook burgers in oil over medium heat for 5-6 minutes on each side or until a thermometer reads 160°.

3. Meanwhile, combine mayonnaise and wasabi; spread over buns. Serve burgers on buns with cabbage.

EAT SMART
ONE-POT MEATY SPAGHETTI

I used to help my mom make this when I was growing up, and the recipe stuck. It was a beloved comfort food at college, and now it's a weeknight staple for my fiance and me.

—**KRISTIN MICHALENKO** SEATTLE, WA

START TO FINISH: 30 MIN.
MAKES: 6 SERVINGS

- 1 **pound extra-lean ground beef (95% lean)**
- 2 **garlic cloves, minced**
- 1 **teaspoon sugar**
- 1 **teaspoon dried basil**
- ½ **teaspoon dried oregano**
- ¼ **teaspoon salt**
- ¼ **teaspoon paprika**
- ¼ **teaspoon pepper**
- 1 **can (28 ounces) diced tomatoes, undrained**
- 1 **can (15 ounces) tomato sauce**
- 2 **cups water**
- ¼ **cup chopped fresh parsley**
- 8 **ounces uncooked whole wheat spaghetti, broken in half**
- ¼ **cup grated Parmesan cheese Additional chopped parsley**

1. In a 6-qt. stockpot, cook and crumble beef with garlic over medium heat until no longer pink, 5-7 minutes; drain. Stir in sugar and seasonings. Add tomatoes, tomato sauce, water and ¼ cup parsley; bring to a boil. Reduce heat; simmer, covered, 5 minutes.

2. Stir in spaghetti, a little at a time; return to a boil. Reduce heat to medium-low; cook, uncovered, until spaghetti is al dente, 8-10 minutes, stirring occasionally. Stir in cheese. Sprinkle with additional parsley.

Per 1⅓ cups: 292 cal., 6g fat (2g sat. fat), 46mg chol., 737mg sod., 40g carb. (6g sugars, 8g fiber), 24g pro.
Diabetic Exchanges: 3 starch, 2 lean meat.

ONE-POT MEATY
SPAGHETTI

Poultry

TURKEY NOODLE STEW

If you are looking for a hearty stew that comes together in a jiffy, try this recipe. It's chock-full of vegetables, turkey and tender noodles, and it's delicious on a chilly day.

—**TRACI MALONEY** TOMS RIVER, NJ

START TO FINISH: 30 MIN.
MAKES: 6 SERVINGS

- 1 **pound turkey breast tenderloins, cut into ¼-inch slices**
- 1 **medium onion, chopped**
- 1 **tablespoon canola oil**
- 1 **can (14½ ounces) reduced-sodium chicken broth**
- 1 **can (10¾ ounces) reduced-fat reduced-sodium condensed cream of chicken soup, undiluted**
- 2 **cups frozen mixed vegetables**
- ½ **to 1 teaspoon lemon-pepper seasoning**
- 3 **cups uncooked extra-wide egg noodles**

1. In a large skillet, cook turkey and onion in oil for 5-6 minutes or until turkey is no longer pink; drain.
2. In a large bowl, combine the broth, soup, vegetables and lemon-pepper. Add to the skillet; bring to a boil. Stir in noodles. Reduce heat; cover and simmer for 10 minutes or until noodles and vegetables are tender.
Per 1 cup: 259 cal., 6g fat (1g sat. fat), 50mg chol., 566mg sod., 29g carb. (6g sugars, 4g fiber), 24g pro.
Diabetic Exchanges: 3 lean meat, 2 starch, ½ fat.

CHORIZO
PUMPKIN PASTA

CHORIZO PUMPKIN PASTA

I'm a busy student, and this spicy-sweet pasta makes a perfect quick dinner. Even better, it works on a bigger scale to feed a bunch of friends.

—**CHRISTINE YANG** SYRACUSE, NY

START TO FINISH: 30 MIN.
MAKES: 6 SERVINGS

- 3 **cups uncooked gemelli or spiral pasta (about 12 ounces)**
- 1 **package (12 ounces) fully cooked chorizo chicken sausage links or flavor of choice, sliced**
- 1 **cup canned pumpkin**
- 1 **cup half-and-half cream**
- ¾ **teaspoon salt**
- ¼ **teaspoon pepper**
- 1½ **cups shredded manchego or Monterey Jack cheese**
  Minced fresh cilantro, optional

1. Cook pasta according to package directions. Drain, reserving ¾ cup pasta water.
2. Meanwhile, in a large skillet, saute sausage over medium heat until lightly browned; reduce heat to medium-low. Add pumpkin, cream, salt and pepper; cook and stir until heated through. Toss with pasta and enough pasta water to moisten; stir in cheese. If desired, sprinkle with cilantro.

ASIAN GLAZED
CHICKEN THIGHS

TURKEY IN COGNAC CREAM SAUCE

I found this recipe in a magazine and over the years have adjusted it to suit my family's taste. It is special enough for company and easy enough for a weeknight meal.

—**VIRGINIA ANTHONY** JACKSONVILLE, FL

PREP: 20 MIN. • **COOK:** 20 MIN.
MAKES: 4 SERVINGS

- 1 **package (17.6 ounces) turkey breast cutlets**
- ¼ **teaspoon plus ⅛ teaspoon salt, divided**
- ¼ **teaspoon coarsely ground pepper**
- 2 **tablespoons mustard seeds, crushed**
- 4½ **teaspoons olive oil, divided**
- 1½ **cups sliced fresh mushrooms**
- 1 **shallot, finely chopped**
- 1 **garlic clove, minced**
- ⅓ **cup reduced-sodium chicken broth**
- 3 **tablespoons Cognac or 3 tablespoons brandy**
- 1 **plum tomato, seeded and chopped**
- ¼ **cup half-and-half cream**
- 4½ **teaspoons minced fresh basil**

1. Sprinkle turkey with ¼ teaspoon salt and pepper; press on mustard seeds. In a large nonstick skillet over medium heat, cook turkey in 3 teaspoons oil in batches for 2-3 minutes on each side or until no longer pink. Remove and keep warm.
2. In the same skillet, saute mushrooms and shallot in remaining oil until tender. Add garlic; cook 1 minute longer. Remove from the heat; stir in broth and Cognac, stirring to loosen browned bits from pan. Add tomato and cream. Bring to a boil; cook until liquid is reduced by half. Stir in basil and remaining salt. Serve with turkey.

EAT SMART
ASIAN GLAZED CHICKEN THIGHS

Everyone goes for this super moist, garlicky chicken, including my fussy kids. For your holiday buffet or family gathering, serve it with rice or noodles.

—**CAROLE LOTITO** HILLSDALE, NJ

START TO FINISH: 25 MIN.
MAKES: 4 SERVINGS

- ¼ **cup rice vinegar**
- 3 **tablespoons reduced-sodium soy sauce**
- 2 **tablespoons honey**
- 2 **teaspoons canola oil**
- 4 **boneless skinless chicken thighs (about 1 pound)**
- 3 **garlic cloves, minced**
- 1 **teaspoon minced fresh gingerroot or ½ teaspoon ground ginger**
  Toasted sesame seeds, optional

1. In a small bowl, whisk vinegar, soy sauce and honey until blended. In a large nonstick skillet, heat oil over medium-high heat. Brown chicken on both sides.
2. Add garlic and ginger to skillet; cook and stir for 1 minute (do not allow garlic to brown). Stir in vinegar mixture; bring to a boil. Reduce heat; simmer, covered, 8-10 minutes or until a thermometer inserted in chicken reads 170°.
3. Uncover; simmer for 1-2 minutes longer or until the sauce is slightly thickened. If desired, cut into bite-size pieces and sprinkle with sesame seeds before serving.
Per serving: 247 cal., 11g fat (2g sat. fat), 76mg chol., 735mg sod., 15g carb. (14g sugars, 0 fiber), 22g pro.
Diabetic Exchanges: 3 lean meat, 1 starch, ½ fat.

"I'm a new mom, and my schedule is very dependent upon our young son. So I like meals that can be ready in as little time as possible. This all-in-one stir-fry with a hint of sweetness from honey is a big time-saver."
—CAROLINE SPERRY ALLENTOWN, MI

HONEY CHICKEN
STIR-FRY

HONEY CHICKEN STIR-FRY

START TO FINISH: 30 MIN.
MAKES: 4 SERVINGS

- 2 teaspoons cornstarch
- 1 tablespoon cold water
- 3 teaspoons olive oil, divided
- 1 pound boneless skinless chicken breasts, cut into 1-inch pieces
- 1 garlic clove, minced
- 3 tablespoons honey
- 2 tablespoons reduced-sodium soy sauce
- ⅛ teaspoon salt
- ⅛ teaspoon pepper
- 1 package (16 ounces) frozen broccoli stir-fry vegetable blend
  Hot cooked rice

1. Mix cornstarch and water until smooth. In a large nonstick skillet, heat 2 teaspoons oil over medium-high heat; stir-fry chicken and garlic for 1 minute. Stir in honey, soy sauce, salt and pepper; cook until chicken is no longer pink, 2-3 minutes, stirring occasionally. Remove from pan.
2. In same pan, stir-fry the vegetable blend in remaining oil just until tender, 4-5 minutes. Stir cornstarch mixture and add to pan, along with chicken. Bring to a boil; cook and stir until thickened, about 1 minute. Serve with rice.
Per 1 cup: 249 cal., 6g fat (1g sat. fat), 63mg chol., 455mg sod., 21g carb. (15g sugars, 3g fiber), 25g pro.
Diabetic Exchanges: 3 lean meat, 2 vegetable, ½ starch.

TOP TIP

QUICK SLICING BONELESS CHICKEN

"It's easier to slice boneless chicken or beef steak for a stir-fry or a casserole if it's slightly frozen."

—BRENDA HUFF SOMERSET, CO

WEEKNIGHT CABBAGE KIELBASA SKILLET

WEEKNIGHT CABBAGE KIELBASA SKILLET

I like the challenge of cooking lighter meals that pack big flavor. This one, which came from a dear friend, fits the bill. My son rated it a 10 out of 10!
—BEVERLY BATTY FOREST LAKE, MN

START TO FINISH: 30 MIN.
MAKES: 4 SERVINGS

- 1½ teaspoons cornstarch
- ¼ cup cider vinegar
- 1 tablespoon honey
- 1 teaspoon Dijon mustard
- ¼ teaspoon salt
- ¼ teaspoon pepper
- 1 tablespoon canola oil
- 1 package (14 ounces) smoked turkey kielbasa, cut into ¼-inch slices
- 2 medium red potatoes (about 8 ounces), cut into ½-inch cubes
- ½ cup sliced sweet onion
- ½ cup chopped sweet red pepper
- 4 bacon strips, cooked and crumbled
- ½ cup water
- 1 teaspoon beef bouillon granules
- 1 package (14 ounces) coleslaw mix

1. In a small bowl, whisk the first six ingredients until smooth. In a large skillet, heat oil over medium-high heat. Add kielbasa, potatoes, onion, red pepper and bacon; cook and stir for 3-5 minutes or until kielbasa is lightly browned.
2. Add water and bouillon; bring to a boil. Reduce heat; simmer, covered, 6-8 minutes or until potatoes are almost tender. Add coleslaw; cook, covered, 4-6 minutes longer or until tender, stirring occasionally.
3. Stir cornstarch mixture and add to pan. Bring to a boil; cook and stir for 1-2 minutes or until sauce is thickened.

COUSCOUS &
SAUSAGE-STUFFED
ACORN SQUASH

TURKEY CUTLETS IN LEMON WINE SAUCE

After I tried something similar to this recipe while dining out, I put together my own version at home for my family. Now I serve this dish a lot since it's so quick to make—and my family is so happy I do.

—KATHIE WILSON WARRENTON, VA

START TO FINISH: 25 MIN.
MAKES: 4 SERVINGS

- ½ cup all-purpose flour
- ½ teaspoon salt
- ½ teaspoon paprika
- ¼ teaspoon pepper
- 4 turkey breast cutlets (2½ ounces each)
- 1 tablespoon olive oil
- 1 cup white wine or chicken broth
- ¼ cup lemon juice

1. In a shallow bowl, mix flour, salt, paprika and pepper. Dip turkey in flour mixture to coat both sides; shake off excess.
2. In a large skillet, heat oil over medium heat. Add turkey and cook in batches for 1-2 minutes on each side or until no longer pink. Remove from pan.
3. Add wine and lemon juice to skillet, stirring to loosen browned bits. Bring to a boil; cook until liquid is reduced by half. Return cutlets to pan; turn to coat and heat through.

Per 1 turkey cutlet with 2 tablespoons sauce: 145 cal., 4g fat (1g sat. fat), 44mg chol., 110mg sod., 5g carb. (1g sugars, 0 fiber), 18g pro.
Diabetic Exchanges: 2 lean meat, 1 fat.

COUSCOUS & SAUSAGE-STUFFED ACORN SQUASH

With a tiny apartment, zero counter space and only two people to feed, hefty meals are out. This acorn squash with couscous is just the right size.

—JESSICA LEVINSON NYACK, NY

START TO FINISH: 25 MIN.
MAKES: 2 SERVINGS

- 1 medium acorn squash (about 1½ pounds)
- ¼ teaspoon salt
- ¼ teaspoon pepper
- 1 tablespoon olive oil
- 1 medium onion, chopped
- 2 fully cooked spinach and feta chicken sausage links (3 ounces each), sliced
- ½ cup chicken stock
- ½ cup uncooked couscous
  Crumbled feta cheese, optional

1. Cut squash lengthwise in half; remove and discard seeds. Sprinkle squash with salt and pepper; place in a microwave-safe dish, cut side down. Microwave, covered, on high for 10-12 minutes or until tender.
2. Meanwhile, in a large skillet, heat oil over medium heat. Add onion; cook and stir for 5-7 minutes or until tender and lightly browned. Add sausage; cook and stir for 2-3 minutes or until lightly browned.
3. Add stock; bring to a boil. Stir in couscous. Remove from heat; let stand, covered, 5 minutes or until stock is absorbed. Spoon over squash. If desired, top with feta cheese.

THAI CHICKEN
PEANUT NOODLES

THAI CHICKEN PEANUT NOODLES

My husband enjoys the spicy Thai flavors in this speedy, simple dish and breaks out the chopsticks for a more immersed experience.

—JENNIFER FISHER AUSTIN, TX

START TO FINISH: 30 MIN.
MAKES: 6 SERVINGS

- ¼ **cup creamy peanut butter**
- ½ **cup reduced-sodium chicken broth**
- ¼ **cup lemon juice**
- ¼ **cup reduced-sodium soy sauce**
- 4 **teaspoons Sriracha Asian hot chili sauce**
- ¼ **teaspoon crushed red pepper flakes**
- 12 **ounces uncooked multigrain spaghetti**
- 1 **pound lean ground chicken**
- 1½ **cups julienned carrots**
- 1 **medium sweet red pepper, chopped**
- 1 **garlic clove, minced**
- ½ **cup finely chopped unsalted peanuts**
- 4 **green onions, chopped**

1. In a small bowl, whisk the first six ingredients until blended. Cook spaghetti according to package directions; drain.
2. Meanwhile, in a large skillet, cook chicken, carrots, pepper and garlic over medium heat for 5-6 minutes or until chicken is no longer pink, breaking up chicken into crumbles; drain.
3. Stir in peanut butter mixture; bring to a boil. Reduce heat; simmer, uncovered, 3-5 minutes or until sauce is slightly thickened. Serve with spaghetti. Top with peanuts and green onions.

CHICKEN SAUSAGE GYROS

I surprised my family with this fast, filling meal after a day at the beach. Casual and hearty, these whole wheat pitas are packed with veggies.

—KERRI GEORGE BERNE, IN

START TO FINISH: 20 MIN.
MAKES: 4 SERVINGS

- 1 **package (12 ounces) fully cooked spinach and feta chicken sausage links or flavor of your choice, cut into ¼-inch slices**
- 1 **cup (8 ounces) reduced-fat sour cream**
- ¼ **cup finely chopped cucumber**
- 1½ **teaspoons red wine vinegar**
- 1½ **teaspoons olive oil**
- ½ **teaspoon garlic powder**
- 4 **whole wheat pita breads (6 inches)**
- 1 **plum tomato, sliced**
- ½ **small onion, thinly sliced**

1. In a large skillet coated with cooking spray, cook sausage over medium heat until heated through.
2. Meanwhile, in a small bowl, combine the sour cream, cucumber, vinegar, oil and garlic powder. Serve chicken sausage on pita breads with tomato, onion and cucumber sauce.

> **TOP TIP**
>
> ### SLICING TOMATOES
> The best way to cut through the skin of a tomato is with a serrated, not a straight-edged, knife. Cut a tomato vertically, from stem end to blossom end, for slices that will be less juicy and hold their shape better.

CHICKEN TACOS
WITH AVOCADO SALSA

CHICKEN TACOS WITH AVOCADO SALSA

My family has special dietary needs, and these zesty tacos suit everyone. For extra toppings, add cilantro, red onion, jalapeno, black olives and lettuce.

—CHRISTINE SCHENHER EXETER, CA

START TO FINISH: 30 MIN.
MAKES: 4 SERVINGS

- 1 **pound boneless skinless chicken breasts, cut into ½-inch strips**
- ⅓ **cup water**
- 1 **teaspoon sugar**
- 1 **tablespoon chili powder**
- 1 **teaspoon onion powder**
- 1 **teaspoon dried oregano**
- 1 **teaspoon ground cumin**
- 1 **teaspoon paprika**
- ½ **teaspoon salt**
- ½ **teaspoon garlic powder**
- 1 **medium ripe avocado, peeled and cubed**
- 1 **cup fresh or frozen corn, thawed**
- 1 **cup cherry tomatoes, quartered**
- 2 **teaspoons lime juice**
- 8 **taco shells, warmed**

1. Place a large nonstick skillet coated with cooking spray over medium-high heat. Brown chicken. Add water, sugar and seasonings. Cook for 4-5 minutes or until chicken is no longer pink, stirring occasionally.

2. Meanwhile, in a small bowl, gently mix avocado, corn, tomatoes and lime juice. Spoon chicken mixture into taco shells; top with avocado salsa.

Freeze option: Freeze cooled meat mixture in freezer containers. To use, partially thaw in refrigerator overnight. Heat through in a saucepan, stirring occasionally and adding a little water if necessary.

Per 2 tacos: 354 cal., 15g fat (3g sat. fat), 63mg chol., 474mg sod., 30g carb. (4g sugars, 6g fiber), 27g pro.
Diabetic Exchanges: 3 lean meat, 2 starch, 1 fat.

CHICKEN WITH CELERY ROOT PUREE

CHICKEN WITH CELERY ROOT PUREE

Celeriac, or celery root, is a root veggie than combines well with other seasonal ingredients and adds nice texture and flavor to this puree.

—TASTE OF HOME TEST KITCHEN

PREP: 30 MIN.
COOK: 15 MIN.
MAKES: 4 SERVINGS

- 4 **boneless skinless chicken breast halves (6 ounces each)**
- ½ **teaspoon pepper**
- ¼ **teaspoon salt**
- 3 **teaspoons canola oil, divided**
- 1 **large celery root, peeled and chopped (about 3 cups)**
- 2 **cups chopped peeled butternut squash**
- 1 **small onion, chopped**
- 2 **garlic cloves, minced**
- ⅔ **cup unsweetened apple juice**

1. Sprinkle chicken with pepper and salt. In a large nonstick skillet coated with cooking spray, heat 2 teaspoons oil over medium heat. Brown chicken on both sides. Remove chicken from pan.

2. In same pan, heat remaining oil over medium-high heat. Add celery root, squash and onion; cook and stir until squash is crisp-tender. Add garlic; cook for 1 minute longer.

3. Return chicken to pan; add apple juice. Bring to a boil. Reduce heat; simmer, covered, 12-15 minutes or until a thermometer inserted in chicken reads 165°.

4. Remove chicken; keep warm. Cool vegetable mixture slightly. Process in a food processor until smooth. Return to pan and heat through. Serve with chicken.

Per 1 chicken breast half with ⅔ cup puree: 328 cal., 8g fat (1g sat. fat), 94mg chol., 348mg sod., 28g carb. (10g sugars, 5g fiber), 37g pro.
Diabetic Exchanges: 5 lean meat, 2 starch, ½ fat.

SHORTCUT SAUSAGE JAMBALAYA

This quick and easy dinner is one of my husband's top picks. Secret ingredient alert: A pinch of coffee crystals gives my jambalaya its roasty, toasty flavor.

—**BETTY HENAGIN** MEDFORD, OR

START TO FINISH: 20 MIN.
MAKES: 4 SERVINGS

- 1 package (8.8 ounces) ready-to-serve long grain rice
- 1 tablespoon butter
- 1 small onion, chopped
- 1 celery rib, chopped
- 1 small green pepper, chopped
- 1 package (14 ounces) smoked turkey kielbasa, sliced
- ¼ teaspoon salt
- ¼ teaspoon garlic powder
- ¼ teaspoon pepper
- ⅛ teaspoon cayenne pepper, optional
- 1 can (14½ ounces) no-salt-added diced tomatoes, undrained
- 1 cup salsa
  Dash instant coffee granules

1. Heat rice according to package directions. Meanwhile, in a large skillet, heat butter over medium-high heat. Add onion, celery and green pepper; cook and stir for 4-6 minutes or until tender. Stir in kielbasa, salt, garlic powder, pepper and, if desired, cayenne; cook and stir for 2-3 minutes or until kielbasa is browned.

2. Add tomatoes, salsa and coffee granules; heat through. Stir in rice.

Freeze option: Do not heat or add rice. Freeze cooled meat mixture in a freezer container. To use, partially thaw in refrigerator overnight. Heat rice according to package directions. Place meat mixture in a large skillet; heat through, stirring occasionally and adding a little water if necessary. Proceed as directed.

SHORTCUT SAUSAGE JAMBALAYA

BBQ CHICKEN SANDWICHES

These tasty sandwiches are a cinch to make. For a spicier taste, eliminate the ketchup and increase the amount of salsa to 1 cup.

—**LETICIA LEWIS** KENNEWICK, WA

PREP: 20 MIN. • **COOK:** 15 MIN.
MAKES: 6 SERVINGS

- ½ cup chopped onion
- ½ cup diced celery
- 1 garlic clove, minced
- 1 tablespoon butter
- ½ cup salsa
- ½ cup ketchup
- 2 tablespoons brown sugar
- 2 tablespoons cider vinegar
- 1 tablespoon Worcestershire sauce
- ½ teaspoon chili powder
- ¼ teaspoon salt
- ⅛ teaspoon pepper
- 2 cups shredded cooked chicken
- 6 hamburger buns, split and toasted

1. In a large saucepan, saute the onion, celery and garlic in butter until tender. Stir in the salsa, ketchup, brown sugar, vinegar, Worcestershire sauce, chili powder, salt and pepper.

2. Stir in chicken. Bring to a boil. Reduce heat; cover and simmer for 15 minutes. Serve about ⅓ cup chicken mixture on each bun.

Freeze option: Freeze cooled meat mixture in freezer containers. To use, partially thaw in refrigerator overnight. Heat through in a saucepan, stirring occasionally and adding a little water if necessary. Serve in buns.

Per sandwich: 284 cal., 8g fat (3g sat. fat), 47mg chol., 770mg sod., 35g carb. (12g sugars, 3g fiber), 18g pro.

Diabetic Exchanges: 2 starch, 2 lean meat.

BBQ CHICKEN
SANDWICHES

CASHEW-CHICKEN
ROTINI SALAD

CASHEW-CHICKEN ROTINI SALAD

I've tried many chicken salad recipes over the years, but this is my very favorite. It's fresh, fruity and refreshing, and the cashews add wonderful crunch. Every time I serve it at a potluck or picnic, I get rave reviews...and I always come home with an empty bowl!

—**KARA COOK** ELK RIDGE, UT

PREP: 30 MIN. + CHILLING
MAKES: 12 SERVINGS

- 1 package (16 ounces) spiral or rotini pasta
- 4 cups cubed cooked chicken
- 1 can (20 ounces) pineapple tidbits, drained
- 1½ cups sliced celery
- ¾ cup thinly sliced green onions
- 1 cup seedless red grapes
- 1 cup seedless green grapes
- 1 package (5 ounces) dried cranberries
- 1 cup ranch salad dressing
- ¾ cup mayonnaise
- 2 cups salted cashews

1. Cook pasta according to package directions. Meanwhile, in a large bowl, combine the chicken, pineapple, celery, onions, grapes and cranberries. Drain pasta and rinse in cold water; stir into chicken mixture.

2. In a small bowl, whisk the ranch dressing and mayonnaise. Pour over salad and toss to coat. Cover and refrigerate for at least 1 hour. Just before serving, stir in cashews.

ROTISSERIE CHICKEN RAGOUT

Deli-roasted chicken is the secret to this super-quick family favorite. It's especially good after a long day of shopping, when you're tired or the kids have a game and time's tight. I like to serve this fail-proof meal-in-one with crusty Italian bread. That's all it needs!

—**PAULA MARCHESI** LENHARTSVILLE, PA

START TO FINISH: 25 MIN.
MAKES: 5 SERVINGS

- 1 cup chopped yellow summer squash
- 1 cup chopped zucchini
- ½ cup chopped onion
- 2 tablespoons olive oil
- 1½ teaspoons minced garlic
- 2 cups cubed cooked rotisserie chicken
- 1 can (15 ounces) cannellini beans, rinsed and drained
- 1 tablespoon heavy whipping cream
- 1 tablespoon minced fresh thyme
- ⅛ teaspoon salt
- ⅛ teaspoon pepper
- ½ cup shredded Parmesan cheese

1. In a large skillet, saute the yellow squash, zucchini and onion in oil for 4-6 minutes or until tender. Add garlic; cook for 1 minute longer.

2. Add the chicken, beans, cream, thyme, salt and pepper. Cook and stir for 3-4 minutes longer or until heated through. Sprinkle with cheese.

SPICY BUFFALO CHICKEN WRAPS

This recipe has a real kick and it's one of my husband's favorites. It's ready in a flash, is easily doubled, and is the closest thing to restaurant Buffalo wings I've ever tasted—in a light version.

—**JENNIFER BECK** MERIDIAN, ID

START TO FINISH: 25 MIN.
MAKES: 2 SERVINGS

- ½ pound boneless skinless chicken breast, cubed
- ½ teaspoon canola oil
- 2 tablespoons Louisiana-style hot sauce
- 1 cup shredded lettuce
- 2 flour tortillas (6 inches), warmed
- 2 teaspoons reduced-fat ranch salad dressing
- 2 tablespoons crumbled blue cheese

1. In a large nonstick skillet coated with cooking spray, cook chicken in oil over medium heat for 6 minutes; drain. Stir in hot sauce. Bring to a boil. Reduce heat; simmer, uncovered, for 3-5 minutes or until sauce is thickened and chicken is no longer pink.

2. Place lettuce on tortillas; drizzle with ranch dressing. Top with chicken mixture and blue cheese; roll up.

Per wrap: 273 cal., 11g fat (3g sat. fat), 70mg chol., 453mg sod., 15g carb. (1g sugars, 1g fiber), 28g pro.

Diabetic Exchanges: 3 lean meat, 1½ fat, 1 starch.

READER RAVE

"I will be making these chicken wraps again soon. I just started a low-carb regimen under advisement of my doctor, and the recipe was my first attempt at a low-carb dish. I loved it, and so did my husband! It's full of flavor, and with low-carb tortillas it's even better!"

—**MAY_BABY21** TASTEOFHOME.COM

LEMON-OLIVE CHICKEN
WITH ORZO

LEMON-OLIVE CHICKEN WITH ORZO

A fantastic combo of lemon and Greek olives really brightens up a weeknight chicken dinner. Cooking the orzo in the same pan saves so much time. Toss up a leafy salad while it simmers, and you're ready to go.

—**NANCY BROWN** DAHINDA, IL

START TO FINISH: 30 MIN.
MAKES: 4 SERVINGS

- 1 tablespoon olive oil
- 4 boneless skinless chicken thighs (about 1 pound)
- 1 can (14½ ounces) reduced-sodium chicken broth
- ⅔ cup uncooked whole wheat orzo pasta
- ½ medium lemon, cut into 4 wedges
- ½ cup pitted Greek olives, sliced
- 1 tablespoon lemon juice
- 1 teaspoon dried oregano
- ¼ teaspoon pepper

1. In a large nonstick skillet, heat oil over medium heat. Brown chicken on both sides; remove from pan.

2. Add broth to skillet; increase heat to medium-high. Cook for 1-2 minutes, stirring to loosen browned bits from pan. Stir in remaining ingredients; bring to a boil. Reduce heat; simmer, uncovered, 5 minutes, stirring occasionally.

3. Return chicken to pan. Cook, covered, 5-8 minutes or until pasta is tender and a thermometer inserted in chicken reads 170°.

Per serving: 345 cal., 17g fat (3g sat. fat), 76mg chol., 636mg sod., 22g carb. (1g sugars, 5g fiber), 26g pro.
Diabetic Exchanges: 3 lean meat, 2 fat, 1 starch.

MEDITERRANEAN CHICKEN & BEANS

Not only does this cooking method make really juicy chicken thighs, it saves you time scrubbing an extra pan.

—**MARIE RIZZIO** INTERLOCHEN, MI

PREP: 25 MIN. • **COOK:** 20 MIN.
MAKES: 6 SERVINGS

- 2 tablespoons all-purpose flour
- 1 teaspoon garlic salt
- 1 teaspoon dried rosemary, crushed
- ½ teaspoon pepper
- 6 bone-in chicken thighs (about 2¼ pounds), skin removed
- 2 tablespoons olive oil
- 1 can (15 ounces) cannellini beans, rinsed and drained
- 1 can (14½ ounces) diced tomatoes, undrained
- 6 slices provolone cheese

1. In a large resealable plastic bag, combine the flour, garlic salt, rosemary and pepper. Add chicken, a few pieces at a time, and shake to coat.

2. In a large skillet, brown chicken in oil. Stir in beans and tomatoes; bring to a boil. Reduce heat. Cover and simmer for 20-25 minutes or until chicken juices run clear. Remove from the heat. Top with cheese. Cover and let stand for 5 minutes or until cheese is melted.

QUICK CHICKEN
CACCIATORE

SAUSAGE & VEGETABLE SKILLET DINNER

EAT SMART

I threw this together one night trying to use up produce before going out of town. Who knew it was going to be such a hit! Now it's a go-to recipe that I use when I don't have much time to cook or wash dishes.

—**ELIZABETH KELLEY** CHICAGO, IL

START TO FINISH: 30 MIN.
MAKES: 4 SERVINGS

- 1   tablespoon olive oil
- 1   package (12 ounces) fully cooked Italian chicken sausage links, cut into 1-inch pieces
- 1   large onion, chopped
- 3   garlic cloves, minced
- ¼   teaspoon crushed red pepper flakes
- 1½ pounds red potatoes (about 5 medium), thinly sliced
- 1   package (10 ounces) frozen corn
- ¼   teaspoon pepper
- 1¼ cups vegetable broth
- 2   cups fresh baby spinach

1. In a 12-in. skillet, heat the oil over medium-high heat; saute sausage and onion until onion is tender. Add garlic and pepper flakes; cook and stir for 1 minute.
2. Add potatoes, corn, pepper and broth; bring to a boil. Reduce heat; simmer, covered, until potatoes are tender, 15-20 minutes. Stir in spinach until wilted.
Per 1½ cups: 371 cal., 11g fat (3g sat. fat), 65mg chol., 715mg sod., 48g carb. (6g sugars, 5g fiber), 22g pro.
Diabetic Exchanges: 3 starch, 3 lean meat, 1 fat.

TOP TIP

HEALTHY CHOICE
Italian chicken sausage has less than half the fat of regular sausage. It's lean, but adds a lot of flavor. Give it a try!

QUICK CHICKEN CACCIATORE

This is a colorful and flavorful fast-to-fix main dish. Serve it with a crisp lettuce and tomato salad topped with your favorite bottled dressing.

—**MARCIA HOSTETTER** CANTON, NY

PREP: 10 MIN. • **COOK:** 30 MIN.
MAKES: 4 SERVINGS

- 1   medium green pepper, cut into strips
- 1   medium onion, sliced into rings
- 8   ounces fresh mushrooms, sliced
- 1   tablespoon olive oil
- 4   boneless skinless chicken breast halves (4 ounces each)
- 1   can (15 ounces) tomato sauce
- 1   can (4 ounces) chopped green chilies
- ¼ to ½ teaspoon dried basil
- ¼ to ½ teaspoon dried oregano
- ⅛ to ¼ teaspoon garlic powder
      Dash cayenne pepper
      Cooked spaghetti or rice, optional

1. In a large skillet, saute green pepper, onion and mushrooms in olive oil for 4-5 minutes or until crisp-tender. Place the chicken breasts over the vegetables.
2. In a small bowl, combine tomato sauce, chilies and seasonings. Pour over the chicken; cover and simmer for 20 minutes or until a meat thermometer reads 170°. Serve with spaghetti or rice if desired.

CURRY TURKEY
STIR-FRY

TANGY CRANBERRY CHICKEN

My husband loves chicken when it's nice and moist, like it is in this autumn recipe. I serve it over hot fluffy rice with a salad and warm rolls on the side. The ruby-red sauce has a tart cinnamony flavor.
—**DOROTHY BATEMAN** CARVER, MA

PREP: 20 MIN. • **COOK:** 20 MIN.
MAKES: 6 SERVINGS

- ½ cup all-purpose flour
- ½ teaspoon salt
- ¼ teaspoon pepper
- 6 boneless skinless chicken breast halves (4 ounces each)
- 3 tablespoons butter
- 1 cup water
- 1 cup fresh or frozen cranberries
- ½ cup packed brown sugar
  Dash ground nutmeg
- 1 tablespoon red wine vinegar, optional
  Hot cooked rice

1. In a shallow dish, combine flour, salt and pepper; dredge chicken. In a skillet, melt butter over medium heat. Brown the chicken on both sides. Remove and keep warm.
2. Add water, cranberries, brown sugar, nutmeg and, if desired, vinegar to the pan; cook and stir until the berries burst, about 5 minutes. Return chicken to skillet. Cover and simmer for 20-30 minutes or until chicken is tender, basting occasionally with the sauce. Serve with rice.

Freeze option: Place chicken in freezer containers; top with sauce. If desired, place rice in separate freezer containers. Cool and freeze. To use, partially thaw in refrigerator overnight. Microwave, covered, on high in a microwave-safe dish until heated through, gently stirring and adding a little water to chicken if necessary.

CURRY TURKEY STIR-FRY

Just open the fridge and go to town making this throw-together curry. My family prefers turkey, but if you like chicken, shrimp, even bean sprouts and carrots, by all means, add them.
—**LAUREN RUSH** CLARK, NJ

START TO FINISH: 20 MIN.
MAKES: 4 SERVINGS

- ½ teaspoon cornstarch
- 2 tablespoons reduced-sodium soy sauce
- 1 tablespoon minced fresh cilantro
- 1 tablespoon honey
- 1 teaspoon curry powder
- 1 teaspoon sesame or canola oil
- 1 garlic clove, minced
- ⅛ teaspoon crushed red pepper flakes, optional
- 1 tablespoon canola oil
- 1 large sweet red pepper, julienned
- 3 green onions, cut into 2-inch pieces
- 2 cups cubed cooked turkey breast
- 2 cups hot cooked brown rice

1. Mix first seven ingredients and, if desired, pepper flakes. In a large skillet, heat 1 tablespoon canola oil over medium-high heat; stir-fry red pepper until crisp-tender, about 2 minutes. Add green onions; stir-fry until tender, 1-2 minutes.
2. Stir cornstarch mixture and add to pan. Bring to a boil; cook and stir until thickened, 1-2 minutes. Stir in turkey; heat through. Serve with rice.
Per ¾ cup turkey mixture with ½ cup rice: 287 cal., 7g fat (1g sat. fat), 60mg chol., 351mg sod., 31g carb. (7g sugars, 3g fiber), 25g pro.
Diabetic Exchanges: 3 lean meat, 2 starch, 1 fat.

TANGY
CRANBERRY
CHICKEN

TURKEY REUBENS

I have always enjoyed traditional Reuben sandwiches. Then I gave them a try with smoked turkey a few years ago and I loved the taste. This recipe is terrific to make in summer, when you don't want to heat up the kitchen.

—JO ANN DALRYMPLE CLAREMORE, OK

START TO FINISH: 15 MIN.
MAKES: 2 SERVINGS

- 4 slices pumpernickel or rye bread
- 2 tablespoons Thousand Island salad dressing
- 6 ounces sliced deli smoked turkey
- ½ cup sauerkraut, rinsed and well drained
- 2 slices Swiss cheese
- 2 teaspoons butter, softened

1. Spread two slices of bread with salad dressing. Layer with turkey, sauerkraut and cheese; top with remaining bread. Butter the outsides of sandwiches.
2. In a large skillet, toast sandwiches for 3-4 minutes on each side or until heated through.

IN-A-PINCH CHICKEN & SPINACH

I needed a fast supper while babysitting my grandchild. I used what my daughter-in-law had in the fridge and turned it into what's now one of our favorite recipes.

—SANDRA ELLIS STOCKBRIDGE, GA

START TO FINISH: 25 MIN.
MAKES: 4 SERVINGS

- 4 boneless skinless chicken breast halves (6 ounces each)
- 2 tablespoons olive oil
- 1 tablespoon butter
- 1 package (6 ounces) fresh baby spinach
- 1 cup salsa

1. Pound chicken with a meat mallet to ½-in. thickness. In a large skillet, heat oil and butter over medium heat. Cook chicken for 5-6 minutes on each side or until no longer pink. Remove and keep warm.
2. Add spinach and salsa to pan; cook and stir for 3-4 minutes or just until spinach is wilted. Serve with chicken.

SOUTHWEST TURKEY LETTUCE WRAPS

EAT SMART FREEZE IT
SOUTHWEST TURKEY LETTUCE WRAPS

If you're tired of the same old taco routine, give these wraps a try. I tweaked a friend's recipe to suit our tastes and my family loves it. These are so yummy and easy to make.

—ALLY BILLHORN WILTON, IA

START TO FINISH: 25 MIN.
MAKES: 6 SERVINGS

- 2 pounds extra-lean ground turkey
- 1 small onion, finely chopped
- 2 tablespoons chili powder
- ¾ teaspoon ground cumin
- ½ teaspoon salt
- ½ teaspoon pepper
- 1 can (15 ounces) tomato sauce
- 18 Bibb or iceberg lettuce leaves
- ¾ cup shredded cheddar cheese
  Optional toppings: sour cream, salsa and guacamole

1. In a large skillet, cook and crumble turkey with onion over medium-high heat until no longer pink, 8-10 minutes.
2. Stir in seasonings and tomato sauce; bring to a boil. Reduce heat; simmer, covered, until flavors are blended, about 10 minutes. Serve in lettuce with cheese and toppings as desired.

Freeze option: Freeze cooled meat mixture in freezer containers. To use, partially thaw in refrigerator overnight. Heat through in a saucepan, stirring occasionally and adding a little water if necessary.

Per 3 filled lettuce wraps: 251 cal., 7g fat (3g sat. fat), 75mg chol., 806mg sod., 7g carb. (2g sugars, 2g fiber), 43g pro.
Diabetic Exchanges: 5 lean meat, 1 vegetable.

BLACK BEAN CHICKEN WITH RICE

This family favorite only requires a few ingredients, so it's quick to fix on a weeknight.

—**MOLLY NEWMAN** PORTLAND, OR

PREP/TOTAL: 25 MIN.
MAKES: 4 SERVINGS

- 3 **teaspoons chili powder**
- 1 **teaspoon ground cumin**
- 1 **teaspoon pepper**
- ¼ **teaspoon salt**
- 4 **boneless skinless chicken breast halves (4 ounces each)**
- 2 **teaspoons canola oil**
- 1 **can (15 ounces) black beans, rinsed and drained**
- 1 **cup frozen corn**
- 1 **cup salsa**
- 2 **cups hot cooked brown rice**

1. In a small bowl, mix seasonings; sprinkle over both sides of chicken. In a large nonstick skillet coated with cooking spray, heat oil over medium heat. Brown chicken on both sides.

2. Add beans, corn and salsa to skillet; cook, covered, 10-15 minutes or until a thermometer inserted in chicken reads 165°. Remove chicken from pan; cut into slices. Serve with bean mixture and rice.

Per 1 chicken breast half with ¾ cup bean mixture and ½ cup cooked rice: 400 cal., 7g fat (1g sat. fat), 63mg chol., 670mg sod., 52g carb. (4g sugars, 8g fiber), 32g pro.

BLACK BEAN
CHICKEN WITH RICE

CHICKEN FETTUCCINE ALFREDO

You need only two pans to make this family favorite. My son does the dishes in our house, so the fewer dishes for him to clean, the happier he is!

—**SANDY SCHMITZER** SWARTZ CREEK, MI

START TO FINISH: 30 MIN.
MAKES: 6 SERVINGS

- 1 **package (12 ounces) fettuccine**
- 8 **bacon strips, cut into 1-inch pieces**
- 1 **pound boneless skinless chicken breasts, cubed**
- 2 **cups sliced fresh mushrooms**
- 6 **green onions, thinly sliced**
- 1 **garlic clove, minced**
- 1½ **cups half-and-half cream**
- ½ **cup shredded Parmesan cheese**
- 1 **teaspoon paprika**
- ½ **teaspoon coarsely ground pepper**
  Additional shredded Parmesan cheese

1. Cook fettuccine according to package directions. Meanwhile, in a large skillet, cook bacon until crisp. Remove to paper towels to drain, reserving 1-2 tablespoons of drippings.

2. Saute chicken in drippings until no longer pink. Add mushrooms and green onions; cook until mushrooms are tender. Add garlic; cook for 1 minute longer. Stir in the cream, cheese, paprika and pepper. Reduce heat; simmer, uncovered, for 5-10 minutes. Stir in reserved bacon.

3. Drain fettuccine; place in a serving bowl. Add chicken mixture; toss to coat. Garnish with additional cheese.

READER RAVE

"Totally delicious, especially with the bacon flavor. My family really enjoyed this version of fettuccine Alfredo, even my husband, who is not that crazy about pasta."

—**RROHRER** TASTEOFHOME.COM

POTLUCK SLOPPY JOES

For a change of pace, consider swapping out the green pepper in these tasty sloppy joes for an Anaheim, if available. Long and lighter green in color than a bell pepper, Anaheim peppers have just a hint of a bite.

—**RICK BOLTE** MONTCLAIR, CA

PREP: 30 MIN. • **COOK:** 15 MIN.
MAKES: 12 SERVINGS

- 3 pounds lean ground turkey
- 3 celery ribs, chopped
- 2 medium onions, chopped
- 1 large green pepper, chopped
- 1¾ cups ketchup
- 1 can (8 ounces) no-salt-added tomato sauce
- 3 tablespoons all-purpose flour
- 3 tablespoons sugar
- 3 tablespoons cider vinegar
- 1 tablespoon prepared mustard
- 12 whole wheat hamburger buns, split and toasted

1. In a large nonstick skillet, cook the turkey, celery, onions and pepper over medium heat until meat is no longer pink; drain.

2. Stir in the ketchup, tomato sauce, flour, sugar, vinegar and mustard. Bring to a boil. Reduce heat; cover and simmer for 10-15 minutes or until heated through. Spoon ⅔ cup turkey mixture onto each bun.

Freeze option: Cool turkey mixture and freeze in freezer containers for up to 3 months. To use frozen turkey mixture, thaw in the refrigerator; place in a saucepan and heat through. Spoon ⅔ cup turkey mixture onto each bun.

Per serving: 360 cal., 11g fat (3g sat. fat), 90mg chol., 785mg sod., 41g carb. (19g sugars, 4g fiber), 24g pro.
Diabetic Exchanges: 3 lean meat, 2½ starch.

SUMMER TURKEY SALADS

Tender turkey is treated to a yummy walnut coating in this dressy salad that just begs to be served outside. Add a cold glass filled with Arnold Palmer mix—lemonade and iced tea—and enjoy!

—**TASTE OF HOME** TEST KITCHEN

START TO FINISH: 25 MIN.
MAKES: 4 SERVINGS

- ¼ cup all-purpose flour
- ½ teaspoon salt
- 1 large egg, beaten
- ¾ cup finely chopped walnuts
- ½ teaspoon dried rosemary, crushed
- ½ pound turkey breast cutlets, cut into strips
- 1 tablespoon olive oil
- 1 package (5 ounces) spring mix salad greens
- 2 plum tomatoes, cut into wedges
- 1 cup fresh blueberries
- ½ cup mandarin oranges
- 2 green onions, thinly sliced

BLUEBERRY VINAIGRETTE
- ¼ cup red wine vinegar
- ½ cup fresh blueberries
- 1 tablespoon honey
- 2 teaspoons Dijon mustard
- ¼ cup olive oil

1. Combine flour and salt in a shallow bowl. Place egg in a separate shallow bowl. Combine walnuts and rosemary in another shallow bowl. Coat turkey in flour mixture, then dip in egg and coat with walnut mixture.

2. In a large skillet over medium heat, cook turkey in oil in batches for 2-3 minutes on each side or until meat is no longer pink.

3. Divide salad greens among four serving plates; top with tomatoes, blueberries, oranges, onions and turkey strips.

4. In a blender, combine the vinegar, blueberries, honey and mustard. While processing, gradually add oil in a steady stream. Serve with salad.

CAZUELA

I learned to make Cazuela while living in Chile for a few months. I grow extra butternut squash in our garden just for this recipe.

—**LOUISE SCHMID** MARSHALL, MN

PREP: 5 MIN. • **COOK:** 30 MIN.
MAKES: 6-8 SERVINGS

- 6 chicken drumsticks or thighs
- 3 cups cubed peeled butternut squash (1-inch cubes)
- 6 small potatoes, peeled
- 6 pieces of fresh or frozen corn on the cob (2 inches each)
- 3 carrots, cut into 1-inch chunks
- 3 cans (14½ ounces each) chicken broth
  Hot cooked rice
  Hot pepper sauce to taste
  Salt and pepper to taste
  Minced fresh cilantro or parsley

1. In a large soup kettle or Dutch oven, place the chicken, squash, potatoes, corn, carrots and broth; bring to a boil. Reduce heat; cover and simmer for 25 minutes or until chicken is done and vegetables are tender.

2. Serve over rice in a shallow soup bowl. Serve with hot pepper sauce, salt, pepper and cilantro or parsley.

TOP TIP

REMOVING CORN SILK

"I use a crumpled paper towel to gently brush the silk from corn. This works better for me than a vegetable brush, and the towel isn't abrasive to the kernels."

—**HILDA NEWCOMER** HAGERSTOWN, MD

"Microwave each ear of corn on high for 1 minute. While still warm, grab husk and silks from the top of the ear and peel downward. For any remaining silks, take a dry paper towel and rub the ear till they're gone."

—**BETH PARKER** GRAYSVILLE, AL

CAZUELA

Pork

ASPARAGUS HAM DINNER

I've been making this light meal for my family for years now, and it's always well received. With asparagus, tomato, pasta and chunks of ham, it's a tempting blend of tastes and textures.

—RHONDA ZAVODNY DAVID CITY, NE

START TO FINISH: 25 MIN.
MAKES: 6 SERVINGS

- 2 **cups uncooked corkscrew or spiral pasta**
- ¾ **pound fresh asparagus, cut into 1-inch pieces**
- 1 **medium sweet yellow pepper, julienned**
- 1 **tablespoon olive oil**
- 6 **medium tomatoes, diced**
- 6 **ounces boneless fully cooked ham, cubed**
- ¼ **cup minced fresh parsley**
- ½ **teaspoon salt**
- ½ **teaspoon dried oregano**
- ½ **teaspoon dried basil**
- ⅛ **to ¼ teaspoon cayenne pepper**
- ¼ **cup shredded Parmesan cheese**

Cook the pasta according to the package directions. Meanwhile, in a large nonstick skillet, saute asparagus and yellow pepper in oil until crisp-tender. Add the tomatoes and ham; heat through. Drain pasta; add to vegetable mixture. Stir in parsley and seasonings. Sprinkle with cheese.

Per 1⅓ cups: 204 cal., 5g fat (1g sat. fat), 17mg chol., 561mg sod., 29g carb. (5g sugars, 3g fiber), 12g pro.
Diabetic Exchanges: 1½ starch, 1 lean meat, 1 vegetable, ½ fat.

ASPARAGUS
HAM DINNER

PORK PANCIT

MOZZARELLA-STUFFED MEATBALLS

It's fun to watch my friends eat these meatballs for the first time. They're pleasantly surprised to find melted cheese in the middle. These meatballs are also great in a hot sub sandwich.

—**MICHAELA ROSENTHAL** INDIO, CA

PREP: 20 MIN. • **COOK:** 15 MIN.
MAKES: 6 SERVINGS

- 1 large egg, lightly beaten
- ¼ cup prepared Italian salad dressing
- 1½ cups cubed bread
- 2 tablespoons minced fresh parsley
- 2 garlic cloves, minced
- ½ teaspoon dried oregano
- ½ teaspoon pepper
- ¼ teaspoon salt
- ½ pound ground pork
- ½ pound ground sirloin
- 3 ounces fresh mozzarella cheese
- 2 tablespoons canola oil
- 1 jar (26 ounces) marinara sauce
  Hot cooked pasta

1. In a large bowl, combine the first eight ingredients. Crumble pork and beef over the mixture; mix well. Cut mozzarella into eighteen ½-in. cubes. Divide the meat mixture into 18 portions; shape each around a cheese cube.

2. In a large skillet, cook the meatballs in oil in batches until a thermometer inserted in the meat reads 160°; drain. In a large saucepan, heat marinara sauce; add the meatballs and heat through. Serve over pasta.

Freeze option: Freeze cooled meatball mixture in freezer containers. To use, partially thaw in refrigerator overnight. Heat through in a covered saucepan, gently stirring and adding a little water if necessary.

MAKE MEATBALLS OF EQUAL SIZE

Pat the meat mixture into a 1-in.-thick rectangle. Cut the rectangle into the same number of squares as meatballs in the recipe; form each square into a ball.

PORK PANCIT

A dear friend gave me a pork recipe so tempting, we never have leftovers. Try it with meats like chicken, sausage or Spam.

—**PRISCILLA GILBERT**

INDIAN HARBOUR BEACH, FL

START TO FINISH: 30 MIN.
MAKES: 6 SERVINGS

- 8 ounces uncooked vermicelli or angel hair pasta
- 1 pound boneless pork loin chops (½ inch thick), cut into thin strips
- 3 tablespoons canola oil, divided
- 4 garlic cloves, minced
- 1½ teaspoons salt, divided
- 1 medium onion, halved and thinly sliced
- 2½ cups shredded cabbage
- 1 medium carrot, julienned
- 1 cup fresh snow peas
- ¼ teaspoon pepper

1. Break the vermicelli in half; cook it according to package directions. Drain.

2. Meanwhile, in a bowl, toss pork with 2 tablespoons oil, garlic and ½ teaspoon salt. Place a large skillet over medium-high heat. Add half of the pork mixture; stir-fry 2-3 minutes or until browned. Remove from the pan. Repeat with the remaining pork mixture.

3. In the same skillet, heat the remaining oil over medium-high heat. Add onion; stir-fry for 1-2 minutes or until tender. Add the remaining vegetables; stir-fry 3-5 minutes or until crisp-tender. Stir in pepper and the remaining salt. Return the pork to pan. Add vermicelli; heat through, tossing to combine.

Per 1⅓ cups: 326 cal., 12g fat (2g sat. fat), 36mg chol., 627mg sod., 34g carb. (3g sugars, 3g fiber), 21g pro.

Diabetic Exchanges: 2 starch, 2 lean meat, 1 vegetable, 1 fat

"This hearty, flavorful dish is great on cold winter nights. I love the sweetness of the apples, the heat of the curry, and the bit of almond crunch."

—MARY MARLOWE LEVERETTE COLUMBIA, SC

PORK CHOPS WITH
TOMATO CURRY

PORK CHOPS WITH TOMATO CURRY

PREP: 15 MIN. • **COOK:** 25 MIN.
MAKES: 6 SERVINGS

- 4 teaspoons butter, divided
- 6 boneless pork loin chops (6 ounces each)
- 1 small onion, finely chopped
- 3 medium apples, thinly sliced (about 5 cups)
- 1 can (28 ounces) whole tomatoes, undrained
- 4 teaspoons sugar
- 2 teaspoons curry powder
- ½ teaspoon salt
- ½ teaspoon chili powder
- 4 cups hot cooked brown rice
- 2 tablespoons toasted slivered almonds, optional

1. In a 6-qt. stockpot, heat 2 teaspoons butter over medium-high heat. Brown pork chops in batches. Remove from pan.
2. In same pan, heat the remaining butter over medium heat. Add onion; cook and stir 2-3 minutes or until tender. Stir in apples, tomatoes, sugar, curry powder, salt and chili powder. Bring to a boil, stirring to break up the tomatoes.
3. Return the chops to pan. Reduce heat; simmer, uncovered, 5 minutes. Turn chops; cook 3-5 minutes longer or until a thermometer inserted in pork reads 145°. Let stand 5 minutes before serving. Serve with rice and, if desired, sprinkle with almonds.

Test Kitchen Note: To toast nuts, bake in a shallow pan in a 350° oven for 5-10 minutes or cook in a skillet over low heat until lightly browned, stirring occasionally.
Per 1 pork chop with ¾ cup tomato mixture and ⅔ cup rice: 478 cal., 14g fat (5g sat. fat), 89mg chol., 475mg sod., 50g carb. (15g sugars, 7g fiber), 38g pro.
Diabetic Exchanges: 5 lean meat, 2 starch, 2 vegetable, ½ fruit, ½ fat.

FRESH CORN FETTUCCINE

FRESH CORN FETTUCCINE

I love corn, so it wasn't much of a leap to figure out that with the help of a food processor, I could turn fresh corn kernels into a best-of-the-season sauce that's delicious over pasta.
—LILY JULOW LAWRENCEVILLE, GA

START TO FINISH: 30 MIN.
MAKES: 6 SERVINGS

- 12 ounces uncooked fettuccine
- 4 thick-sliced bacon strips, chopped
- 4 cups fresh or frozen corn, thawed
- 3 garlic cloves, minced
- ¼ teaspoon salt
- ⅛ teaspoon pepper
- ½ cup grated Parmesan cheese
- ⅓ cup blanched almonds
- ⅓ cup olive oil
- 1 cup thinly sliced fresh basil, divided
  Halved grape tomatoes and additional grated Parmesan cheese, optional

1. Cook fettuccine according to the package directions.
2. Meanwhile, in a large skillet, cook bacon over medium heat until crisp. Remove with a slotted spoon; drain on paper towels. Discard drippings, reserving 2 teaspoons.
3. Add corn, garlic, salt and pepper to the drippings; cook and stir over medium-high heat until corn is tender. Remove ¾ cup corn from pan. Transfer the remaining corn to a food processor; add cheese, almonds and oil. Process until blended. Return to skillet; add the reserved corn and heat through.
4. Drain fettuccine, reserving ½ cup pasta water. Add fettuccine, three-fourths of the bacon and ¾ cup of the basil to the corn mixture. Add enough of the reserved pasta water to reach the desired consistency, tossing to coat. Sprinkle with the remaining bacon and basil. If desired, top with tomatoes and additional cheese.

CRANBERRY-ORANGE PORK CHOPS

My family loves the taste of these moist and spicy pork chops. In a pinch, I've substituted diced drained peaches for the mandarin oranges with equally delicious results.

—MARGARET WILSON SAN BERNARDINO, CA

START TO FINISH: 25 MIN
MAKES: 6 SERVINGS

- 6 boneless pork loin chops (6 ounces each)
- ¼ teaspoon salt
- ¼ teaspoon pepper
- 1 tablespoon canola oil
- ½ cup chicken broth
- 1 can (11 ounces) mandarin oranges, drained
- ⅓ cup dried cranberries
- ¼ teaspoon ground allspice
- ¼ teaspoon paprika

1. Sprinkle pork chops with salt and pepper. In a large skillet, brown chops in oil on both sides.
2. Add the remaining ingredients. Bring to a boil. Reduce heat; cover and simmer for 8-10 minutes or until a thermometer reads 145°.

HAM SLICES WITH PINEAPPLE

My husband is so fond of this dish that I often have to double the recipe. I mix the leftovers with macaroni and cheese and add a can of cheddar cheese soup for a quick casserole.

—DONNA WARNER TAVARES, FL

START TO FINISH: 20 MIN.
MAKES: 2 SERVINGS

- 1 can (8¼ ounces) sliced pineapple
- 2 slices fully cooked ham (3 ounces each)
- 1 tablespoon butter
- 1½ teaspoons cornstarch
- ¾ teaspoon ground mustard
- 3 tablespoons sherry or apple juice

1. Drain pineapple, reserving juice. Add enough water to juice to measure ½ cup; set aside. In a large nonstick skillet, lightly brown pineapple and ham. Remove and keep warm.

2. Using the same skillet, melt the butter. Whisk in cornstarch and mustard until smooth. Stir in sherry or apple juice and the reserved pineapple juice. Bring to a boil; cook and stir for 2 minutes or until thickened. Serve with ham and pineapple.

FREEZE IT
MAPLE-PECAN PORK CHOPS

To make a standout supper, start with these sweet and savory chops. They're guaranteed to make any occasion special. Simmer the pork chops in apple juice, then drizzle with sweet maple syrup and top with crunchy pecans.

—TASTE OF HOME TEST KITCHEN

START TO FINISH: 30 MIN.
MAKES: 4 SERVINGS (1¼ CUPS SAUCE)

- 2 tablespoons spicy brown mustard
- ½ teaspoon pepper
- ½ cup maple syrup, divided
- 4 bone-in pork loin chops (¾ inch thick and 8 ounces each)
- 1 tablespoon butter
- ½ cup unsweetened apple juice
- 1 cup pecan halves

1. Mix mustard, pepper and 2 teaspoons of the maple syrup. Lightly drizzle over both sides of pork chops.
2. In a large nonstick skillet, heat butter over medium heat. Brown the pork chops 2-3 minutes on each side. Add apple juice. Reduce the heat; simmer, covered, until a thermometer reads 145°, 15-20 minutes. Remove chops; let stand 5 minutes, keeping them warm.
3. Add pecans and the remaining syrup to the skillet; cook and stir until blended, 1-2 minutes. Serve with pork chops.
Freeze option: Cool the pork chops. Prepare maple sauce, but do not add pecans. Freeze pecans and pork chops with sauce in separate freezer containers. To use, thaw pecans; partially thaw pork chop mixture in refrigerator overnight. Heat through slowly in a covered skillet, turning occasionally, until a thermometer inserted in pork reads 145°. Remove the chops to a platter. Add the pecans to the sauce; serve with chops.

SKILLET CASSOULET

This quick skillet version of the French classic is chock-full of flavor. Kielbasa, ham and cannellini beans make the stew a hearty meal-in-one dinner.

—BARBARA BRITTAIN SANTEE, CA

START TO FINISH: 30 MIN.
MAKES: 3 SERVINGS

- 2 teaspoons canola oil
- ¼ pound smoked turkey kielbasa, cut into ½-inch slices
- ¼ pound fully cooked boneless ham, cubed
- 2 medium carrots, sliced
- 1 celery rib, sliced
- ½ medium red onion, sliced
- 2 garlic cloves, minced
- 1 can (15 ounces) no-salt-added white kidney or cannellini beans, rinsed and drained
- 1 can (14½ ounces) no-salt-added diced tomatoes, undrained
- ¾ teaspoon dried thyme
- ⅛ teaspoon pepper

1. In a large skillet, heat oil over medium-high heat. Add kielbasa, ham, carrots, celery and onion; cook and stir until the sausage is browned and vegetables are tender. Add garlic; cook 1 minute longer.
2. Stir in remaining ingredients. Bring to a boil. Reduce heat; simmer, uncovered, 4-5 minutes or until heated through.

TOP TIP

ALWAYS HAVE VEGGIES ON HAND

"When I buy fresh carrots, celery and onions, I chop them up, use what I need, and then freeze the rest in small amounts. That way, I always have vegetables on hand for when I want to make stews, soups and casseroles."

—JOAN FRALEY COLUMBUS, OH

MAPLE-PECAN
PORK CHOPS

ROSEMARY PORK MEDALLIONS WITH PEAS

PORK CHOPS WITH MUSHROOM-TARRAGON SAUCE

Nothing says decadent like fresh mushrooms, wine and tarragon. Garlic salt and pepper boost flavor without adding any unwanted calories in this special entree.

—**MELISSA JELINEK** APPLE VALLEY, MN

START TO FINISH: 30 MIN.
MAKES: 4 SERVINGS

- 4 **boneless pork loin chops (¾ inch thick and 6 ounces each)**
- ¼ **teaspoon garlic salt**
- ¼ **teaspoon pepper**
- 2 **teaspoons olive oil, divided**
- ¾ **pound sliced fresh mushrooms**
- 1 **medium onion, chopped**
- 2 **garlic cloves, minced**
- ⅓ **cup white wine or reduced-sodium chicken broth**
- ¼ **cup all-purpose flour**
- 1 **cup reduced-sodium chicken broth**
- 2 **teaspoons minced fresh tarragon or ½ teaspoon dried tarragon**
- 2 **teaspoons butter**

1. Sprinkle pork chops with garlic salt and pepper. In a large nonstick skillet coated with cooking spray, brown the chops in 1 teaspoon oil. Remove and keep warm. In the same pan, saute the mushrooms and onion in the remaining oil until almost tender. Add garlic; cook 1 minute longer.

2. Stir in wine. Bring to a boil; cook until the liquid is almost evaporated. Combine flour and broth until smooth then stir into the pan. Bring to a boil; cook and stir for 2 minutes or until thickened. Return the pork chops to the pan and add the tarragon. Cover and cook for 6-8 minutes or until a thermometer reads 145°. Stir in the butter.

Per 1 pork chop with ½ cup sauce: 342 cal., 14g fat (5g sat. fat), 87mg chol., 322mg sod., 14g carb. (4g sugars, 2g fiber), 37g pro.

Diabetic Exchanges: 5 lean meat, 1 vegetable, 1 fat, ½ starch.

ROSEMARY PORK MEDALLIONS WITH PEAS

It's nice to have a quick meal to fix after coming home from work. This pork dish is simple to prepare and doesn't use a lot of ingredients, so it works very well for beginner cooks.

—**LAURA MCALLISTER** MORGANTON, NC

START TO FINISH: 25 MIN.
MAKES: 4 SERVINGS

- 1 **pound pork tenderloin, cut into ½-inch slices**
- ½ **teaspoon salt**
- ¼ **teaspoon pepper**
- ¼ **cup all-purpose flour**
- 1 **tablespoon olive oil**
- 2 **teaspoons butter**
- 1 **cup reduced-sodium chicken broth**
- 1 **garlic clove, minced**
- 1 **teaspoon dried rosemary, crushed**
- 2 **cups frozen peas**

1. Sprinkle pork with salt and pepper. Toss with flour to coat lightly; shake off the excess.

2. In a large skillet, heat oil and butter over medium heat. Add the pork; cook 1-2 minutes on each side or until tender. Remove from pan; keep warm.

3. In the same pan, add the broth, garlic and rosemary; bring to a boil, stirring to loosen browned bits from pan. Cook for 2-3 minutes or until liquid is reduced by a third. Stir in peas; cook 2-3 minutes longer or until heated through. Serve with pork.

Per 3 ounces cooked pork with ⅓ cup peas: 260 cal., 10g fat (3g sat. fat), 69mg chol., 571mg sod., 15g carb. (4g sugars, 3g fiber), 28g pro.

Diabetic Exchanges: 3 lean meat, 1 starch, ½ fat.

PORK & POTATO SUPPER

If you're looking for a comforting one-dish dinner that can be easily made on a busy night, this recipe is for you. My husband made sure that I added it to the list of our family's favorites.

—MACEY ALLEN GREEN FOREST, AR

START TO FINISH: 30 MIN.
MAKES: 4 SERVINGS

- 2 tablespoons butter, divided
- 1 pork tenderloin (1 pound), cut into ¼-inch slices
- 1 cup sliced fresh mushrooms
- 2 garlic cloves, minced
- 8 small red potatoes, quartered
- 1 can (14½ ounces) reduced-sodium chicken broth, divided
- 2 teaspoons Worcestershire sauce
- ¼ teaspoon salt
- ¼ teaspoon pepper
- 2 tablespoons all-purpose flour
- 4 green onions, sliced

1. In a 12-in. skillet, heat 1 tablespoon butter over medium heat. Cook pork 2-4 minutes on each side or until tender. Remove from pan.
2. In same pan, heat the remaining butter over medium-high heat. Add mushrooms; cook and stir until almost tender. Add garlic; cook 1 minute longer. Stir in potatoes, 1½ cups of the broth, Worcestershire sauce, salt and pepper. Bring to a boil. Reduce heat; simmer, covered, 10-15 minutes or until the potatoes are tender.
3. In a small bowl, mix flour and the remaining broth until smooth. Stir into the mushroom mixture. Bring to a boil; cook and stir until the sauce is thickened. Stir in green onions. Return pork to pan and heat through.
Per 1½ cups: 282 cal., 10g fat (5g sat. fat), 78mg chol., 565mg sod., 21g carb. (2g sugars, 2g fiber), 27g pro.
Diabetic Exchanges: 3 lean meat, 1½ fat, 1 starch.

MOM'S PAELLA

MOM'S PAELLA

I enjoy cooking ethnic foods, especially those that call for lots of rice. Like my mom, I often prepare this dish for special Sunday-get-togethers.

—ENA QUIGGLE GOODHUE, MN

PREP: 10 MIN. • **COOK:** 40 MIN.
MAKES: 6-8 SERVINGS

- 1½ cups cubed cooked chicken
- 1 cup cubed fully cooked ham
- ½ cup sliced fully cooked smoked sausage (¼-inch slices)
- 1 medium onion, chopped
- 1 small green pepper, chopped
- 4 tablespoons olive oil, divided
- ¼ cup pimiento-stuffed olives, halved
- ½ cup raisins, optional
- 1 cup uncooked converted rice
- 2 garlic cloves, minced
- 3 teaspoons ground turmeric
- 1½ teaspoons curry powder
- 2¼ cups chicken broth
- 1½ cups frozen mixed vegetables

1. In a large skillet, saute the chicken, ham, sausage, onion and green pepper in 2 tablespoons oil for 3-5 minutes or until the onion is tender. Add olives and raisins if desired. Cook for 2-3 minutes longer or until heated through, stirring occasionally; remove meat and vegetable mixture from pan and keep warm.
2. In the same skillet, saute the rice in the remaining oil for 2-3 minutes or until it is lightly browned. Stir in the garlic, turmeric and curry. Return the meat and vegetables to the pan; toss lightly. Add broth and mixed vegetables; bring to a boil. Reduce heat; cover and simmer for 25-30 minutes or until the rice is tender.

SKILLET PORK CHOPS WITH APPLES & ONION

SKILLET PORK CHOPS WITH APPLES & ONION

Simple recipes that land on the table fast are a lifesaver. I serve these with veggies and, if time allows, cornbread stuffing.

—**TRACEY KARST** PONDERAY, ID

START TO FINISH: 20 MIN.
MAKES: 4 SERVINGS

- 4 **boneless pork loin chops (6 ounces each)**
- 3 **medium apples, cut into wedges**
- 1 **large onion, cut into thin wedges**
- ¼ **cup water**
- ⅓ **cup balsamic vinaigrette**
- ½ **teaspoon salt**
- ¼ **teaspoon pepper**

1. In a large nonstick skillet over medium heat, brown pork chops on both sides, about 4 minutes. Remove from pan.
2. In the same skillet, combine apples, onion and water. Place pork chops over the apple mixture; drizzle chops with vinaigrette. Sprinkle with salt and pepper. Reduce the heat; simmer, covered, for 3-5 minutes or until a thermometer inserted in chops reads 145°.

OUR FAVORITE PORK CHOPS

My husband raves about these tender sweet-and-sour chops that top my list of best quick dinners.

—**LINDA FOREMAN** LOCUST GROVE, OK

START TO FINISH: 20 MIN.
MAKES: 4 SERVINGS

- 4 **bone-in pork loin chops**
- 2 **tablespoons all-purpose flour**
- 2 **tablespoons olive oil**
- 1 **cup picante sauce**
- 1 **medium tart apple, peeled and chopped**
- 2 **tablespoons brown sugar**

1. Coat pork chops with flour. In a large skillet over medium-high heat, cook the chops in oil for 2-3 minutes on each side or until chops are lightly browned; drain. In a small bowl, combine picante sauce, apple and brown sugar; add to the pan.
2. Reduce heat; cover and cook for 4-6 minutes or until a thermometer reads 145°. Let stand for 5 minutes before serving.

SKILLET
HAM & RICE

SKILLET HAM & RICE

Ham, rice and mushrooms make a tasty combination in this homey stovetop dish that's on the table in under 30 minutes.

—**SUSAN ZIVEC** REGINA, SK

START TO FINISH: 25 MIN.
MAKES: 2 SERVINGS

- 1 **teaspoon olive oil**
- 1 **medium onion, chopped**
- 1 **cup sliced fresh mushrooms**
- 1 **cup cubed fully cooked ham**
- ⅛ **teaspoon pepper**
- ½ **cup reduced-sodium chicken broth**
- ¼ **cup water**
- ¾ **cup uncooked instant rice**
- 2 **green onions, sliced**
- ¼ **cup shredded Parmesan cheese**

1. In a large nonstick skillet, heat the oil over medium-high heat; saute onion and mushrooms until tender. Stir in the ham, pepper, broth and water; bring to a boil. Stir in the rice. Reduce the heat; simmer, covered, until the rice is tender, about 5 minutes.
2. Fluff the rice with a fork. Top the dish with green onions and cheese.
Health Tip: Look for lower-sodium ham in the meat and deli sections. This variety typically contains 25%-30% less sodium.

HAY & STRAW

BLACKENED PORK CAESAR SALAD

START TO FINISH: 30 MIN.
MAKES: 2 SERVINGS

- 2 **tablespoons mayonnaise**
- 1 **tablespoon olive oil**
- 1 **tablespoon lemon juice**
- 1 **garlic clove, minced**
- ⅛ **teaspoon seasoned salt**
- ⅛ **teaspoon pepper**

SALAD
- ¾ **pound pork tenderloin, cut into 1-inch cubes**
- 1 **tablespoon blackened seasoning**
- 1 **tablespoon canola oil**
- 6 **cups torn romaine**
    Salad croutons and shredded Parmesan cheese, optional

1. For dressing, in a small bowl, mix the first six ingredients until blended.
2. Toss pork with blackened seasoning. In a large skillet, heat oil over medium-high heat. Add pork; cook and stir for 5-7 minutes or until tender.
3. To serve, place romaine in a large bowl; add dressing and toss to coat. Top with pork, and, if desired, croutons and cheese.

BASIL PORK CHOPS

These tender pork chops get a kick from basil, chili powder and a little brown sugar. Serve with your favorite roasted veggies and you've got a super comforting meal bursting with flavor.
—**LISA GILLILAND** FORT COLLINS, CO

START TO FINISH: 25 MIN.
MAKES: 4 SERVINGS

- ¼ **cup packed brown sugar**
- 1½ **teaspoons dried basil**
- ½ **teaspoon salt**
- ½ **teaspoon chili powder**
- 2 **tablespoons canola oil, divided**
- 4 **boneless pork loin chops (½ inch thick and 4 ounces each)**

1. Mix first four ingredients; gradually stir in 1 tablespoon oil (the mixture will be crumbly). Rub over both sides of chops.
2. In a large skillet, heat the remaining oil over medium heat; cook the chops until a thermometer reads 145°, about 4-6 minutes per side. Let stand 5 minutes before serving.

HAY & STRAW

This recipe is not only quick and easy to prepare, but it is colorful, too. Start cooking the ham about 5 minutes before the linguine is supposed to be done; that way, all the ingredients will be ready at the same time.
—**PRISCILLA WEAVER** HAGERSTOWN, MD

START TO FINISH: 20 MIN.
MAKES: 8 SERVINGS

- 1 **package (16 ounces) linguine**
- 2 **cups julienned fully cooked ham**
- 1 **tablespoon butter**
- 3 **cups frozen peas**
- 1½ **cups shredded Parmesan cheese**
- ⅓ **cup heavy whipping cream**

Cook linguine according to the package directions. In a large skillet, saute ham in butter for 3 minutes. Add peas; heat through. Drain linguine; toss with the ham mixture, Parmesan cheese and cream. Serve immediately.

TOP TIP

CUT THE CREAM
For a heavy cream substitute, blend 1 tablespoon flour into 1 cup low-fat milk. In soups, sauces and casseroles, it provides the consistency of heavy cream without the fat.

BLACKENED PORK CAESAR SALAD

HONEY-MUSTARD PORK SCALLOPINI

My family loves honey and mustard. Paired with crispy pork, it's even more mouthwatering. Pounding the boneless chops tenderizes them and makes them cook quickly. It's wonderful to have something as tasty as this when time is short.

—STEPHANIE MOON BOISE, ID

START TO FINISH: 20 MIN.
MAKES: 4 SERVINGS

- 4 boneless butterflied pork chops (4 ounces each)
- 2 tablespoons honey
- 2 tablespoons spicy brown mustard
- ⅓ cup crushed Ritz crackers (about 8 crackers)
- ⅓ cup dry bread crumbs
- 1 tablespoon canola oil
- 1 tablespoon butter

1. Flatten pork to ⅛-in. thickness. In a small bowl, combine honey and mustard; brush over both sides of the pork. In a shallow bowl, combine the cracker and bread crumbs; add pork and turn to coat.
2. In a large skillet, cook pork over medium heat in oil and butter for 2-3 minutes on each side or until crisp and juices run clear.

CURLY NOODLE PORK SUPPER

This hearty meal-in-one is loaded with tender pork and ramen noodles. Broccoli and red pepper add a fresh-from-the-garden flavor.

—CARMEN CARLSON KENT, WA

START TO FINISH: 25 MIN.
MAKES: 4 SERVINGS

- 1 pound pork tenderloin, cut into ¼-inch strips
- 1 medium sweet red pepper, cut into 1-inch pieces
- 1 cup fresh broccoli florets
- 4 green onions, cut into 1-inch pieces
- 1 tablespoon canola oil
- 1½ cups water
- 2 packages (3 ounces each) pork ramen noodles
- 1 tablespoon minced fresh parsley
- 1 tablespoon soy sauce

SWEET & SOUR PORK

1. In a large skillet, cook the pork, red pepper, broccoli and onions in oil until meat is no longer pink.
2. Add the water, noodles with contents of seasoning packets, parsley and soy sauce. Bring this to a boil. Reduce the heat; cook for 3-4 minutes or until the noodles are tender.

SWEET & SOUR PORK

My grandmother made this for me on Valentine's Day when I was a child. Now I make it for my children. I usually make brown rice or rice noodles and add sliced bok choy to up the vegetable intake.

—BARBARA HINTERBERGER BUFFALO, NY

PREP: 20 MIN. • **COOK:** 15 MIN.
MAKES: 4 SERVINGS

- 1 can (20 ounces) unsweetened pineapple chunks
- ⅓ cup water
- ⅓ cup cider vinegar
- 3 tablespoons brown sugar
- 2 tablespoons cornstarch
- 1 tablespoon reduced-sodium soy sauce
- 1 teaspoon Worcestershire sauce
- ½ teaspoon salt
- 1 pound pork tenderloin, cut into ½-inch pieces
- 1 teaspoon paprika
- 1 tablespoon canola oil
- 1 medium green pepper, thinly sliced
- 1 small onion, thinly sliced
- 2 cups hot cooked brown rice

1. Drain pineapple, reserving ⅔ cup juice; set the pineapple aside. In a small bowl, mix the water, vinegar, brown sugar, cornstarch, soy sauce, Worcestershire sauce, salt and reserved pineapple juice until smooth; set aside.
2. Sprinkle pork with paprika. In a large nonstick skillet coated with cooking spray, brown pork in oil.
3. Stir the cornstarch mixture and add it to the pan. Bring to a boil; cook and stir for 1 minute or until thickened. Add green pepper, onion and pineapple. Reduce the heat; simmer, covered, for 6-8 minutes or until the pork is tender. Serve with rice.

PORK SCHNITZEL WITH DILL SAUCE

Schnitzel is one of my husband's favorites. It reminds him of his German roots, and I like the fact it's easy to make for a group.
—JOYCE FOLKER PAROWAN, UT

PREP: 20 MIN. • **COOK:** 20 MIN.
MAKES: 6 SERVINGS

- ½ cup all-purpose flour
- 2 teaspoons seasoned salt
- ½ teaspoon pepper
- 2 large eggs
- ¼ cup 2% milk
- 1½ cups dry bread crumbs
- 2 teaspoons paprika
- 6 pork sirloin cutlets (4 ounces each)
- 6 tablespoons canola oil

DILL SAUCE
- 2 tablespoons all-purpose flour
- 1½ cups chicken broth, divided
- 1 cup (8 ounces) sour cream
- ½ teaspoon dill weed

1. In a shallow bowl, mix flour, seasoned salt and pepper. In a second shallow bowl, whisk the eggs and milk until they are blended. In a third bowl, mix the bread crumbs and paprika.
2. Pound pork cutlets with a meat mallet to ¼-in. thickness. Dip cutlets in the flour mixture to coat both sides; shake off the excess. Dip in the egg mixture , then in the crumb mixture, patting to help the coating adhere.
3. In a large skillet, heat oil over medium heat. Add the pork in batches; cook for 2-3 minutes on each side or until golden brown. Remove to a serving plate; keep warm. Wipe skillet clean if necessary.
4. In a small bowl, whisk flour and broth until smooth; add to the same skillet. Bring to a boil, stirring constantly; cook and stir 2 minutes or until thickened.
5. Reduce the heat to low. Stir in sour cream and dill; heat through (do not boil). Serve with the pork.

MOM'S FRIED RICE

I sometimes add pea pods to this dish for added color and crunch. Or if you want to turn this into a main dish, you can add chopped shrimp, chicken or steak.
—CAREY HUNT PORTLAND, OR

START TO FINISH: 25 MIN.
MAKES: 4 SERVINGS

- 1 teaspoon canola oil
- 1 large egg, beaten
- 8 bacon strips, chopped
- 1 cup chopped fresh mushrooms
- 8 green onions, thinly sliced
- 3 cups leftover cooked rice
- 1 cup bean sprouts
- 1 cup frozen peas, thawed
- ¼ cup reduced-sodium soy sauce

1. In a large skillet, heat oil over medium-high heat. Pour egg into the pan. As egg sets, lift edges, letting uncooked portion flow underneath. When egg is completely cooked, remove to a plate. Set aside.
2. In the same skillet, cook bacon over medium heat until crisp. Using a slotted spoon, remove to paper towels; drain, reserving 2 tablespoons drippings. Saute mushrooms and onions in the drippings. Stir in the rice, bean sprouts, peas, soy sauce and bacon. Chop the egg into small pieces; stir into the pan and heat through.

PORK SCHNITZEL WITH DILL SAUCE

> **TOP TIP**
>
> ### COOKED RICE TIME-SAVER
>
> "Sometimes on a weekend, I make a good-sized pot of rice. Having the cooked rice in the refrigerator is quite a time-saver during the week. I can quickly make fried rice, Spanish rice, rice pudding and even add it to soups."
>
> —**GRACE R.** WRIGHTWOOD, CA

Fish & Seafood

TOMATO-ARTICHOKE TILAPIA

TOMATO-ARTICHOKE TILAPIA

My mom and I really like tomatoes, capers and artichokes, so I used them together in this one-pan meal. The best part is that, on a busy night, all of the ingredients are ready and waiting.

—**DENISE KLIBERT** SHREVEPORT, LA

START TO FINISH: 15 MIN.
MAKES: 4 SERVINGS

- 1 **tablespoon olive oil**
- 1 **can (14½ ounces) diced tomatoes with roasted garlic, drained**
- 1 **can (14 ounces) water-packed quartered artichoke hearts, drained**
- 2 **tablespoons drained capers**
- 4 **tilapia fillets (6 ounces each)**

1. In a large skillet, heat oil over medium heat. Add tomatoes, artichoke hearts and capers; cook 3-5 minutes or until heated through, stirring occasionally.

2. Arrange tilapia over tomato mixture. Cook, covered, 6-8 minutes or until fish begins to flake easily with a fork.

Italian Fish Fillets: Substitute 1 medium julienned green pepper, 1 small julienned onion, ½ cup Italian salad dressing and ½ teaspoon Italian seasoning for the first four ingredients. Cook 5 minutes or until tender. Add 2 cans (14½ ounces each) diced tomatoes; bring to a boil. Add fish and cook as directed.

BASIL-LEMON
CRAB LINGUINE

SALMON & DILL SAUCE WITH LEMON RISOTTO

I love the classic combination of lemon and fish, and this dish is delicious and easy enough to throw together at the end of a long day.

—**AMANDA REED** NASHVILLE, TN

PREP: 20 MIN. • **COOK:** 30 MIN.
MAKES: 4 SERVINGS

SAUCE
- ½ cup mayonnaise
- ¼ cup sour cream
- 1 tablespoon chopped green onion
- 1 tablespoon lemon juice
- 1½ teaspoons snipped fresh dill or ½ teaspoon dill weed

RISOTTO
- 3 to 3½ cups chicken broth
- 2 tablespoons olive oil
- 1 shallot, finely chopped
- 1 cup uncooked arborio rice
- 1 garlic clove, minced
- 2 teaspoons grated lemon peel
- ¼ teaspoon pepper

SALMON
- 4 salmon fillets (6 ounces each)
- ½ teaspoon salt
- ¼ teaspoon pepper
- 2 tablespoons olive oil

1. In a small bowl, mix sauce ingredients. Refrigerate, covered, until serving.
2. In a small saucepan, bring broth to a simmer; keep hot. In a large saucepan, heat oil over medium heat. Add shallot; cook and stir 1-2 minutes or until tender. Add rice and garlic; cook and stir for 1-2 minutes or until rice is coated.
3. Stir in ½ cup hot broth. Reduce heat to maintain a simmer; cook and stir until broth is absorbed. Add remaining broth, ½ cup at a time, cooking and stirring until the broth has been absorbed after each addition, until rice is tender but firm to the bite, and risotto is creamy. Remove from heat; stir in lemon peel and pepper.
4. Meanwhile, sprinkle fillets with salt and pepper. In a large skillet, heat oil over medium heat. Add the fillets; cook for 6-8 minutes on each side or until fish just begins to flake easily with a fork. Serve with sauce and risotto.

BASIL-LEMON CRAB LINGUINE

I love using fresh herbs to punch up pasta dishes. This linguine looks and tastes as if it's from a five-star restaurant.

—**TONYA BURKHARD** PALM COAST, FL

START TO FINISH: 25 MIN.
MAKES: 4 SERVINGS

- 1 package (9 ounces) refrigerated linguine
- ⅓ cup butter, cubed
- 1 jalapeno pepper, seeded and finely chopped
- 1 garlic clove, minced
- 1 teaspoon grated lemon peel
- 3 tablespoons lemon juice
- 2 cans (6 ounces each) lump crabmeat, drained
- ¼ cup loosely packed basil leaves, thinly sliced
- ½ teaspoon sea salt
- ¼ teaspoon freshly ground pepper

1. Cook linguine according to package directions. Meanwhile, in a large skillet, heat butter over medium heat. Add jalapeno and garlic; cook and stir for 1-2 minutes or until tender. Stir in lemon peel and juice. Add crab; heat through, stirring gently.
2. Drain linguine; add to skillet. Sprinkle with basil, salt and pepper; toss to combine.

Test Kitchen Note: Wear disposable gloves when cutting hot peppers; the oils can burn skin. Avoid touching your face.

CONFETTI PASTA

Our Christmas Eve tradition is to make linguine with red and green peppers and shrimp. We serve it with a snappy salad and garlic bread.
—**ELLEN FIORE** MONTVALE, NJ

START TO FINISH: 25 MIN.
MAKES: 8 SERVINGS

- 1 package (16 ounces) linguine
- 1 cup chopped sweet red pepper
- 1 cup chopped green pepper
- ⅓ cup chopped onion
- 3 garlic cloves, peeled and thinly sliced
- ¼ teaspoon salt
- ¼ teaspoon dried oregano
- ⅛ teaspoon crushed red pepper flakes
- ⅛ teaspoon pepper
- ¼ cup olive oil
- 2 pounds peeled and deveined cooked shrimp (61-70 per pound)
- ½ cup shredded Parmesan cheese

1. Cook linguine according to package directions. In a Dutch oven, saute the peppers, onion, garlic and seasonings in oil until vegetables are tender.
2. Add shrimp; cook and stir 2-3 minutes longer or until heated through. Drain the linguine; toss with the shrimp mixture. Sprinkle with Parmesan cheese.
Per 1⅓ cups: 418 cal., 11g fat (2g sat. fat), 176mg chol., 331mg sod., 46g carb. (3g sugars, 3g fiber), 33g pro.
Diabetic Exchanges: 3 starch, 3 lean meat, 1½ fat.

SOUTHERN SHRIMP & GRITS

We sometimes call this dish "breakfast shrimp." Serve it for brunch, dinner or when company's coming—it's down-home comfort food at its finest.
—**MANDY RIVERS** LEXINGTON, SC

PREP: 15 MIN. • **COOK:** 20 MIN.
MAKES: 4 SERVINGS

- 2 cups reduced-sodium chicken broth
- 2 cups 2% milk
- ⅓ cup butter, cubed
- ¾ teaspoon salt
- ½ teaspoon pepper
- ¾ cup uncooked old-fashioned grits
- 1 cup shredded cheddar cheese

SHRIMP
- 8 thick-sliced bacon strips, chopped
- 1 pound uncooked medium shrimp, peeled and deveined
- 3 garlic cloves, minced
- 1 teaspoon Cajun or blackened seasoning
- 4 green onions, chopped

1. In a large saucepan, bring the broth, milk, butter, salt and pepper to a boil. Slowly stir in grits. Reduce heat. Cover and cook for 12-14 minutes or until thickened, stirring occasionally. Stir in cheese until melted. Set aside and keep warm.
2. In a large skillet, cook bacon over medium heat until crisp. Remove to paper towels with a slotted spoon; drain, reserving 4 teaspoons drippings. Saute the shrimp, garlic and seasoning in drippings until shrimp turn pink. Serve with grits and sprinkle with onions.

LEMON-PEPPER TILAPIA WITH MUSHROOMS

My husband and I are trying to add more fish and healthier entrees to our diet and this one makes it easy. It comes together in less than 30 minutes, so it's perfect for hectic weeknights.
—**DONNA MCDONALD** LAKE ELSINORE, CA

START TO FINISH: 25 MIN.
MAKES: 4 SERVINGS

- 2 tablespoons butter
- ½ pound sliced fresh mushrooms
- ¾ teaspoon lemon-pepper seasoning, divided
- 3 garlic cloves, minced
- 4 tilapia fillets (6 ounces each)
- ¼ teaspoon paprika
- ⅛ teaspoon cayenne pepper
- 1 medium tomato, chopped
- 3 green onions, thinly sliced

1. In a 12-in. skillet, heat butter over medium heat. Add mushrooms and ¼ teaspoon lemon pepper; cook and stir for 3-5 minutes or until tender. Add garlic; cook 30 seconds longer.
2. Place fillets over mushrooms; sprinkle with paprika, cayenne and remaining lemon pepper. Cook, covered, for 5-7 minutes or until fish just begins to flake easily with a fork. Top with tomato and green onions.
Per fillet: 216 cal., 8g fat (4g sat. fat), 98mg chol., 173mg sod., 5g carb. (2g sugars, 1g fiber), 34g pro.
Diabetic Exchanges: 4 lean meat, 1½ fat.

HOW-TO

TIPS ON BUYING FISH

- When buying fresh fish fillets or steaks, look for firm flesh that has a moist appearance. Don't purchase fish that looks dry. Fresh fish should have a mild smell, not a strong odor.
- When buying frozen fish, look for packages that are solidly frozen, tightly sealed and free of freezer burn and odor.
- Fresh fish is highly perishable and should be prepared within a day or two after it is caught or purchased.

LEMON-PEPPER TILAPIA
WITH MUSHROOMS

LOUISIANA JAMBALAYA

LOUISIANA JAMBALAYA

My husband helped add a little spice to my life. He grew up on Cajun cooking, while I ate mostly meat-and-potatoes meals. The flavors have been a revelation!
—**SANDI PICHON** MEMPHIS, TN

PREP: 10 MIN. • **COOK:** 30 MIN.
MAKES: 12 SERVINGS

- ¼ **cup canola oil**
- ½ **pound smoked sausage, halved and sliced**
- 2 **cups cubed fully cooked ham**
- 2 **celery ribs, chopped**
- 1 **large onion, chopped**
- 1 **medium green pepper, chopped**
- 5 **green onions, thinly sliced**
- 2 **garlic cloves, minced**
- 1 **can (14½ ounces) diced tomatoes, undrained**
- 1 **teaspoon dried thyme**
- 1 **teaspoon salt**
- ½ **teaspoon pepper**
- ¼ **teaspoon cayenne pepper**
- 2 **cans (14½ ounces each) chicken broth**
- 1 **cup uncooked long grain rice**
- ⅓ **cup water**
- 4½ **teaspoons Worcestershire sauce**
- 2 **pounds peeled and deveined cooked shrimp (31–40 per pound)**

1. In a Dutch oven, heat oil over medium-high heat. Add sausage and ham; saute until lightly browned. Remove and keep warm. In drippings, saute celery, onion, green pepper and green onions until tender. Add garlic; cook and stir 1 minute longer. Stir in tomatoes, thyme, salt, pepper and cayenne; cook 5 minutes longer.

2. Stir in chicken broth, rice, water and Worcestershire sauce. Bring to a boil. Reduce heat; simmer, covered, until the rice is tender, about 20 minutes. Stir in the sausage mixture and shrimp; heat through.

Freeze option: Prepare jambalaya as directed, omitting rice and shrimp. Freeze shrimp and cooled jambalaya in separate freezer containers. Store rice in an airtight container at room temperature. To use, partially thaw jambalaya in the refrigerator overnight. Place jambalaya in a 6-qt. stockpot; heat through. Add rice; cook, covered, about 10 minutes. Add frozen shrimp; continue cooking until shrimp are heated through and rice is tender, 5-7 minutes.

PEKING SHRIMP

In the summer, we spend as much time as possible at our vacation home in a beach town. I prepare lots of seafood because it's so fresh and readily available there, but this main dish is a year-round favorite.
—**JANET EDWARDS** BEAVERTON, OR

START TO FINISH: 25 MIN.
MAKES: 4 SERVINGS

- 1 **tablespoon cornstarch**
- ¼ **cup cold water**
- ¼ **cup corn syrup**
- 2 **tablespoons reduced-sodium soy sauce**
- 2 **tablespoons sherry or chicken broth**
- 1 **garlic clove, minced**
- ¼ **teaspoon ground ginger**
- 1 **small green pepper, cut into 1-inch pieces**
- 2 **tablespoons canola oil**
- 1 **pound uncooked medium shrimp, peeled and deveined**
- 1 **medium tomato, cut into wedges Hot cooked rice, optional**

1. In a small bowl, combine cornstarch and water until smooth. Stir in the corn syrup, soy sauce, sherry, garlic and ginger; set aside.

2. In a nonstick skillet or wok, stir-fry green pepper in oil for 3 minutes. Add shrimp; cook 3 minutes longer or until shrimp turn pink.

3. Stir cornstarch mixture and add to pan. Bring to a boil; cook and stir for 2 minutes or until thickened. Add tomato; heat through. Serve with rice if desired.
Per ¾ cup: 237 cal., 8g fat (1g sat. fat), 168mg chol., 532mg sod., 21g carb. (9g sugars, 1g fiber), 19g pro.
Diabetic Exchanges: 2 lean meat, 1½ fat, 1 starch, 1 vegetable.

CATFISH WITH SAVORY STRAWBERRY SAUCE

Friends and family will love the delicate balance between spicy and sweet in this entree. Serve it with red beans and rice to complete the Cajun theme.

—**HEATHER SAPP** ALEXANDRIA, VA

START TO FINISH: 25 MIN.
MAKES: 4 SERVINGS

- 4 **catfish fillets (6 ounces each)**
- ¼ **teaspoon salt**
- ¼ **teaspoon pepper**
- 1 **teaspoon hot pepper sauce**
- ¼ **cup strawberry spreadable fruit**
- 2 **tablespoons red wine vinegar**
- 1 **tablespoon seafood cocktail sauce**
- ¾ **teaspoon reduced-sodium soy sauce**
- ½ **teaspoon grated horseradish**
- 1 **garlic clove, minced**
- ⅓ **cup all-purpose flour**
- ⅓ **cup cornmeal**
- 1 **tablespoon olive oil**

1. Sprinkle catfish with salt, pepper and hot pepper sauce; set aside. In a small saucepan, combine spreadable fruit, vinegar, seafood sauce, soy sauce, horseradish and garlic. Cook over low heat until heated through, stirring occasionally.
2. Meanwhile, in a large resealable plastic bag, combine flour and cornmeal. Add catfish, one fillet at a time, and shake to coat. In a large nonstick skillet, cook fillets in oil over medium-high heat 2-3 minutes on each side or until the fish flakes easily with a fork. Drain on paper towels. Serve with strawberry sauce.

PECAN-COCONUT CRUSTED TILAPIA

PECAN-COCONUT CRUSTED TILAPIA

When I have guests with dietary restrictions, tilapia coated in pecans and coconut makes everyone happy. It's gluten-free and loaded with flavor.

—**CAITLIN ROTH** CHICAGO, IL

START TO FINISH: 25 MIN.
MAKES: 4 SERVINGS

- 2 **large eggs**
- ½ **cup unsweetened finely shredded coconut**
- ½ **cup finely chopped pecans**
- ½ **teaspoon salt**
- ¼ **teaspoon crushed red pepper flakes**
- 4 **tilapia fillets (6 ounces each)**
- 2 **tablespoons canola oil**

1. In a shallow bowl, whisk eggs. In a separate shallow bowl, combine coconut, pecans, salt and pepper flakes. Dip fillets in eggs, then in coconut mixture, patting to help the coating adhere.
2. In a large skillet, heat oil over medium heat. In batches, add tilapia and cook for 2-3 minutes on each side or until lightly browned and fish just begins to flake easily with a fork.

Parmesan-Crusted Tilapia: Omit coconut, pecans and pepper flakes. In a shallow bowl, combine ½ cup crushed Ritz crackers, ¼ cup grated Parmesan cheese and salt. Proceed as directed.

Test Kitchen Note: Look for unsweetened coconut in the baking, bulk or health food section.

> **TOP TIP**
>
> **FREEZING FISH**
> For long-term storage, wrap fish in freezer paper, heavy-duty foil or heavy-duty plastic bags and freeze no longer than 3 months for fatty or oily fish (such as salmon, whitefish and mackerel) or 6 months for lean fish (such as catfish, sole, cod and tilapia).

"Searching for a lighter substitute to fried fish tacos, I came up with this entree. It's been a hit with friends and family. These fillets are so mild that even those who don't like fish are pleasantly surprised."
—JENNIFER PALMER RANCHO CUCAMONGA, CA

FANTASTIC FISH TACOS

FANTASTIC FISH TACOS

START TO FINISH: 30 MIN.
MAKES: 4 SERVINGS

- ½ cup fat-free mayonnaise
- 1 tablespoon lime juice
- 2 teaspoons fat-free milk
- 1 large egg
- 1 teaspoon water
- ⅓ cup dry bread crumbs
- 2 tablespoons salt-free lemon-pepper seasoning
- 1 pound mahi mahi or cod fillets, cut into 1-inch strips
- 4 corn tortillas (6 inches), warmed

TOPPINGS

- 1 cup coleslaw mix
- 2 medium tomatoes, chopped
- 1 cup shredded reduced-fat Mexican cheese blend
- 1 tablespoon minced fresh cilantro

1. For sauce, in a small bowl, mix the mayonnaise, lime juice and milk; refrigerate until serving.

2. In a shallow bowl, whisk together egg and water. In another bowl, toss bread crumbs with lemon pepper. Dip fish in the egg mixture, then in the crumb mixture, patting to help coating adhere.

3. Place a large nonstick skillet coated with cooking spray over medium-high heat. Add fish; cook 2-4 minutes per side or until golden brown and fish just begins to flake easily with a fork. Serve in tortillas with toppings and sauce.

Per taco: 321 cal., 10g fat (5g sat. fat), 148mg chol., 632mg sod., 29g carb. (5g sugars, 4g fiber), 34g pro.
Diabetic Exchanges: 4 lean meat, 2 starch.

TOP TIP

MAHI MAHI SWAPS

Mahi mahi has a thick, meat-like texture and a flavor that's not too strong. Good substitutes include halibut, sturgeon and swordfish. Cod, catfish, haddock and whitefish are a good match for the flavor, with body that is slightly less dense; they'll work nicely, too.

MAHI MAHI & VEGGIE SKILLET

MAHI MAHI & VEGGIE SKILLET

Cooking mahi mahi and ratatouille may seem complex, but I developed a skillet recipe to bring out the wow without the worry.
—**SOLOMON WANG** ARLINGTON, TX

START TO FINISH: 30 MIN.
MAKES: 4 SERVINGS

- 3 tablespoons olive oil, divided
- 4 mahi mahi or salmon fillets (6 ounces each)
- 3 medium sweet red peppers, cut into thick strips
- ½ pound sliced baby portobello mushrooms
- 1 large sweet onion, cut into thick rings and separated
- ⅓ cup lemon juice
- ¾ teaspoon salt, divided
- ½ teaspoon pepper
- ¼ cup minced fresh chives
- ⅓ cup pine nuts, optional

1. In a large skillet, heat 2 tablespoons oil over medium-high heat. Add fillets; cook 4-5 minutes on each side or until fish just begins to flake easily with a fork. Remove from pan.

2. Add the remaining oil, the peppers, mushrooms, onion, lemon juice and ¼ teaspoon salt. Cook, covered, over medium heat 6-8 minutes or until the vegetables are tender; stir occasionally.

3. Place fish over vegetables; sprinkle with pepper and remaining salt. Cook, covered, 2 minutes longer or until heated through. Sprinkle with chives and, if desired, pine nuts before serving.

Per serving: 307 cal., 12g fat (2g sat. fat), 124mg chol., 606mg sod., 15g carb. (9g sugars, 3g fiber), 35g pro.
Diabetic Exchanges: 4 lean meat, 3 vegetable, 2 fat.

COD WITH HEARTY
TOMATO SAUCE

HALIBUT STEAKS WITH PAPAYA MINT SALSA

The combination of zesty fruit salsa and tender halibut makes this dish the catch of the day!

—**SONYA LABBE** WEST HOLLYWOOD, CA

START TO FINISH: 20 MIN.
MAKES: 4 SERVINGS

- 1 medium papaya, peeled, seeded and chopped
- ¼ cup chopped red onion
- ¼ cup fresh mint leaves
- 1 teaspoon finely chopped chipotle pepper in adobo sauce
- 2 tablespoons olive oil, divided
- 1 tablespoon honey
- 4 halibut steaks (6 ounces each)

1. In a small bowl, combine the papaya, onion, mint, chipotle pepper, 1 tablespoon oil and honey. Cover and refrigerate until serving.
2. In a large skillet, cook halibut in the remaining oil for 4-6 minutes on each side or until fish flakes easily with a fork. Serve with salsa.

SPEEDY SALMON PATTIES

When I was a girl growing up on the farm, my mom often fixed these seasoned patties when we were working late in the field. They're also tasty with chopped green peppers added to the mixture.

—**BONNIE EVANS** CAMERON, NC

START TO FINISH: 25 MIN.
MAKES: 3 SERVINGS

- ⅓ cup finely chopped onion
- 1 large egg, beaten
- 5 saltines, crushed
- ½ teaspoon Worcestershire sauce
- ¼ teaspoon salt
- ⅛ teaspoon pepper
- 1 can (14¾ ounces) salmon, drained, bones and skin removed
- 2 teaspoons butter

1. In a large bowl, combine the first six ingredients. Crumble salmon over mixture and mix well. Shape into six patties.
2. In a large skillet over medium heat, fry the patties in butter 3-4 minutes on each side or until set and golden brown.

COD WITH HEARTY TOMATO SAUCE

My father made this sweet, flavorful recipe for my mother when he would cook for the night. We serve it with whole wheat pasta or brown rice.

—**ANN MARIE EBERHART** GIG HARBOR, WA

START TO FINISH: 30 MIN.
MAKES: 4 SERVINGS

- 2 cans (14½ ounces each) diced tomatoes with basil, oregano and garlic, undrained
- 4 cod fillets (6 ounces each)
- 2 tablespoons olive oil, divided
- 2 medium onions, halved and thinly sliced (about 1½ cups)
- ½ teaspoon dried oregano
- ¼ teaspoon pepper
- ¼ teaspoon crushed red pepper flakes
  Hot cooked whole wheat pasta
  Minced fresh parsley, optional

1. Place tomatoes in a blender or food processor. Cover and process until pureed.
2. Pat fish dry with paper towels. In a large skillet, heat 1 tablespoon oil over medium-high heat. Add cod fillets; cook 2-4 minutes on each side or until surface of fish begins to color. Remove from pan.
3. In the same skillet, heat the remaining oil over medium-high heat. Add onions; cook and stir 2-4 minutes or until tender. Stir in seasonings and pureed tomatoes; bring to a boil. Add cod; return just to a boil, spooning sauce over tops. Reduce heat; simmer, uncovered, 5-7 minutes or until fish just begins to flake easily with a fork. Serve with pasta. If desired, sprinkle with parsley.

Per fillet with ¾ cup sauce: 271 cal., 8g fat (1g sat. fat), 65mg chol., 746mg sod., 17g carb. (9g sugars, 4g fiber), 29g pro.
Diabetic Exchanges: 3 lean meat, 2 vegetable, 1½ fat.

SCALLOPS
WITH WILTED
SPINACH

SCALLOPS WITH WILTED SPINACH

Two of my favorite foods are bacon and seafood. In this dish, I get them together with white wine, shallots and baby spinach. Serve with bread to soak up the tasty broth.
—**DEBORAH WILLIAMS** PEORIA, AZ

START TO FINISH: 25 MIN.
MAKES: 4 SERVINGS

- 4 **bacon strips, chopped**
- 12 **sea scallops (about 1½ pounds), side muscles removed**
- 2 **shallots, finely chopped**
- ½ **cup white wine or chicken broth**
- 8 **cups fresh baby spinach (about 8 ounces)**

1. In a large nonstick skillet, cook bacon over medium heat until crisp, stirring occasionally. Remove with a slotted spoon; drain on paper towels. Discard drippings, reserving 2 tablespoons. Wipe skillet clean if necessary.
2. Pat scallops dry with paper towels. In same skillet, heat 1 tablespoon drippings over medium-high heat. Add scallops; cook 2-3 minutes on each side or until golden brown and firm. Remove from pan; keep warm.

3. Heat the remaining drippings in the same pan over medium-high heat. Add shallots; cook and stir 2-3 minutes or until tender. Add wine; bring to a boil, stirring to loosen browned bits from pan. Add the spinach; cook and stir for 1-2 minutes or until wilted. Stir in bacon. Serve with scallops.

BLACKENED CATFISH WITH MANGO AVOCADO SALSA

A delightful and tasty rub makes this quick recipe fantastic. While the fish is marinating, you can assemble the salsa. My family thinks this is marvelous.
—**LAURA FISHER** WESTFIELD, MA

PREP: 20 MIN. + CHILLING
COOK: 10 MIN.
MAKES: 4 SERVINGS (2 CUPS SALSA)

- 2 **teaspoons dried oregano**
- 2 **teaspoons ground cumin**
- 2 **teaspoons paprika**
- 2¼ **teaspoons pepper, divided**
- ¾ **teaspoon salt, divided**
- 4 **catfish fillets (6 ounces each)**
- 1 **medium mango, peeled and cubed**
- 1 **medium ripe avocado, peeled and cubed**
- ⅓ **cup finely chopped red onion**
- 2 **tablespoons minced fresh cilantro**
- 2 **tablespoons lime juice**
- 2 **teaspoons olive oil**

1. Combine the oregano, cumin, paprika, 2 teaspoons pepper and ½ teaspoon salt; rub over fillets. Refrigerate for at least 30 minutes.
2. In a small bowl, combine the mango, avocado, red onion, cilantro, lime juice and remaining salt and pepper. Chill until serving.
3. In a large cast-iron skillet, cook fillets in oil over medium heat for 5-7 minutes on each side or until the fish flakes easily with a fork. Serve with salsa.

SOLE WITH CUCUMBER SAUCE

Cucumbers and dill lend a mild pickle flavor to the sauce for this sole.
—**EMILY CHANEY** BLUE HILL, ME

START TO FINISH: 25 MIN.
MAKES: 4 SERVINGS

- 2 **medium cucumbers, peeled and thinly sliced**
- ½ **cup chopped green onions**
- ¼ **cup chopped celery**
- 1 **tablespoon minced fresh parsley**
- 1 **teaspoon dill weed**
- 1 **cup chicken broth**
- 4 **sole or flounder fillets (about 1½ pounds)**
- 2 **teaspoon cornstarch**
- ½ **cup heavy whipping cream**
- 1 **teaspoon prepared horseradish**

1. In a large skillet, layer the cucumbers, onions, celery, parsley and dill; pour broth over all. Top with fillets; bring to a boil. Cover and simmer 8-10 minutes or until fish flakes easily with a fork.
2. Transfer fish to a serving platter and keep warm; reserve cucumber mixture in skillet. Combine cornstarch and cream until smooth; add horseradish. Stir into the skillet. Simmer for 2 minutes or until thickened. Pour over fish; serve immediately.

SHRIMP
FRIED RICE

SEARED SALMON WITH STRAWBERRY BASIL RELISH

START TO FINISH: 20 MIN.
MAKES: 6 SERVINGS

- 6 **salmon fillets (4 ounces each)**
- 1 **tablespoon butter, melted**
- ¼ **teaspoon salt**
- ⅛ **teaspoon freshly ground pepper**

RELISH
- 1¼ **cups finely chopped fresh strawberries**
- 1 **tablespoon minced fresh basil**
- 1 **tablespoon honey**
  Dash freshly ground pepper

1. Brush the fillets with melted butter; sprinkle with salt and pepper. Heat a large skillet over medium-high heat. Add fillets, skin side up, in batches if necessary; cook 2-3 minutes on each side or until fish just begins to flake easily with a fork.
2. In a small bowl, toss strawberries with basil, honey and pepper. Serve salmon with the relish.

EASTERN SHORE CRAB CAKES

In Delaware, we're surrounded by an abundance of fresh seafood, particularly terrific crab. The secret to great crab cakes is fresh crab meat, not too much filler and not breaking up the crab too much. This recipe does all that.

—**CYNTHIA BENT** NEWARK, DE

START TO FINISH: 25 MIN.
MAKES: 3 SERVINGS

- 1 **large egg, lightly beaten**
- ½ **cup dry bread crumbs**
- ½ **cup mayonnaise**
- ¾ **teaspoon seafood seasoning**
- ½ **teaspoon lemon juice**
- ½ **teaspoon Worcestershire sauce**
- ⅛ **teaspoon white pepper**
- 1 **pound fresh lump crabmeat**
- 2 **tablespoons canola oil**

1. In a large bowl, combine the egg, bread crumbs, mayonnaise, seafood seasoning, lemon juice, Worcestershire sauce and pepper. Fold in crab. Shape into six patties.
2. In a large skillet, cook the crab cakes in oil for 4-5 minutes on each side or until browned.

SHRIMP FRIED RICE

Our family of four can't get enough of this bright and colorful shrimp dish. Bacon adds crispness and heartiness. Consider it when you need a different entree or brunch item.

—**SANDRA THOMPSON** WHITE HALL, AR

START TO FINISH: 20 MIN.
MAKES: 8 SERVINGS

- 4 **tablespoons butter, divided**
- 4 **large eggs, lightly beaten**
- 3 **cups cold cooked rice**
- 1 **package (16 ounces) frozen mixed vegetables**
- 1 **pound uncooked medium shrimp, peeled and deveined**
- ½ **teaspoon salt**
- ¼ **teaspoon pepper**
- 8 **bacon strips, cooked and crumbled, optional**

1. In a large skillet, melt 1 tablespoon butter over medium-high heat. Pour eggs into skillet. As eggs set, lift edges, letting uncooked portion flow underneath. Remove eggs and keep warm.
2. Melt the remaining butter in the skillet. Add rice, vegetables and shrimp; cook and stir for 5 minutes or until shrimp turn pink. Meanwhile, chop the eggs into small pieces. Return the eggs to the pan; sprinkle with salt and pepper. Cook until heated through, stirring occasionally. If desired, sprinkle with bacon.

SEARED SALMON
WITH STRAWBERRY
BASIL RELISH

HOISIN-PINEAPPLE
SALMON

MEDITERRANEAN FISH SKILLET

This simple, healthy meal has lots of flavor, is quick to prepare and only uses one pan. If you prefer, skip making the salsa and just toss in a can of diced tomatoes with green chilies and a splash of wine.

—**SARAH CHRISTENSON** SAN DIEGO, CA

START TO FINISH: 30 MIN.
MAKES: 2 SERVINGS

- 1 **large tomato, seeded and finely chopped**
- 1 **small green pepper, finely chopped**
- 1 **jalapeno pepper, seeded and minced**
- 3 **tablespoons minced fresh basil**
- 3 **tablespoons white wine or chicken broth**
- 1 **shallot, sliced**
- 1 **garlic clove, minced**
- ½ **teaspoon chili powder, divided**
- 2 **whitefish fillets (5 ounces each)**
- 1 **tablespoon olive oil**

1. In a small bowl, combine tomato, peppers, basil, wine, shallot, garlic and ¼ teaspoon chili powder; set aside.
2. Sprinkle fillets with the remaining chili powder. In a large skillet, cook fillets in oil over medium-high heat for 4-5 minutes on each side or until fish flakes easily with a fork; add tomato mixture during the last 3 minutes of cooking.

Test Kitchen Note: Wear disposable gloves when cutting hot peppers; the oils can burn skin. Avoid touching your face.

HOISIN-PINEAPPLE SALMON

My mouth waters when I think of this sweet, tangy flavor. The pairing of orange and pineapple provides a delicious contrast to the hoisin-glazed salmon. A sprinkle of cilantro adds freshness.

—**NAYLET LAROCHELLE** MIAMI, FL

START TO FINISH: 20 MIN.
MAKES: 4 SERVINGS

- 4 **salmon fillets (6 ounces each)**
- 2 **tablespoons hoisin sauce**
- ¼ **teaspoon pepper**
- ½ **cup unsweetened crushed pineapple**
- ¼ **cup orange marmalade**
- 2 **tablespoons chopped fresh cilantro**

1. Preheat oven to 400°. Spread salmon with hoisin sauce; sprinkle with pepper. Place on a greased foil-lined baking sheet, skin side down. Bake 12-15 minutes or until fish begins to flake easily with a fork.
2. In a small saucepan, combine the pineapple and marmalade. Bring to a boil, stirring occasionally; cook and stir for 4-6 minutes or until slightly thickened. Spoon over salmon; sprinkle with chopped fresh cilantro.

PESTO SCALLOPS VERMICELLI

Quick and easy with a gourmet flavor, tender bay scallops shine in a simple sauce made with pesto and white wine.

—**MARILYN LUSTGARTEN** WENTZVILLE, MO

START TO FINISH: 15 MIN.
MAKES: 2 SERVINGS

- 4 **ounces uncooked vermicelli**
- 2 **tablespoons butter**
- ½ **teaspoon garlic powder**
- ¼ **teaspoon dried oregano**
- ⅛ **teaspoon pepper**
- ½ **pound bay scallops**
- 2 **tablespoons white wine or chicken broth**
- 3 **tablespoons prepared pesto**

1. Cook vermicelli according to package directions. Meanwhile, in a large skillet, melt butter. Stir in the garlic powder, oregano and pepper. Add scallops and wine; cook and stir over medium heat for 5-6 minutes or until scallops are firm and opaque.
2. Reduce heat to low. Stir in pesto; heat through. Drain vermicelli; toss with the scallop mixture.

TOP TIP

SPICE UP OR DOWN

Up to 80% of the fiery factor in peppers is found in the seeds and membranes, so you can raise or lower the heat in your dishes by cutting the seeds out entirely, or including one or two—or more— to suit your individual taste.

SOUTHWESTERN FRIED PERCH

This is one of my favorite ways to prepare perch. Taco seasoning and cornmeal make the coating zesty and unexpected.

—JIM LORD MANCHESTER, NH

START TO FINISH: 30 MIN.
MAKES: 4 SERVINGS

- 1 **envelope taco seasoning**
- 1 **pound lake perch fillets**
- 1 **large egg**
- ½ **cup yellow cornmeal**
- ¼ **cup all-purpose flour**
- 3 **tablespoons canola oil**

1. Place taco seasoning in a large resealable bag; add perch fillets, one at a time, and shake to coat. In a shallow bowl, lightly beat the egg. In another shallow bowl, combine cornmeal and flour. Dip fillets in egg, then coat with cornmeal mixture. Place in a single layer on a plate; refrigerate for 15 minutes.
2. In a large skillet, heat oil over medium-high heat. Fry fillets for 2-3 minutes on each side or until fish flakes easily with a fork.

ORANGE-GLAZED SALMON

The very first time I made this, it became my husband's favorite meal. That's really saying something, because normally his favorite meals involve having most of a cow on his plate!

—TAMMY HAYDEN QUINCY, MI

START TO FINISH: 20 MIN.
MAKES: 4 SERVINGS

- 2 **tablespoons Cajun seasoning**
- 1 **teaspoon brown sugar**
- 4 **salmon fillets (6 ounces each), skin removed**
- ½ **cup orange marmalade**
- ¼ **cup lime juice**

Combine Cajun seasoning and brown sugar; rub over fillets. In a large nonstick skillet coated with cooking spray, cook fillets over medium heat for 3-4 minutes on each side or until fish flakes easily with a fork. Add marmalade and lime juice to the skillet; heat through.

EAT SMART

SHRIMP ORZO WITH FETA

Tender, hearty and flavorful, this recipe is one of my favorites! Garlic and a splash of lemon add to the fresh taste and heart-healthy benefits of shrimp.

—SARAH HUMMEL MOON TOWNSHIP, PA

START TO FINISH: 25 MIN.
MAKES: 4 SERVINGS

- 1¼ **cups uncooked whole wheat orzo pasta**
- 2 **tablespoons olive oil**
- 2 **garlic cloves, minced**
- 2 **medium tomatoes, chopped**
- 2 **tablespoons lemon juice**
- 1¼ **pounds uncooked shrimp (26-30 per pound), peeled and deveined**
- 2 **tablespoons minced fresh cilantro**
- ¼ **teaspoon pepper**
- ½ **cup crumbled feta cheese**

1. Cook orzo according to package directions. Meanwhile, in a large skillet, heat oil over medium heat. Add garlic; cook and stir 1 minute. Add tomatoes and lemon juice. Bring to a boil. Stir in shrimp. Reduce heat; simmer, uncovered, 4-5 minutes or until shrimp turn pink.
2. Drain orzo. Add orzo, cilantro and pepper to shrimp mixture; heat through. Sprinkle with feta cheese.
Per cup: 406 cal., 12g fat (3g sat. fat), 180mg chol., 307mg sod., 40g carb. (2g sugars, 9g fiber), 33g pro.
Diabetic Exchanges: 4 lean meat, 2 starch, 1 fat.

SHRIMP ORZO WITH FETA

SOUTHWESTERN
CASSEROLE, PAGE 180

Oven Entrees

Call everyone to the table and dig in to the **comforting goodness** oven-baked dinners have to offer. From bubbing casseroles and cheesy pizzas to roasted chicken and hearty roasts, these **meal-in-one** classics promise to **make the most** of your time in the kitchen—and at the family dinner table!

Beef & Ground Beef

BEEF & BULGUR-STUFFED
ZUCCHINI BOATS

BEEF & BULGUR-STUFFED ZUCCHINI BOATS

My mom frequently cooked giant zucchini that she grew in her garden. I adapted this recipe from one of her favorite weeknight meals. Though I love the taste of fresh-picked zucchini, ones from the grocery store work great, too.

—SUSAN PETERSON BLAINE, MN

PREP: 35 MIN. • **BAKE:** 30 MIN.
MAKES: 4 SERVINGS

- 4 **medium zucchini**
- 1 **pound lean ground beef (90% lean)**
- 1 **large onion, finely chopped**
- 1 **small sweet red pepper, chopped**
- 1½ **cups tomato sauce**
- ½ **cup bulgur**
- ¼ **teaspoon pepper**
- ½ **cup salsa**
- ½ **cup shredded reduced-fat cheddar cheese**

1. Preheat oven to 350°. Cut each zucchini lengthwise in half. Scoop out pulp, leaving a ¼-in. shell; chop pulp.
2. In a large skillet, cook beef, onion and red pepper over medium heat for 6-8 minutes or until meat is no longer pink, breaking into crumbles; drain. Stir in tomato sauce, bulgur, pepper and zucchini pulp. Bring to a boil. Reduce heat; simmer, uncovered, 12-15 minutes or until bulgur is tender. Stir in salsa. Spoon into zucchini shells.
3. Place in a 13x9-in. baking dish coated with cooking spray. Bake, covered, 20 minutes. Sprinkle with cheese. Bake, uncovered, 10-15 minutes longer or until zucchini is tender and filling is heated through.

BEEF & BISCUIT STEW

This easy-to-prepare dish is a meal in itself. That made it a real favorite of my mother's—she had to cook for nine children! Better yet, my brothers, sisters and I loved it.

—SYLVIA SONNEBORN YORK, PA

PREP: 2¾ HOURS • **BAKE:** 20 MIN.
MAKES: 8-10 SERVINGS

- 2 pounds beef stew meat, cut into 1-inch cubes
  All-purpose flour
- 2 tablespoons vegetable oil
- 2 beef bouillon cubes
- 2 cups boiling water
  Salt and pepper to taste
- 6 to 8 small potatoes, peeled and quartered
- 3 small onions, quartered
- 4 carrots, sliced
- 1 package (9 ounces) frozen cut green beans, thawed
- 2 tablespoons cornstarch
- ¼ cup water

BISCUIT DOUGH

- 2 cups all-purpose flour
- 4 teaspoons baking powder
- ½ teaspoon salt
- 2 tablespoons vegetable oil
- ¾ to 1 cup milk
  Melted butter

1. Coat beef cubes with flour. Brown beef on all sides in oil in a large Dutch oven. Meanwhile, dissolve bouillon in boiling water; add to Dutch oven. Season with salt and pepper. Simmer, covered, for 1½ hours to 2 hours or until the meat is tender. Add the potatoes, onions, carrots and beans; cook until vegetables are tender, about 30-45 minutes. Mix cornstarch and water; stir into stew and cook until thickened and bubbly.

2. For biscuits, combine flour, baking powder, salt, oil and milk in a large bowl. Stir to form a light, soft dough, adding more milk if necessary. Drop by tablespoonfuls on top of stew. Brush top of biscuits with melted butter. Bake, uncovered, at 350° for 20-30 minutes or until the biscuits are done.

SPICED POT ROAST

I always looked forward to Sunday dinner at my grandparents' house. My grandmother's meals were delicious, and I especially loved her savory pot roast. It's wonderful with garden-fresh vegetables on the side and a dessert made with apples.

—FRANCES WILSON TULSA, OK

PREP: 15 MIN. • **BAKE:** 3 HOURS
MAKES: 6-8 SERVINGS

- ⅓ cup all-purpose flour
- 1 teaspoon salt
- ¼ teaspoon pepper
- 1 boneless beef rump or chuck roast (3 pounds)
- 2 tablespoons vegetable oil
- 1½ cups beef broth
- ½ cup chutney
- ½ cup raisins
- ½ cup chopped onion
- 1½ teaspoons curry powder
- ½ teaspoon garlic powder
- ½ teaspoon ground ginger

1. Combine flour, salt and pepper; rub over entire roast. In a Dutch oven, brown roast in oil on all sides. Combine remaining ingredients and pour over roast.

2. Cover and bake at 325° for 3 hours or until meat is tender. Thicken gravy if desired.

EAT SMART
TENDERLOIN WITH CREMINI-APRICOT STUFFING

Simple but special is an ideal description of this dish. The sweet and savory stuffing complements the beef tenderloin well. Your guests will be giving you kudos!

—MARIE RIZZIO INTERLOCHEN, MI

PREP: 35 MIN. • **BAKE:** 35 MIN. + STANDING
MAKES: 10 SERVINGS

- 1 cup sliced baby portobello (cremini) mushrooms
- ⅓ cup chopped onion
- ⅓ cup chopped celery
- 2 tablespoons butter
- ½ cup chopped dried apricots
- 1 tablespoon minced fresh rosemary
- 1 beef tenderloin roast (2½ pounds)

- 1 tablespoon olive oil
- 3 garlic cloves, minced
- ½ teaspoon salt
- ¼ teaspoon pepper

1. In a large skillet, saute the mushrooms, onion and celery in butter until tender. Transfer to a small bowl; stir in apricots and rosemary. Cool slightly.

2. Cut a lengthwise slit down the center of the tenderloin to within ½ in. of bottom. Open tenderloin so it lies flat. On each half, make another lengthwise slit down the center to within ½ in. of bottom; open roast and cover with plastic wrap. Flatten to ½-in. thickness. Remove plastic.

3. Spread mushroom mixture over meat. Roll up jelly-roll style, starting with a long side. Tie at 1½-in. to 2-in. intervals with kitchen string.

4. Combine the oil, garlic, salt and pepper; rub over roast. In a large ovenproof skillet, brown roast on all sides.

5. Bake at 425° for 35-50 minutes or until meat reaches desired doneness (for medium-rare, a thermometer should read 145°; medium, 160°; well-done, 170°). Let stand 10 minutes before slicing. Place slices on a platter and spoon pan juices over the top.

Ham & Cheese Stuffed Tenderloin: Omit stuffing. Prepare roast as directed. Layer with ¼ pound sliced provolone, 6 cups fresh spinach and ½ pound thinly sliced deli ham; press down gently. Roll up, starting with a long side; secure with string. Proceed as directed.

Per serving: 219 cal., 10g fat (4g sat. fat), 56mg chol., 143mg sod., 6g carb. (3g sugars, 1g fiber), 25g pro.
Diabetic Exchanges: 3 lean meat, 1 fat, ½ starch.

BEEF
NACHO PIE

BEEF NACHO PIE

I like to spend time in the garden, so I look for recipes that don't require hours in the kitchen. This Southwestern pie is quick to put together and makes a tasty meal with a lettuce salad.

—**DORIS GILL** SARGENT, NE

PREP: 25 MIN. • **BAKE:** 20 MIN.
MAKES: 6-8 SERVINGS

- 1 **pound ground beef**
- ½ **cup chopped onion**
- 1 **can (8 ounces) tomato sauce**
- 2 **tablespoons taco seasoning**
- 1 **tube (8 ounces) refrigerated crescent rolls**
- 1½ **cups crushed nacho-flavored tortilla chips, divided**
- 1 **cup (8 ounces) sour cream**
- 1 **cup shredded Mexican cheese blend**

1. In a large skillet, cook beef and onion over medium heat until meat is no longer pink; drain. Stir in tomato sauce and taco seasoning. Bring to a boil. Reduce heat; simmer, uncovered, for 5 minutes.
2. Meanwhile, separate crescent dough into eight triangles; place in a greased 9-in. pie plate with points toward the center. Press onto the bottom and up the sides to form a crust; seal perforations.
3. Sprinkle 1 cup chips over crust. Top with meat mixture. Carefully spread sour cream over meat mixture. Sprinkle with cheese and remaining chips. Bake at 350° for 20-25 minutes or until cheese is melted and crust is golden brown. Let stand for 5 minutes before cutting.

> **TOP TIP**
>
> ### SPICE-IT-UP SUBS
>
> If you like meals that bring the heat, substitute chorizo for half of the ground beef in the Beef Nacho Pie recipe. Zip up the meat mixture's spice level with a sprinkling of cumin, chili powder or additional taco seasoning. Or add a few pickled jalapeno slices to the meat before spreading on the sour cream layer.

BRISKET WITH CHUNKY TOMATO SAUCE

When I treat dinner guests to this impressive brisket, they agree it's the best beef they've ever tasted. A savory tomato sauce adds the finishing touch.

—**LINDA BLASKA** ATLANTA, GA

PREP: 15 MIN.
BAKE: 3½ HOURS + CHILLING
MAKES: 12 SERVINGS

- 1 **fresh beef brisket (4½ pounds)**
- 1 **teaspoon salt**
- ¼ **to ½ teaspoon pepper**
- 1 **tablespoon olive oil**
- 3 **large onions, chopped**
- 2 **garlic cloves, minced**
- 1 **cup dry red wine or beef broth**
- 1 **can (14½ ounces) diced tomatoes, undrained**
- 2 **celery ribs with leaves, chopped**
- ½ **teaspoon dried thyme**
- ½ **teaspoon dried rosemary, crushed**
- 1 **bay leaf**
- 1 **pound carrots, cut into ½-inch slices**

1. Season brisket with salt and pepper. In a Dutch oven, brown brisket in oil over medium-high heat. Remove and keep warm. In the same pan, saute onions and garlic until tender. Place brisket over onions. Add the wine or broth, tomatoes, celery, thyme, rosemary and bay leaf.
2. Cover and bake at 325° for 2 hours, basting occasionally. Add carrots; bake for 1 hour longer or until meat is tender. Discard bay leaf. Cool for 1 hour; cover and refrigerate overnight.
3. Trim visible fat from brisket and skim fat from tomato mixture. Thinly slice beef across the grain. In a saucepan, warm tomato mixture; transfer to a shallow roasting pan. Top with sliced beef. Cover and bake at 325° for 30 minutes or until heated through. Serve sauce over beef.
Test Kitchen Note: This is a fresh beef brisket, not corned beef.

HAMBURGER NOODLE CASSEROLE

People have a hard time believing this homey and hearty casserole uses lighter ingredients. The taste is so rich and creamy. It's a great weeknight family entree!

—**MARTHA HENSON** WINNSBORO, TX

PREP: 30 MIN. • **BAKE:** 35 MIN.
MAKES: 10 SERVINGS

- 5 **cups uncooked egg noodles**
- 1½ **pounds lean ground beef (90% lean)**
- 2 **garlic cloves, minced**
- 3 **cans (8 ounces each) tomato sauce**
- ½ **teaspoon sugar**
- ½ **teaspoon salt**
- ⅛ **teaspoon pepper**
- 1 **package (8 ounces) reduced-fat cream cheese**
- 1 **cup reduced-fat ricotta cheese**
- ¼ **cup reduced-fat sour cream**
- 3 **green onions, thinly sliced, divided**
- ⅔ **cup shredded reduced-fat cheddar cheese**

1. Preheat oven to 350°. Cook noodles according to package directions.
2. Meanwhile, in a large nonstick skillet over medium heat, cook beef until no longer pink. Add garlic; cook for 1 minute longer. Drain. Stir in tomato sauce, sugar, salt and pepper; heat through. Drain noodles; stir into beef mixture.
3. In a small bowl, beat cream cheese, ricotta cheese and sour cream until blended. Stir in half of the onions.
4. Spoon half the noodle mixture into a 13x9-in. baking dish coated with cooking spray. Top with cheese mixture and remaining noodle mixture.
5. Cover and bake for 30 minutes. Uncover; sprinkle with cheddar cheese. Bake for 5-10 minutes longer or until heated through and cheese is melted. Sprinkle with remaining onions.

VEGETABLE &
BEEF STUFFED
RED PEPPERS

tomato sauce, mozzarella cheese
and salt.

4. Place red peppers in a greased
8-in. square baking dish. Fill with
meat mixture. Bake, covered,
35-40 minutes or until peppers are
tender. Top with provolone cheese;
bake, uncovered, 5 minutes or until
cheese is melted.

Per stuffed pepper: 287 cal., 13g fat
(5g sat. fat), 57mg chol., 555mg sod.,
21g carb. (8g sugars, 5g fiber), 23g pro.
Diabetic Exchanges: 3 lean meat,
2 vegetable, 1 fat, ½ starch.

CRAB & HERB CHEESE FILET MIGNON

Save the money you'd spend on going out
for surf and turf. Instead, treat yourself to
thick-cut steaks stuffed with garlic-herb
cheese spread and fresh crabmeat. It's a
home-cooked meal that looks and tastes
like it came from a four-star restaurant!
—*TASTE OF HOME* TEST KITCHEN

PREP: 15 MIN. • **BROIL:** 20 MIN.
MAKES: 4 SERVINGS

- 1½ **cups fresh crabmeat**
- 1 **package (6½ ounces) garlic-herb spreadable cheese, divided**
- 4 **beef tenderloin steaks (1 inch thick and 8 ounces each)**
- ¼ **teaspoon salt**
- ¼ **teaspoon pepper**

1. Combine crab and ¾ cup spreadable
cheese in a small bowl. Cut a horizontal
pocket in each steak. Fill each pocket
with ⅓ cup crab mixture. Place steaks
on a greased broiler pan. Sprinkle with
salt and pepper.

2. Broil 4 in. from the heat for 10 minutes
on each side or until meat reaches
desired doneness (for medium-rare, a
thermometer should read 145°; medium,
160°; well-done, 170°), spooning the
remaining cheese over steaks during the
last 2 minutes of broiling. Let stand for
5 minutes before serving.

EAT SMART

VEGETABLE & BEEF STUFFED RED PEPPERS

I love this recipe because it's one of the
few ways I can get my husband to eat
veggies! For a meatless version, replace
the beef with eggplant and add more
vegetables, like mushrooms or squash.
You can also replace the rice with barley,
couscous or even orzo.
—**JENNIFER ZIMMERMAN** AVONDALE, AZ

PREP: 35 MIN. • **BAKE:** 40 MIN.
MAKES: 6 SERVINGS

- 6 **medium sweet red peppers**
- 1 **pound lean ground beef (90% lean)**
- 1 **tablespoon olive oil**
- 1 **medium zucchini, chopped**
- 1 **medium yellow summer squash, chopped**
- 1 **medium onion, finely chopped**
- ⅓ **cup finely chopped green pepper**
- 2 **cups coarsely chopped fresh spinach**
- 4 **garlic cloves, minced**
- 1 **cup ready-to-serve long grain and wild rice**
- 1 **can (8 ounces) tomato sauce**
- ½ **cup shredded part-skim mozzarella cheese**
- ¼ **teaspoon salt**
- 3 **slices reduced-fat provolone cheese, halved**

1. Preheat oven to 350°. Cut and
discard tops from red peppers;
remove seeds. In a 6-qt. stockpot,
cook peppers in boiling water for
3-5 minutes or until crisp-tender;
drain and rinse in cold water.

2. In a large skillet, cook beef over
medium heat for 6-8 minutes or until
no longer pink, breaking into crumbles.
Remove with a slotted spoon; pour
off drippings.

3. In same pan, heat oil over medium
heat; saute zucchini, yellow squash,
onion and green pepper for 4-5 minutes
or until tender. Add spinach and garlic;
cook and stir for 1 minute or until
wilted. Stir in cooked beef, rice,

HEARTY BEEF & CABBAGE POCKETS

I found this recipe many years ago and the only ingredients listed were hamburger, cabbage, onion, salt and pepper. After a bit of experimenting, I decided this is one for the books. If you have the time, use a homemade dough. Or you can use a 48-ounce package of frozen whole wheat bread dough if you can't find the frozen rolls. Just cut the bread into 24 pieces.

—**ELAINE CLARK** WELLINGTON, KS

PREP: 1 HOUR + RISING • **BAKE:** 15 MIN.
MAKES: 2 DOZEN

- 24 **frozen dough Texas-size whole wheat dinner rolls (3 pounds total), thawed**
- 1½ **pounds lean ground beef (90% lean)**
- ½ **pound reduced-fat bulk pork sausage**
- 1 **large onion, chopped**
- 1 **pound carrots, grated**
- 2 **cans (4 ounces each) chopped green chilies**
- 2 **tablespoons prepared mustard**
- ½ **teaspoon salt**
- ½ **teaspoon pepper**
- 1 **small head cabbage, shredded**
- 2 **large egg whites**
- 2 **teaspoons water**
  Caraway seeds

1. Let dough stand at room temperature for 30-40 minutes or until softened. In a Dutch oven, cook beef, sausage and onion over medium heat 12-15 minutes or until meat is no longer pink, breaking meat into crumbles; drain. Stir in carrots, chilies, mustard, salt and pepper. Add cabbage in batches; cook and stir until tender.

2. On a lightly floured surface, press or roll each dinner roll into a 5-in. circle. Top with a heaping ⅓ cup filling; bring edges of dough up over filling and pinch to seal.

3. Place on baking sheets coated with cooking spray, seam side down. Cover with kitchen towels; let rise in a warm place until almost doubled, about 45 minutes. Preheat oven to 350°.

4. Whisk egg whites and water; brush over tops. Sprinkle with caraway seeds. Bake for 15-20 minutes or until pockets are golden brown.

Freeze option: Freeze baked and cooled pockets in resealable plastic freezer bags. To use, reheat pockets on a baking sheet coated with cooking spray in a preheated 350° oven for 30-35 minutes or until heated through; cover loosely with foil if needed to prevent overbrowning.

FRENCH VEAL CHOPS

Perfectly portioned for two, here's an easy dish that can easily be doubled to serve four. Try it the next time you're entertaining another couple or whenever you'd like to prepare a meal that's just a bit special.

—**BETTY BIEHL** MERTZTOWN, PA

PREP: 15 MIN. • **BAKE:** 30 MIN.
MAKES: 2 SERVINGS

- 2 **veal chops (1 inch thick)**
- ½ **teaspoon salt**
  Dash pepper
- 1 **tablespoon canola oil**
- ½ **cup chopped onion**
- 2 **tablespoons butter, divided**
- ¼ **cup chicken broth**
- ⅓ **cup dry bread crumbs**
- 2 **tablespoons grated Parmesan cheese**

1. Sprinkle veal chops with salt and pepper. In a skillet, brown chops on both sides in oil. Sprinkle onion into a greased shallow baking dish; dot with 1 tablespoon butter. Top with chops; drizzle with broth. Melt remaining butter; toss with bread crumbs and Parmesan cheese. Sprinkle over top.

2. Bake, uncovered, at 350° for 30-35 minutes or until meat is no longer pink and a meat thermometer reads 160°.

HEARTY BEEF & CABBAGE POCKETS

"Here's a twist on classic meat loaf that can be made ahead and will last for a few days afterward. Make sandwiches with the leftovers, buns and a little Monterey Jack cheese."
—**TASHA TULLY** OWINGS MILLS, MD

SASSY SALSA
MEAT LOAVES

SASSY SALSA MEAT LOAVES

PREP: 25 MIN.
BAKE: 1 HOUR 5 MIN. + STANDING
MAKES: 2 LOAVES (6 SERVINGS EACH)

- ¾ cup uncooked instant brown rice
- 1 can (8 ounces) tomato sauce
- 1½ cups salsa, divided
- 1 large onion, chopped
- 1 large egg, lightly beaten
- 1 celery rib, finely chopped
- ¼ cup minced fresh parsley
- 2 tablespoons minced fresh cilantro
- 2 garlic cloves, minced
- 1 tablespoon chili powder
- 1½ teaspoons salt
- ½ teaspoon pepper
- 2 pounds lean ground beef (90% lean)
- 1 pound ground turkey
- ½ cup shredded reduced-fat Monterey Jack cheese or Mexican cheese blend

1. Preheat oven to 350°. Cook rice according to the package directions; cool slightly. In a large bowl, combine tomato sauce, ½ cup salsa, onion, egg, celery, parsley, cilantro, garlic and seasonings; stir in the rice. Add beef and turkey; mix lightly but thoroughly.

2. Shape into two 8x4-in. loaves on a greased rack in a broiler pan. Bake 1-1¼ hours or until a thermometer reads 165°.

3. Spread with the remaining salsa; sprinkle with cheese; bake 5 minutes or until the cheese is melted. Let stand 10 minutes before slicing.

Freeze option: Bake meat loaves without topping. Cool; securely wrap in plastic, then foil. To use, partially thaw in refrigerator overnight. Unwrap meat loaves; place in a greased 15x10x1-in. baking pan. Reheat in a preheated 350° oven for 40-45 minutes or until a thermometer inserted in the center reads 165°; top as directed.

Per serving: 237 cal., 11g fat (4g sat. fat), 91mg chol., 634mg sod., 9g carb. (2g sugars, 1g fiber), 25g pro.
Diabetic Exchanges: 3 lean meat, ½ starch, ½ fat.

BEEF BRISKET ON BUNS

BEEF BRISKET ON BUNS

With its slightly smoky flavor, this beef turns out tender and delicious every time! Plus, it slices well so it looks great included in a buffet.
—**DEBRA WAGGONER** GRAND ISLAND, NE

PREP: 25 MIN. + STANDING
BAKE: 5 HOURS
MAKES: 16 SERVINGS

- ½ teaspoon ground ginger
- ½ teaspoon ground mustard
- 1 fresh beef brisket (4 to 5 pounds)
- 2 cups water
- 1 cup ketchup
- ½ cup Worcestershire sauce
- 2 tablespoons brown sugar
- 2 teaspoons liquid smoke, optional
- 1 teaspoon chili powder
- 16 to 20 sandwich buns, split, optional

1. Combine the ginger and the mustard; rub over brisket. Place on a rack in a shallow roasting pan. Bake, uncovered, at 325° for 2 hours.

2. Let stand for 20 minutes. Thinly slice meat across the grain. Place in a foil-lined 13x9-in. baking dish. In a bowl, combine the water, ketchup, Worcestershire sauce, brown sugar, liquid smoke if desired and chili powder; pour over meat. Cover tightly with foil; bake for 3 hours longer or until tender. Serve on buns if desired.

Test Kitchen Note: This is a fresh beef brisket, not corned beef.

SWISS STEAK WITH DUMPLINGS

My mother was a great cook, and I learned so much from her. Ten years ago, I entered this hearty recipe in a contest and I won. It's great all year round and a favorite when I take it to our field workers during harvest.
—**PAT HABIGER** SPEARVILLE, KS

PREP: 25 MIN. • **BAKE:** 70 MIN.
MAKES: 6-8 SERVINGS

- 2 pounds beef top round steak
- ⅓ cup all-purpose flour
- 2 tablespoons canola oil
- 2 cans (10¾ ounces each) condensed cream of chicken soup, undiluted
- 1⅓ cups water
- ½ teaspoon salt
- ⅛ teaspoon pepper

DUMPLINGS

- ½ cup dry bread crumbs
- 5 tablespoons butter, melted, divided
- 1⅓ cups all-purpose flour
- 2 teaspoons baking powder
- ½ teaspoon salt
- ¼ teaspoon poultry seasoning
- ⅔ cup milk

1. Cut steaks into six or eight pieces. Place flour in a large resealable bag. Add beef, a few pieces at a time, and shake to coat. In a large skillet, brown meat in oil on both sides. Transfer to a greased 2½-qt. baking dish.
2. In the same skillet, combine the soup, water, salt and pepper; bring to a boil, stirring occasionally. Pour over steak. Cover and bake at 350° for 50-60 minutes or until meat is tender.
3. For dumplings, combine bread crumbs and 2 tablespoons butter in a small bowl; set aside. In another bowl, combine the flour, baking powder, salt and poultry seasoning. Stir in milk and remaining butter just until moistened.
4. Drop by rounded tablespoonfuls into the crumb mixture; roll until coated. Place dumplings over steak. Bake, uncovered, at 425° for 20-30 minutes or until dumplings are lightly browned and a toothpick inserted near the center comes out clean.

WEEKDAY LASAGNA

This lasagna is my husband's favorite dish. I love it because it's low-fat and a real time-saver since you don't cook the noodles before baking.
—**KAREN MCCABE** PROVO, UT

PREP: 35 MIN.
BAKE: 1 HOUR + STANDING
MAKES: 9 SERVINGS

- 1 pound lean ground beef (90% lean)
- 1 small onion, chopped
- 1 can (28 ounces) crushed tomatoes
- 1¾ cups water
- 1 can (6 ounces) tomato paste
- 1 envelope spaghetti sauce mix
- 1 large egg, lightly beaten
- 2 cups (16 ounces) fat-free cottage cheese
- 2 tablespoons grated Parmesan cheese
- 6 uncooked lasagna noodles
- 1 cup shredded part-skim mozzarella cheese

1. In a large saucepan, cook beef and onion over medium heat until meat is no longer pink; drain. Stir in the tomatoes, water, tomato paste and spaghetti sauce mix. Bring to a boil. Reduce heat; cover and simmer for 15-20 minutes, stirring occasionally.
2. In a small bowl, combine the egg, cottage cheese and Parmesan cheese. Spread 2 cups meat sauce in a 13x9-in. baking dish coated with cooking spray. Layer with three noodles, half of the cottage cheese mixture and half of the remaining meat sauce. Repeat layers.
3. Cover and bake at 350° for 50 minutes or until a thermometer reads 160°. Uncover; sprinkle with mozzarella cheese. Bake 10-15 minutes longer or until bubbly and cheese is melted. Let stand for 15 minutes before cutting.

LIL CHEDDAR MEAT LOAVES

PREP: 15 MIN. • **BAKE:** 25 MIN.
MAKES: 8 SERVINGS

- 1 large egg
- ¾ cup whole milk
- 1 cup shredded cheddar cheese
- ½ cup quick-cooking oats
- ½ cup chopped onion
- ½ teaspoon salt
- 1 pound ground beef
- ⅔ cup ketchup
- ½ cup packed brown sugar
- 1½ teaspoons prepared mustard

1. In a large bowl, whisk egg and milk. Stir in the cheese, oats, onion and salt. Crumble beef over mixture and mix well. Shape into eight loaves; place in a greased 13x9-in. baking dish. In a small bowl, combine the ketchup, brown sugar and mustard; spoon over loaves.
2. Bake, uncovered, at 350° for 25-30 minutes or until no pink remains and a meat thermometer reads 160°.

BEEF VEGGIE CASSEROLE

I love this satisfying stew dish because it's a breeze to fix. It uses leftover roast beef and refrigerated biscuits.
—**PATTI KEITH** EBENSBURG, PA

START TO FINISH: 25 MIN.
MAKES: 5 SERVINGS

- 1 envelope mushroom gravy mix
- ¾ cup water
- 2 cups cubed cooked beef
- 2 cups frozen mixed vegetables
- 2 medium potatoes, peeled, cubed and cooked
- 1 tube (12 ounces) refrigerated buttermilk biscuits, separated into 10 biscuits

1. In a large saucepan, combine gravy mix and water, stir until smooth. Bring to a boil; cook and stir for 1 minute or until thickened. Stir in the beef, vegetables and potatoes; heat through.
2. Transfer to a greased 8-in. square baking dish. Top with biscuits. Bake, uncovered, at 400° for 12-16 minutes or until bubbly and the biscuits are golden brown.

"I got this recipe from my aunt when I was a teen and have made these miniature loaves many times since. My husband and three children count this main dish among their favorites."
—**KATHY BOWRON** COCOLALLA, ID

LIL CHEDDAR
MEAT LOAVES

ZUCCHINI PIZZA
CASSEROLE

ZUCCHINI PIZZA CASSEROLE

I grow zucchini by the bushel, so this pizza bake is one of my dinnertime go-to's. My hungry family gobbles it right up.

—LYNN BERNSTETTER WHITE BEAR LAKE, MN

PREP: 20 MIN. • **BAKE:** 40 MIN.
MAKES: 8 SERVINGS

- 4 **cups shredded unpeeled zucchini**
- ½ **teaspoon salt**
- 2 **large eggs**
- ½ **cup grated Parmesan cheese**
- 2 **cups shredded part-skim mozzarella cheese, divided**
- 1 **cup shredded cheddar cheese, divided**
- 1 **pound ground beef**
- ½ **cup chopped onion**
- 1 **can (15 ounces) Italian tomato sauce**
- 1 **medium green pepper, chopped**

1. Preheat oven to 400°. Place zucchini in colander; sprinkle with salt. Let stand 10 minutes, then squeeze out moisture.

2. Combine zucchini with eggs, Parmesan cheese and half of mozzarella and cheddar cheeses. Press into a greased 13x9-in. or 3-qt. baking dish. Bake for 20 minutes.

3. Meanwhile, in a large saucepan, cook beef and onion over medium heat, crumbling beef, until meat is no longer pink; drain. Add tomato sauce; spoon over zucchini mixture. Sprinkle with remaining cheeses; add green pepper. Bake until heated through, about 20 minutes longer.

Freeze option: Cool baked casserole; cover and freeze. To use, partially thaw in refrigerator overnight. Remove from refrigerator for 30 minutes before baking. Preheat oven to 350°. Unwrap casserole; reheat on a lower oven rack until heated through and a thermometer inserted in the center reads 165°.

WINTERTIME
BRAISED BEEF
STEW

4. Bake, covered, 1½ hours. Stir in beans; bake, covered, 30-40 minutes longer or until beef and vegetables are tender. Remove bay leaves and oregano sprigs. If desired, sprinkle with parsley.

Freeze option: Freeze cooled stew in freezer containers. To use, partially thaw stew in refrigerator overnight. Heat through in a saucepan, stirring occasionally and adding a little broth or water if necessary.

Per cup: 310 cal., 9g fat (3g sat. fat), 64mg chol., 373mg sod., 26g carb. (8g sugars, 5g fiber), 25g pro.
Diabetic Exchanges: 3 lean meat, 1 starch, 1 vegetable, 1 fat.

UNSTUFFED CABBAGE

A teacher at the preschool where I work shared the recipe for this delicious ground beef and cabbage casserole. It's a nutritious and economical meal for busy families.

—**JUDY THORN** MARS, PA

PREP: 20 MIN. • **BAKE:** 45 MIN.
MAKES: 4 SERVINGS

- 6 **cups chopped cabbage**
- ½ **pound lean ground beef (90% lean)**
- 1 **small onion, chopped**
- 1 **cup uncooked instant rice**
- ½ **teaspoon salt, optional**
- ¼ **teaspoon pepper**
- 2 **cans (10¾ ounces each) condensed tomato soup, undiluted**
- 1 **cup water**
- ⅓ **cup shredded cheddar cheese**

1. Place the cabbage in a greased 2½-qt. baking dish. In a large skillet, cook beef and onion over medium heat until meat is no longer pink; drain. Stir in the rice, salt if desired and pepper; spoon over the cabbage.
2. Combine soup and water; pour over beef mixture. Cover and bake at 350° for 40-50 minutes or until rice and cabbage are tender. Uncover; sprinkle with cheese. Bake 5-10 minutes longer or until the cheese is melted.

WINTERTIME BRAISED BEEF STEW

This wonderful beef stew makes an easy Sunday meal. It's even better a day or two later, so we make a double batch to make sure we have leftovers.

—**MICHAELA ROSENTHAL**
WOODLAND HILLS, CA

PREP: 40 MIN. • **BAKE:** 2 HOURS
MAKES: 8 SERVINGS (2 QUARTS)

- 2 **pounds boneless beef sirloin steak or chuck roast, cut into 1-inch pieces**
- 2 **tablespoons all-purpose flour**
- 2 **teaspoons Montreal steak seasoning**
- 2 **tablespoons olive oil, divided**
- 1 **large onion, chopped**
- 2 **celery ribs, chopped**
- 2 **medium parsnips, peeled and cut into 1½-inch pieces**
- 2 **medium carrots, peeled and cut into 1½-inch pieces**
- 2 **garlic cloves, minced**
- 1 **can (14½ ounces) diced tomatoes, undrained**
- 1 **cup dry red wine or reduced-sodium beef broth**
- 2 **tablespoons red currant jelly**
- 2 **bay leaves**
- 2 **fresh oregano sprigs**
- 1 **can (15 ounces) cannellini beans, rinsed and drained**
  Minced fresh parsley, optional

1. Preheat oven to 350°. Toss beef with flour and steak seasoning.
2. In an ovenproof Dutch oven, heat 1 tablespoon oil over medium heat. Brown beef in batches; remove with a slotted spoon.
3. In same pan, heat remaining oil over medium heat. Add onion, celery, parsnips and carrots; cook and stir until onion is tender. Add garlic; cook 1 minute longer. Stir in tomatoes, wine, jelly, bay leaves, oregano and beef; bring to a boil.

TINA'S
POT ROAST

TINA'S POT ROAST

If you are looking to make a tender pot roast, this is the recipe for you. It's hearty and also kid-friendly. Even picky eaters gobble it up. The last time I made this for my family, the gravy was so tasty that we poured it over the entire meal—meat, carrots and potatoes!

—TINA MEYER LAKE ORION, MI

PREP: 10 MIN. • **BAKE:** 2¾ HOURS
MAKES: 8 SERVINGS

- 1 tablespoon canola oil
- 1 boneless beef chuck roast (3 pounds)
- 1½ cups water
- 1 envelope brown gravy mix
- 1 envelope Italian salad dressing mix
- 1 envelope onion soup mix
- ½ teaspoon garlic powder
- ½ teaspoon pepper
- 3 pounds potatoes (about 9 medium), peeled and quartered
- 1 pound carrots, cut into 2-inch pieces

1. Preheat oven to 325°. In a Dutch oven, heat oil over medium heat. Brown roast on all sides. In a small bowl, whisk water, gravy mix, dressing mix, soup mix, garlic powder and pepper until blended; add to pan. Bring to a boil. Bake, covered, 1½ hours.

2. Add vegetables; cook 1¼ to 1½ hours longer or until meat and vegetables are tender. Skim fat if necessary.

READER RAVE

"I made this pot roast recipe and my husband loved it. He said it was the best pot roast I have ever made! The meat was so tender it melted in our mouths! This will be a new favorite in our house now."

— PASTORIUS01 TASTEOFHOME.COM

QUICK & EASY
DEEP-DISH PIZZA

FREEZE IT
QUICK & EASY DEEP-DISH PIZZA

I was trying to impress my boyfriend with my cooking, so I made this meaty pizza. I think it worked. Here we are 17 years later, and I still make it for our family at least once a month, if not more!

—STACEY WHITE FUQUAY-VARINA, NC

PREP: 30 MIN. • **BAKE:** 30 MIN.
MAKES: 8 SERVINGS

- 1 pound ground beef
- 1 medium green pepper, chopped
- 1 small onion, chopped
- 1 jar (14 ounces) pizza sauce
- 10 slices Canadian bacon (about 6 ounces), coarsely chopped
- 2 packages (6½ ounces each) pizza crust mix
- 2 cups shredded part-skim mozzarella cheese
- 4 ounces sliced pepperoni

1. Preheat oven to 425°. In a large skillet, cook beef, pepper and onion over medium heat for 8-10 minutes or until beef is no longer pink, breaking up beef into crumbles; drain. Stir in pizza sauce and Canadian bacon; remove from heat.

2. Prepare dough for pizza crust according to package directions. Press dough to fit bottom and 1 in. up sides of a greased 13x9-in. baking pan.

3. Spoon meat sauce into crust. Sprinkle with cheese; top with pepperoni. Bake, covered, 25 minutes. Uncover; bake 5-10 minutes longer or until crust and cheese are golden brown.

Freeze option: Cool meat sauce before assembling pizza. Securely cover and freeze unbaked pizza. To use, bake frozen pizza, covered with foil, in a preheated 425° oven for 25 minutes. Uncover; bake 15-20 minutes longer or until golden brown and heated through.

MEXICAN
LASAGNA

OVEN SWISS STEAK

I was really glad to find this recipe since it's a great way to use economical round steak and it picks up fabulous flavor from one of my favorite herbs— tarragon.

—LORNA DICKAU VANDERHOOF, BC

PREP: 30 MIN. • **BAKE:** 1¼ HOURS
MAKES: 6 SERVINGS

- 8 **bacon strips**
- 2 **pounds beef top round steak (¾ inch thick)**
- 2 **cups sliced fresh mushrooms**
- 1 **can (14½ ounces) diced tomatoes, undrained**
- ½ **cup chopped onion**
- 1 **to 2 teaspoons dried tarragon**
- 2 **tablespoons cornstarch**
- 2 **tablespoons water**
- 1 **cup heavy whipping cream**
  Minced fresh parsley, optional

1. In a large ovenproof skillet, cook bacon over medium heat until crisp. Remove to paper towels to drain, reserving ¼ cup drippings. Crumble bacon and set aside.

2. Trim beef; cut into serving-size pieces. Brown on both sides in drippings. Top meat with mushrooms, tomatoes and onion. Sprinkle with tarragon and bacon. Cover and bake at 325° for 1¼ to 1¾ hours or until meat is tender, basting twice.

3. Remove meat to a serving platter; keep warm. Combine cornstarch and water until smooth; add to skillet. Bring to a boil; cook and stir for 2 minutes or until thickened. Reduce heat; stir in cream. Simmer, uncovered, 3-4 minutes or until heated through. Return meat to skillet and turn to coat with sauce. If desired, sprinkle with parsley.

MEXICAN LASAGNA

I collect cookbooks and recipes (this one is from my son's mother-in-law). My husband teases me that I won't live long enough to try half the recipes in my files!

—ROSE ANN BUHLE MINOOKA, IL

PREP: 20 MIN.
BAKE: 65 MIN. + STANDING
MAKES: 12 SERVINGS

- 2 **pounds ground beef**
- 1 **can (16 ounces) refried beans**
- 1 **can (4 ounces) chopped green chilies**
- 1 **envelope taco seasoning**
- 2 **tablespoons hot salsa**
- 12 **ounces uncooked lasagna noodles**
- 4 **cups shredded Colby-Monterey Jack cheese, divided**
- 1 **jar (16 ounces) mild salsa**
- 2 **cups water**
- 2 **cups (16 ounces) sour cream**
- 1 **can (2¼ ounces) sliced ripe olives, drained**
- 3 **green onions, chopped**
- 1 **medium tomato, chopped, optional**

1. Preheat oven to 350°. In a large skillet, cook beef over medium heat until no longer pink; drain. Stir in beans, chilies, taco seasoning and hot salsa.

2. In a greased 13x9-in. baking dish, layer a third of the noodles and meat mixture. Sprinkle with 1 cup of cheese. Repeat layers twice.

3. Combine mild salsa and water; pour over top. Cover and bake for 1 hour or until heated through.

4. Top with sour cream, olives, onions, tomatoes if desired and remaining cheese. Bake, uncovered, 5 minutes. Let stand 10-15 minutes before cutting.

BEEFY FRENCH
ONION POTPIE

BEEFY FRENCH ONION POTPIE

I came up with this dish knowing my husband loves French onion soup. It's a good base for this hearty, beefy potpie.
—SARA HUTCHENS DU QUOIN, IL

PREP: 10 MIN. • **BAKE:** 20 MIN.
MAKES: 4 SERVINGS

- 1 pound ground beef
- 1 small onion, chopped
- 1 can (10½ ounces) condensed French onion soup
- 1½ cups shredded part-skim mozzarella cheese
- 1 tube (12 ounces) refrigerated buttermilk biscuits

1. Preheat oven to 350°. In a large skillet, cook beef and onion over medium heat for 6-8 minutes or until beef is no longer pink, breaking beef into crumbles; drain. Stir in soup; bring to a boil.
2. Transfer to an ungreased 9-in. deep-dish pie plate; sprinkle with cheese. Bake for 5 minutes or until cheese is melted. Top with biscuits. Bake 15-20 minutes longer or until biscuits are golden brown.

BROWN SUGAR-GLAZED CORNED BEEF

I serve this delicious entree at St. Patrick's Day celebrations. The meat is so tasty with the simple glaze. Leftovers make excellent Reuben sandwiches.
—PERLENE HOEKEMA LYNDEN, WA

PREP: 3 HOURS
BAKE: 25 MIN. + STANDING
MAKES: 12 SERVINGS

- 1 corned beef brisket with spice packet (3 to 4 pounds), trimmed
- 1 medium onion, sliced
- 1 celery rib, sliced
- ¼ cup butter, cubed
- 1 cup packed brown sugar
- ⅔ cup ketchup
- ⅓ cup white vinegar
- 2 tablespoons prepared mustard
- 2 teaspoons prepared horseradish

1. Place corned beef and contents of seasoning packet in a Dutch oven; cover with water. Add onion and celery; bring to a boil. Reduce heat; cover and simmer for 2½ hours or until meat is tender.
2. Drain and discard liquid and vegetables. Place beef on a greased rack in a shallow roasting pan; set aside.
3. In a small saucepan, melt butter over medium heat. Stir in the remaining ingredients. Cook and stir until sugar is dissolved. Brush over beef.
4. Bake, uncovered, at 350° for 25 minutes. Let stand for 10 minutes before slicing.

FREEZE IT
TACO-FILLED PASTA SHELLS

I've been stuffing pasta shells with different fillings for years, but my family enjoys this version with taco-seasoned meat the most. The frozen shells are so convenient, because you can take out only the number you need for a single-serving lunch or a family dinner.
—MARGE HODEL ROANOKE, IL

PREP: 20 MIN. + CHILLING • **BAKE:** 45 MIN.
MAKES: 2 CASSEROLES (6 SERVINGS EACH)

- 2 pounds ground beef
- 2 envelopes taco seasoning
- 1½ cups water
- 1 package (8 ounces) cream cheese, cubed
- 24 uncooked jumbo pasta shells
- ¼ cup butter, melted

ADDITIONAL INGREDIENTS (FOR EACH CASSEROLE)

- 1 cup salsa
- 1 cup taco sauce
- 1 cup shredded cheddar cheese
- 1 cup shredded Monterey Jack cheese
- 1½ cups crushed tortilla chips
- 1 cup (8 ounces) sour cream
- 3 green onions, chopped

1. In a Dutch oven, cook beef over medium heat until no longer pink; drain. Stir in taco seasoning and water. Bring to a boil. Reduce heat; simmer, uncovered, for 5 minutes. Stir in cream cheese until melted. Transfer to a bowl; cool. Chill for 1 hour.
2. Cook pasta according to package directions; drain. Gently toss with butter. Fill each shell with about 3 tablespoons of meat mixture. Place 12 shells in a freezer container. Cover and freeze for up to 3 months.
3. To prepare remaining shells, spoon salsa into a greased 9-in. square baking dish. Top with stuffed shells and taco sauce. Cover and bake at 350° for 30 minutes. Uncover; sprinkle with cheeses and chips. Bake for 15 minutes longer or until heated through. Serve with sour cream and onions.
To use frozen shells: Thaw in the refrigerator for 24 hours (shells will be partially frozen). Spoon salsa into a greased 9-in. square baking dish; top with shells and taco sauce. Cover and bake at 350° for 40 minutes. Sprinkle with cheeses and chips; proceed as directed.

RYE BREAD-TOPPED REUBEN CASSEROLE

I always get compliments when I take this wonderful casserole to a potluck dinner.
—NITA WHITE CEDAR SPRINGS, MI

START TO FINISH: 30 MIN.
MAKES: 4 SERVINGS

- 1 can (14 ounces) sauerkraut, rinsed and well drained
- 1 cup Thousand Island salad dressing
- 1 pound thinly sliced deli corned beef, cut into strips
- 2 cups shredded Swiss cheese
- 4 to 6 slices rye bread, buttered

1. In a large bowl, combine sauerkraut and salad dressing; spread into a greased 13x9-in. baking dish. Top with corned beef and cheese.
2. Place bread, buttered side up, over the top. Bake, uncovered, at 375° for 25-30 minutes or until heated through and bubbly.

TOP TIP
SHRED & FREEZE CHEESE
"It's usually cheaper to buy cheese in blocks than in shredded form. So I purchase blocks of cheese, then shred them myself in my food processor. I store the cheese in the freezer in heavy-duty resealable plastic bags, so I have it whenever it's needed."
—EVELYN O. PARMA, OH

SOUTHWESTERN
CASEROLE

2-qt. baking dishes. Top with cheese and jalapenos. Cover and bake at 375° for 30 minutes. Uncover; bake until bubbly and heated through, about 10 minutes longer. Serve one casserole. Cool the second; cover and freeze for up to 3 months.

To use frozen casserole: Thaw in refrigerator for 8 hours. Preheat oven to 375°. Remove from refrigerator 30 minutes before baking. Cover and bake, increasing time as necessary to heat through and for a thermometer inserted in center to read 165°, 20-25 minutes.

Test Kitchen Note: Wear disposable gloves when cutting hot peppers; the oils can burn skin. Avoid touching your face.

GARLIC & HERB STEAK PIZZA

My family craves pizza that's super fast, cheesy and original. This one with steak and veggies is for folks who like their pie with everything on top.

—JADE FEARS GRAND RIDGE, FL

START TO FINISH: 30 MIN.
MAKES: 6 SERVINGS

- 1 **beef top sirloin steak (¾ inch thick and 1 pound)**
- ¾ **teaspoon salt**
- ¾ **teaspoon pepper**
- 1 **tablespoon olive oil**
- 1 **prebaked 12-inch thin pizza crust**
- ½ **cup garlic-herb spreadable cheese (about 3 ounces)**
- 2 **cups chopped fresh spinach**
- 1 **cup sliced red onion**
- 1 **cup sliced fresh mushrooms**
- 1½ **cups shredded part-skim mozzarella cheese**

1. Preheat oven to 450°. Season steak with salt and pepper. In a large skillet, heat oil over medium heat. Add steak; cook for 5-6 minutes on each side or until a thermometer reads 145° for medium-rare doneness. Remove from pan.
2. Meanwhile, place pizza crust on an ungreased baking sheet; spread with garlic-herb cheese. Top with spinach and onion.
3. Cut steak into slices; arrange on pizza. Top with mushrooms and cheese. Bake 8-10 minutes or until cheese is melted. Cut into 12 pieces.

FREEZE IT

SOUTHWESTERN CASSEROLE

I've been making this mild family-pleasing casserole recipe for years. It tastes wonderful, fits nicely into our budget, and, best of all, makes a second one to freeze and enjoy later.

—JOAN HALLFORD NORTH RICHLAND HILLS, TX

PREP: 15 MIN. • **BAKE:** 40 MIN.
MAKES: 2 CASSEROLES (6 SERVINGS EACH)

- 2 **cups (8 ounces) uncooked elbow macaroni**
- 2 **pounds ground beef**
- 1 **large onion, chopped**
- 2 **garlic cloves, minced**
- 2 **cans (14½ ounces each) diced tomatoes, undrained**
- 1 **can (16 ounces) kidney beans, rinsed and drained**
- 1 **can (6 ounces) tomato paste**
- 1 **can (4 ounces) chopped green chilies, drained**
- 1½ **teaspoons salt**
- 1 **teaspoon chili powder**
- ½ **teaspoon ground cumin**
- ½ **teaspoon pepper**
- 2 **cups shredded Monterey Jack cheese**
- 2 **jalapeno peppers, seeded and chopped**

1. Cook macaroni according to package directions. Meanwhile, in a large saucepan, cook beef and onion over medium heat, crumbling beef, until meat is no longer pink. Add garlic; cook for 1 minute longer. Drain. Stir in next eight ingredients. Bring to a boil. Reduce heat; simmer, uncovered, for 10 minutes. Drain macaroni; stir into beef mixture.
2. Preheat oven to 375°. Transfer macaroni mixture to two greased

GARLIC & HERB
STEAK PIZZA

"Enchiladas are typically prepared with corn tortillas, but we prefer flour tortillas in this saucy casserole with a subtle kick."
—JENNIFER STANDRIDGE DALLAS, GA

GARLIC BEEF
ENCHILADAS

GARLIC BEEF ENCHILADAS

PREP: 30 MIN. • **BAKE:** 40 MIN.
MAKES: 5 SERVINGS

- 1 pound ground beef
- 1 medium onion, chopped
- 2 tablespoons all-purpose flour
- 1 tablespoon chili powder
- 1 teaspoon salt
- 1 teaspoon garlic powder
- ½ teaspoon ground cumin
- ¼ teaspoon rubbed sage
- 1 can (14½ ounces) stewed tomatoes, cut up

SAUCE
- ⅓ cup butter
- 4 to 6 garlic cloves, minced
- ½ cup all-purpose flour
- 1 can (14½ ounces) beef broth
- 1 can (15 ounces) tomato sauce
- 1 to 2 tablespoons chili powder
- 1 to 2 teaspoons ground cumin
- 1 to 2 teaspoons rubbed sage
- ½ teaspoon salt
- 10 flour tortillas (6 inches), warmed
- 2 cups shredded Colby-Monterey Jack cheese, divided
  Optional toppings: halved grape tomatoes, minced fresh cilantro, sliced jalapeno peppers and medium red onion, chopped or sliced

1. Preheat oven to 350°. In a large skillet, cook beef and onion over medium heat, crumbling meat, until beef is no longer pink, 6-8 minutes; drain. Stir in flour and seasonings. Add tomatoes; bring to a boil. Reduce heat; simmer, covered, 15 minutes.

2. In a saucepan, heat butter over medium-high heat. Add garlic; cook and stir 1 minute or until tender. Stir in flour until blended; gradually whisk in broth. Bring to a boil; cook and stir 2 minutes or until thickened. Add tomato sauce and seasonings; heat through.

3. Pour 1½ cups sauce into an ungreased 13x9-in. baking dish. Place about ¼ cup beef mixture off center on each tortilla; top with 1-2 tablespoons cheese. Roll up and place in dish, seam side down. Top with remaining sauce. Bake, covered, until heated through, 30-35 minutes. Sprinkle with remaining cheese. Bake, uncovered, until cheese is melted, 10-15 minutes. Serve with toppings, if desired.

EAT SMART
CHILI STEAK & PEPPERS

In the mood for steak tonight? Chili sauce, lime juice and brown sugar is a simple combination for kicking up flavor, and the entire entree is under 275 calories.
—*TASTE OF HOME* TEST KITCHEN

START TO FINISH: 30 MIN.
MAKES: 4 SERVINGS

- 2 tablespoons chili sauce
- 1 tablespoon lime juice
- 1 teaspoon brown sugar
- ½ teaspoon crushed red pepper flakes
- ½ teaspoon salt, divided
- 1 beef top sirloin steak (1¼ pounds), cut into four steaks
- 1 medium onion, halved and sliced
- 1 medium green pepper, cut into strips
- 1 medium sweet yellow pepper, cut into strips
- 2 teaspoons olive oil
- 1 small garlic clove, minced
- ⅛ teaspoon pepper
- ¼ cup reduced-fat sour cream
- 1 teaspoon prepared horseradish

1. Combine the chili sauce, lime juice, brown sugar, pepper flakes and ¼ teaspoon salt; brush over steaks. Broil steaks 4-6 in. from the heat for 5-7 minutes on each side or until meat reaches desired doneness (for medium-rare, a meat thermometer should read 145°; medium, 160°; well-done, 170°).

2. Meanwhile, in a large skillet, saute onion and green and yellow peppers in oil until tender. Add the garlic, pepper and remaining salt; cook for 1 minute longer. In a small bowl, combine sour cream and horseradish. Serve steaks with pepper mixture and sauce.

Per steak with ⅓ cup pepper mixture and 1 tablespoon sauce: 265 cal., 9g fat (3g sat. fat), 62mg chol., 491mg sod., 12g carb. (8g sugars, 2g fiber), 32g pro.
Diabetic Exchanges: 4 lean meat, 1 vegetable, 1 fat.

BRAISED SHORT RIBS

Very hearty and very delicious is how I describe these ribs. Instead of baking them, I sometimes finish them in a slow cooker for 8-10 hours on low.
—SUSAN KINSELLA EAST FALMOUTH, MA

PREP: 30 MIN. • **BAKE:** 1½ HOURS
MAKES: 8 SERVINGS

- 4 pounds bone-in beef short ribs
- 1 teaspoon pepper, divided
- ½ teaspoon salt
- 3 tablespoons canola oil
- 3 celery ribs, chopped
- 2 large carrots, chopped
- 1 large yellow onion, chopped
- 1 medium sweet red pepper, chopped
- 1 garlic clove, minced
- 1 cup dry red wine or reduced-sodium beef broth
- 4 cups reduced-sodium beef broth
- 1 fresh rosemary sprig
- 1 fresh oregano sprig
- 1 bay leaf

1. Preheat oven to 325°. Sprinkle ribs with ½ teaspoon pepper and salt. In an ovenproof Dutch oven, brown ribs in oil in batches. Remove and set aside.
2. In the drippings, saute the celery, carrots, onion, red pepper and garlic until tender. Add wine, stirring to loosen browned bits from pan. Bring to a boil; cook until liquid is reduced by half.
3. Return ribs to the pan. Add broth, rosemary, oregano, bay leaf and remaining pepper; bring to a boil.
4. Cover and bake 1½ to 2 hours or until meat is tender. Remove ribs and keep warm. Discard herbs. Skim fat from pan juices; thicken if desired.

TOP TIP

You can purchase fresh bay leaves in the herb section of large supermarkets. Fresh leaves are more aromatic than dried, and you can finely mince them to season kabobs and Mediterranean dishes. To preserve leftover bay leaves, rinse and pat them dry, freeze in a single layer, then store in a freezer container for soups.

Poultry

DELICIOUS OVEN BARBECUED CHICKEN

A friend made this juicy chicken for us when we had our first child. I pared down the recipe to make it a little healthier. It's now a family favorite, and even the kids ask for it.

—MARGE WAGNER ROSELLE, IL

PREP: 20 MIN. • **BAKE:** 35 MIN.
MAKES: 6 SERVINGS

- 6 **bone-in chicken breast halves (8 ounces each)**
- ⅓ **cup chopped onion**
- ¾ **cup ketchup**
- ½ **cup water**
- ⅓ **cup white vinegar**
- 3 **tablespoons brown sugar**
- 1 **tablespoon Worcestershire sauce**
- 1 **teaspoon ground mustard**
- ¼ **teaspoon salt**
- ⅛ **teaspoon pepper**

1. Preheat oven to 350°. In a nonstick skillet coated with cooking spray, brown chicken over medium heat. Transfer to a 13x9-in. baking dish coated with cooking spray.

2. Recoat the skillet with cooking spray. Add onion; cook and stir over medium heat until tender. Stir in the remaining ingredients; bring to a boil. Reduce heat; simmer, uncovered, 15 minutes. Pour over chicken.

3. Bake, uncovered, until a thermometer inserted in the chicken reads 170°, 35-45 minutes.

DELICIOUS OVEN BARBECUED CHICKEN

COCONUT-CRUSTED
TURKEY STRIPS

CHICKEN & DUMPLING CASSEROLE

This savory casserole is one of my husband's favorites. He loves the fluffy dumplings with plenty of gravy poured over them. The basil adds just the right touch and makes the whole house smell so good while this dish cooks.

—SUE MACKEY JACKSON, WI

PREP: 30 MIN. • **BAKE:** 40 MIN.
MAKES: 6-8 SERVINGS

- ½ cup chopped onion
- ½ cup chopped celery
- ¼ cup butter, cubed
- 2 garlic cloves, minced
- ½ cup all-purpose flour
- 2 teaspoons sugar
- 1 teaspoon salt
- 1 teaspoon dried basil
- ½ teaspoon pepper
- 4 cups chicken broth
- 1 package (10 ounces) frozen green peas
- 4 cups cubed cooked chicken

DUMPLINGS
- 2 cups biscuit/baking mix
- 2 teaspoons dried basil
- ⅔ cup 2% milk

1. Preheat oven to 350°. In a large saucepan, saute onion and celery in butter until tender. Add garlic; cook 1 minute longer. Stir in flour, sugar, salt, basil and pepper until blended. Gradually add broth; bring to a boil. Cook and stir 1 minute or until thickened; reduce heat. Add peas and cook 5 minutes, stirring constantly. Stir in chicken. Pour into a greased 13x9-in. baking dish.
2. For dumplings, in a small bowl, combine baking mix and basil. Stir in milk with a fork just until moistened. Drop by tablespoonfuls into 12 mounds over the chicken mixture.
3. Bake, uncovered, 30 minutes. Cover and bake 10 minutes longer or until a toothpick inserted in a dumpling comes out clean.

COCONUT-CRUSTED TURKEY STRIPS

My granddaughter shared these baked turkey strips with plum dipping sauce—they're just the thing for a light dinner.

—AGNES WARD STRATFORD, ON

START TO FINISH: 30 MIN.
MAKES: 6 SERVINGS

- 2 large egg whites
- 2 teaspoons sesame oil
- ½ cup flaked coconut, toasted
- ½ cup dry bread crumbs
- 2 tablespoons sesame seeds, toasted
- ½ teaspoon salt
- 1½ pounds turkey breast tenderloins, cut into ½-inch strips
- Cooking spray

DIPPING SAUCE
- ½ cup plum sauce
- ⅓ cup unsweetened pineapple juice
- 1½ teaspoons prepared mustard
- 1 teaspoon cornstarch

1. Preheat oven to 425°. In a shallow bowl, whisk egg whites and oil. In another shallow bowl, mix coconut, bread crumbs, sesame seeds and salt. Dip turkey in the egg mixture, then in the coconut mixture, patting to help the coating adhere.
2. Place on baking sheets coated with cooking spray; spritz turkey with cooking spray. Bake 10-12 minutes or until turkey is no longer pink, turning once.
3. Meanwhile, in a small saucepan, mix sauce ingredients. Bring to a boil; cook and stir 1-2 minutes or until thickened. Serve turkey with sauce.

Test Kitchen Note: To toast coconut, bake in a shallow pan for 5-10 minutes at 350° or cook in a skillet over low heat until golden brown, stirring occasionally.

Per 3 ounces cooked turkey with 2 tablespoons sauce: 278 cal., 8g fat (3g sat. fat), 56mg chol., 519mg sod., 22g carb. (11g sugars, 1g fiber), 30g pro.
Diabetic Exchanges: 3 lean meat, 1½ starch, ½ fat.

EAT SMART

SAUSAGE & FETA STUFFED TOMATOES

I'm all about eating healthy. In fact, I'm a professional weight loss coach. My clients and blog followers love these tomatoes so much—they're hearty and healthy and still oh so tasty.

—**SHANA CONRADT** GREENVILLE, WI

START TO FINISH: 25 MIN.
MAKES: 4 SERVINGS

- **3 Italian turkey sausage links (4 ounces each), casings removed**
- **1 cup crumbled feta cheese, divided**
- **8 plum tomatoes**
- **¼ teaspoon salt**
- **¼ teaspoon pepper**
- **3 tablespoons balsamic vinegar Minced fresh parsley**

1. Preheat oven to 350°. In a skillet, cook sausage over medium heat for 4-6 minutes or until no longer pink, breaking into crumbles. Transfer to a small bowl; stir in ½ cup feta cheese.
2. Cut tomatoes in half lengthwise. Scoop out pulp, leaving a ½-in. shell; discard the pulp. Sprinkle tomatoes with salt and pepper; transfer to an ungreased 13x9-in. baking dish. Spoon the sausage mixture into the tomato shells; drizzle with vinegar. Sprinkle with the remaining feta cheese.
3. Bake, uncovered, 10-12 minutes or until heated through. Sprinkle with fresh parsley.

Per 4 stuffed tomato halves: 200 cal., 10g fat (4g sat. fat), 46mg chol., 777mg sod., 12g carb. (8g sugars, 3g fiber), 16g pro.
Diabetic Exchanges: 2 medium-fat meat, 1 vegetable, ½ starch.

EAT SMART

SUNDAY ROAST CHICKEN

This recipe proves that comfort food doesn't have to be full of unwanted calories. Mixed with orange and lemon juice, my roast chicken is both flavorful and healthy.

—**ROBIN HAAS** CRANSTON, RI

PREP: 30 MIN.
BAKE: 1¾ HOURS + RESTING
MAKES: 6 SERVINGS

- **1 medium fennel bulb**
- **5 large carrots, cut into 1½-inch pieces**
- **1 large white onion, quartered, divided**
- **1 medium lemon**
- **3 garlic cloves, minced**
- **1 tablespoon honey**
- **1 teaspoon kosher salt**
- **1 teaspoon crushed red pepper flakes**
- **1 teaspoon pepper**
- **1 broiler/fryer chicken (4 pounds)**
- **2 garlic cloves**
- **1 cup orange juice**

1. Preheat oven to 350°. Using a sharp knife, trim stalks and root end of fennel bulb. Cut bulb lengthwise into quarters; cut and remove core. Cut fennel into 1-in. wedges. Place fennel, carrots and three of the onion quarters in a shallow roasting pan, spreading evenly.
2. Cut lemon in half; squeeze juice into a small bowl, reserving lemon halves. Stir minced garlic, honey, salt, pepper flakes and pepper into juice.
3. Place chicken on a work surface, neck side down. With fingers, carefully loosen skin from the tail end of the chicken breast. Spoon the juice mixture under the skin of the breast; secure skin with toothpicks. Place garlic cloves, lemon halves and the remaining onion inside the chicken cavity. Tuck wings under chicken; tie drumsticks together. Place chicken over vegetables, breast side up.
4. Pour orange juice over chicken. Roast 1½-2 hours or until a thermometer inserted in thickest part of thigh reads 170°-175°. (Cover loosely with foil if chicken browns too quickly.)
5. Remove roasting pan from oven; increase oven setting to 450°. Remove chicken from pan; tent with foil and let stand 15 minutes before carving.
6. Meanwhile, return roasting pan to oven; roast vegetables 10-15 minutes longer or until vegetables are tender and lightly browned. Using a slotted spoon, remove vegetables from pan. If desired, skim fat from pan juices and serve with chicken and vegetables.

Per 4 ounces cooked chicken (skin removed) with ½ cup vegetables: 292 cal., 8g fat (2g sat. fat), 98mg chol., 470mg sod., 20g carb. (12g sugars, 4g fiber), 34g pro.
Diabetic Exchanges: 4 lean meat, 1 starch, 1 vegetable.

SAUSAGE & FETA STUFFED TOMATOES

SUNDAY
ROAST
CHICKEN

ITALIAN-STYLE CHICKEN & PEPPERS

I found my mom's well-stained recipe card for chicken and green peppers and was flooded with memories. I'd forgotten how good it was!

—DONNA MILLER GROSSE POINTE, MI

START TO FINISH: 30 MIN.
MAKES: 4 SERVINGS

- 2 **cups meatless pasta sauce**
- 2 **teaspoons olive oil**
- 1 **medium green pepper, finely chopped**
- 4 **ounces cream cheese, softened**
- 4 **boneless skinless chicken breast halves (4 ounces each)**
- ¼ **teaspoon salt**
- ⅛ **teaspoon pepper**
- 4 **slices part-skim mozzarella cheese**

1. Preheat oven to 425°. Place the pasta sauce in a microwave-safe bowl; microwave, covered, on high for 3-4 minutes or until hot, stirring halfway through.
2. Meanwhile, in a large skillet, heat oil over medium-high heat. Add green pepper; cook and stir 3-4 minutes or until tender. Transfer to a small bowl; stir in cream cheese.
3. Arrange chicken in a greased 13x9-in. baking dish; sprinkle with salt and pepper. Spoon the pepper mixture onto chicken. Pour warmed sauce over top. Place cheese over sauce. Bake, covered, for 25-30 minutes or until a thermometer inserted in chicken reads 165°.

TOP TIP

SOFTENING CREAM CHEESE

To quickly soften cream cheese, place it, unwrapped, in a microwave-safe bowl. Heat on high 15-20 seconds, turning it over halfway through the heating time. If the cream cheese isn't soft enough, continue to heat it, 10 seconds at a time, until it's reached the desired softness.

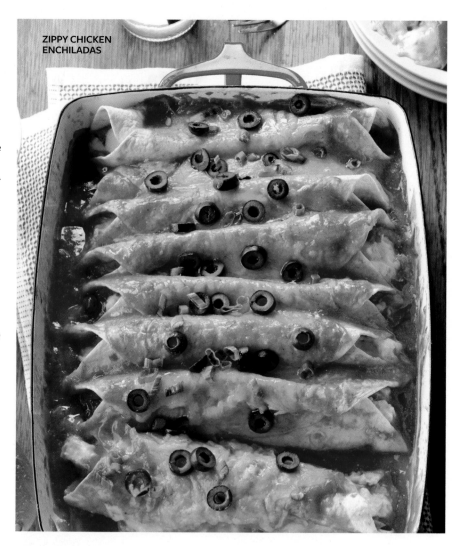

ZIPPY CHICKEN ENCHILADAS

FREEZE IT

ZIPPY CHICKEN ENCHILADAS

Leftover chicken gets a makeover in this rich and creamy casserole. This colorful, flavorful dish is a nice change of pace from beef enchiladas.

—JULIE MOUTRAY WICHITA, KS

PREP: 15 MIN. • **BAKE:** 35 MIN.
MAKES: 10 SERVINGS

- 1 **can (16 ounces) refried beans**
- 10 **flour tortillas (8 inches), warmed**
- 1 **can (10¾ ounces) condensed cream of chicken soup, undiluted**
- 1 **cup sour cream**
- 3 **to 4 cups cubed cooked chicken**
- 3 **cups shredded cheddar cheese, divided**
- 1 **can (15 ounces) enchilada sauce**
- ¼ **cup sliced green onions**
- ¼ **cup sliced ripe olives**
  Shredded lettuce, optional

1. Spread about 2 tablespoons of beans on each tortilla. Combine soup and sour cream; stir in chicken. Spoon ⅓-½ cup of this mixture down the center of each tortilla; top with 1 tablespoon of cheese.
2. Roll up the tortillas and place seam side down in a greased 13x9-in. baking dish. Pour enchilada sauce over top; sprinkle with onions, olives and the remaining cheese.
3. Bake, uncovered, at 350° for 35 minutes or until heated through. Just before serving, sprinkle lettuce around the enchiladas if desired.
Freeze option: Cover and freeze the unbaked casserole. To use, partially thaw in refrigerator overnight. Remove from refrigerator 30 minutes before baking. Preheat oven to 350°. Bake casserole as directed, increasing time as necessary to heat through and for a thermometer inserted in center to read 165°.

CHICKEN SALAD-STUFFED PEPPERS

We love this recipe because it combines the fresh flavor of summer bell peppers and chicken salad.

—**MARY MARLOWE LEVERETTE** COLUMBIA, SC

PREP: 30 MIN. • **BAKE:** 15 MIN.
MAKES: 4 SERVINGS

- 4 green onions, finely chopped
- ½ cup mayonnaise
- 2 tablespoons lemon juice
- ½ teaspoon dried tarragon
- ½ teaspoon pepper
- ¼ teaspoon salt
- 2 cups finely chopped rotisserie chicken
- ½ cup shredded Monterey Jack cheese
- 1 celery rib, finely chopped
- 4 medium sweet red peppers
  Crushed potato chips, optional

1. Preheat oven to 350°. In a small bowl, mix the first six ingredients. Add chicken, cheese and celery; toss to coat.

2. Cut peppers lengthwise in half; remove seeds. In a Dutch oven, cook the peppers in boiling water for 3-4 minutes or until crisp-tender; drain.

3. Place in a greased 13x9-in. baking dish. Fill with chicken mixture. If desired, sprinkle with chips. Bake, uncovered, for 15-20 minutes or until the filling is heated through.

CHICKEN SALAD-STUFFED PEPPERS

ORANGE ROASTED TURKEY

When we roast turkey for the holidays, we use orange marmalade to make a glaze that gives the bird's skin an awesome tangy flavor.

—**LEE BREMSON** KANSAS CITY, MO

PREP: 20 MIN.
BAKE: 3 HOURS + STANDING
MAKES: 16 SERVINGS

- 1 turkey (14 to 16 pounds)
- 1 tablespoon canola oil
- ½ teaspoon salt
- ¼ teaspoon pepper
  Orange and onion wedges, optional

GLAZE
- ½ cup orange juice
- ½ cup orange marmalade
- ¼ cup butter, cubed
- 2 teaspoons grated orange peel
- 2 teaspoons minced fresh thyme or ½ teaspoon dried thyme
  Fresh parsley sprigs, optional

1. Preheat oven to 325°. Place turkey on a rack in a shallow roasting pan, breast side up. Tuck the wings under the turkey; tie the drumsticks together. Rub oil over the turkey, then sprinkle with salt and pepper. If desired, add orange and onion wedges to the roasting pan.

2. Roast, uncovered, for 2¾ hours. For the glaze, in a small saucepan, bring orange juice, marmalade and butter to a boil. Reduce heat; simmer, uncovered, 15-20 minutes or until slightly thickened, stirring occasionally. Stir in orange peel and thyme.

3. Brush turkey with some of the glaze. Roast 15-30 minutes longer or until a thermometer inserted in the thickest part of a thigh reads 170°-175°, brushing occasionally with the remaining glaze. (Cover the turkey loosely with foil if it browns too quickly.) Remove the turkey from the oven; tent with foil. Let stand for 20 minutes before carving. If desired, skim fat and thicken pan drippings for gravy. Serve with turkey and, if desired, orange and onion wedges and parsley.

FAVORITE
BAKED
SPAGHETTI

FAVORITE BAKED SPAGHETTI

This yummy spaghetti casserole will be requested again and again for potlucks and family gatherings. It's especially popular with my grandchildren, who just love all the cheese.

—LOUISE MILLER WESTMINSTER, MD

PREP: 25 MIN. • **BAKE:** 1 HOUR
MAKES: 10 SERVINGS

- 1 package (16 ounces) spaghetti
- 1 pound ground turkey
- 1 medium onion, chopped
- 1 jar (24 ounces) meatless spaghetti sauce
- ½ teaspoon seasoned salt
- 2 large eggs
- ⅓ cup grated Parmesan cheese
- 5 tablespoons butter, melted
- 2 cups (16 ounces) 4% cottage cheese
- 4 cups part-skim shredded mozzarella cheese

1. Cook spaghetti according to package directions. Meanwhile, in a large skillet, cook turkey and onion over medium heat until meat is no longer pink; drain. Stir in spaghetti sauce and seasoned salt; set aside.

2. In a large bowl, whisk the eggs, Parmesan cheese and butter. Drain spaghetti; add to egg mixture and toss to coat.

3. Place half of the spaghetti mixture in a greased 3-qt. baking dish. Top with half of the cottage cheese, meat sauce and mozzarella cheese. Repeat layers.

4. Cover casserole and bake at 350° for 40 minutes. Uncover; bake for 20-25 minutes longer or until cheese is melted.

CANTONESE CHICKEN BURGERS

Onion, chopped peanuts and carrots perk up ground chicken for these delectable chicken burgers that can be served year-round. These may take a little more work than the standard burger, but the taste is worth it!

—BETTY CARR HUNTSVILLE, OH

START TO FINISH: 30 MIN.
MAKES: 4 SERVINGS

- 1 large egg
- 1 teaspoon sesame oil
- 1 teaspoon soy sauce
- ⅓ cup dry bread crumbs
- ¼ cup chopped salted peanuts
- 2 tablespoons sliced green onion
- 2 tablespoons shredded carrot
- ⅛ teaspoon garlic powder
- 1 pound ground chicken
- 4 hamburger buns, split and toasted
- ½ cup plum sauce
- 8 spinach leaves, chopped

1. In a large bowl, whisk egg, oil and soy sauce. Stir in bread crumbs, peanuts, onion, carrot and garlic powder. Crumble ground chicken over the mixture and mix well. Shape into four patties.

2. Broil 3-4 in. from the heat for 8-10 minutes on each side or until juices run clear. Serve on buns; top with plum sauce and spinach.

TOP TIP

STICKY BUNS?

I buy hamburger buns in packs of 12 to keep them on hand in the freezer. But if I freeze the entire bag, the buns stick together. They're easier to work with if, before freezing, I wrap them securely in plastic, two per package, then place them in a freezer bag.

—ARLENE WRAGE TRAER, IA

EASY CHEDDAR CHICKEN POTPIE

My kids love potpie, and I love that this is so easy to put together with frozen veggies and store-bought gravy. To make it even simpler, my friend and I topped it with a biscuit crust instead of homemade pastry. It's delicious!

—LINDA DREES PALESTINE, TX

PREP: 20 MIN. • **BAKE:** 25 MIN.
MAKES: 6 SERVINGS

- 1 package (16 ounces) frozen vegetables for stew, thawed and coarsely chopped
- 1 jar (12 ounces) chicken gravy
- 2 cups shredded cheddar cheese
- 2 cups cubed cooked chicken
- 2 cups biscuit/baking mix
- 1 teaspoon minced fresh or ¼ teaspoon dried thyme
- 2 large eggs
- ¼ cup 2% milk

1. Combine vegetables and gravy in a large saucepan. Bring to a boil. Reduce heat; stir in cheese and chicken. Cook and stir until cheese is melted. Pour into a greased 11x7-in. baking dish.

2. Combine biscuit mix and thyme in a small bowl. In another bowl, whisk eggs and milk; stir into dry ingredients just until moistened. Drop by tablespoonfuls over chicken mixture; spread gently.

3. Bake potpie, uncovered, at 375° for 23-27 minutes or until golden brown. Let stand for 5 minutes before serving.

BAKED MONTEREY CHICKEN WITH ROASTED VEGGIES

BAKED MONTEREY CHICKEN WITH ROASTED VEGGIES

Everyone asks me to make this baked chicken. Roasting the veggies brings out their sweetness. They're delicious with fettuccine, rice or mashed potatoes.
—**GLORIA BRADLEY** NAPERVILLE, IL

PREP: 15 MIN. • **BAKE:** 25 MIN.
MAKES: 6 SERVINGS

- 1 **pound fresh asparagus, trimmed and cut into 2-inch pieces**
- 2 **large sweet red peppers, cut into strips**
- 1 **tablespoon olive oil**
- 1½ **teaspoons salt, divided**
- ¾ **teaspoon coarsely ground pepper, divided**
- 6 **boneless skinless chicken breast halves (6 ounces each)**
- 5 **tablespoons butter, divided**
- ¼ **cup all-purpose flour**
- 1 **cup chicken broth**
- 1 **cup heavy whipping cream**
- ¼ **cup white wine or additional chicken broth**
- 1½ **cups shredded Monterey Jack cheese, divided**

1. Preheat oven to 400°. Place the asparagus and red peppers in a greased 13x9-in. baking dish; toss with oil, ½ teaspoon salt and ¼ teaspoon pepper. Roast for 5-8 minutes or just until crisp-tender, then remove vegetables from dish.
2. Season chicken with the remaining salt and pepper. In a large skillet, heat 1 tablespoon butter over medium heat; brown 3 chicken breasts on both sides. Transfer to the same baking dish. Repeat with an additional 1 tablespoon butter and the remaining chicken. Top chicken with roasted vegetables.
3. In same skillet, melt the remaining butter over medium heat. Stir in flour until smooth; gradually whisk in broth, cream and wine. Bring to a boil over medium heat, stirring constantly; cook and stir 2-3 minutes or until thickened. Stir in 1 cup cheese until melted. Pour over the chicken.
4. Bake, uncovered, for 25-30 minutes or until a thermometer inserted in the chicken reads 165°. Sprinkle with the remaining cheese.

CHIPOTLE TURKEY CHILAQUILES

PREP: 30 MIN. • **BAKE:** 25 MIN.
MAKES: 8 SERVINGS

- 15 **corn tortillas (6 inches), torn into 1½-inch pieces**
- 3 **cups shredded cooked turkey or chicken**
- 1 **large onion, chopped**
- 4 **garlic cloves, minced**
- ⅓ **cup lime juice**
- 2 **chipotle peppers in adobo sauce**
- 2 **cans (15 ounces each) black beans, rinsed and drained**
- 3 **cups crumbled queso fresco or shredded part-skim mozzarella cheese**
- 3 **cups turkey or chicken broth**
  Chopped fresh cilantro
  Hot cooked rice, optional
  Sour cream, optional

1. Preheat oven to 400°. In batches, arrange tortilla pieces in a single layer on an ungreased baking sheet and bake for 6-8 minutes or until crisp.
2. In a large bowl, toss turkey with onion and garlic. Place lime juice and peppers in a blender; cover and process until blended.
3. Arrange half of the tortilla pieces in a greased 13x9-in. baking dish. Layer with the turkey mixture, beans, 1½ cups cheese and chipotle mixture. Top with the remaining tortilla pieces and cheese. Pour broth over top.
4. Bake, uncovered, 25-30 minutes or until cheese is melted. Sprinkle with cilantro. If desired, serve with rice and sour cream.
Per 1½ cups: 364 cal., 8g fat (3g sat. fat), 56mg chol., 766mg sod., 44g carb. (3g sugars, 7g fiber), 29g pro.

"As a frugal mom, I try to use leftovers in a way that provides good nutrition. This recipe does just that—and it's also a great way for my children to learn to enjoy the flavors of their Mexican heritage."

—AIMEE DAY FERNDALE, WA

CHIPOTLE TURKEY CHILAQUILES

LEMONY
CHICKEN
& RICE

FREEZE IT

CREAMY CHICKEN CASSEROLE

I created this noodle casserole when my husband was craving a dish his aunt used to make. It tastes and smells great and is now a staple at our house.

—MARI WARNKE FREMONT, WI

PREP: 20 MIN. • **BAKE:** 40 MIN.
MAKES: 2 CASSEROLES (5 SERVINGS EACH)

- 4 **cups uncooked egg noodles**
- 4 **cups cubed cooked chicken**
- 1 **package (16 ounces) frozen peas and carrots**
- 2 **cups milk**
- 2 **cans (10¾ ounces each) condensed cream of celery soup, undiluted**
- 2 **cans (10¾ ounces each) condensed cream of chicken soup, undiluted**
- 1 **cup chopped onion**
- 2 **tablespoons butter, melted**
- ½ **teaspoon salt**
- ½ **teaspoon pepper**

1. Preheat oven to 350°. Cook the noodles according to package directions. Meanwhile, in a large bowl, combine the remaining ingredients. Drain the noodles; add to the chicken mixture.
2. Transfer to two greased 8-in. square baking dishes. Cover dishes and bake for 30 minutes. Uncover; bake 10-15 minutes longer or until heated through.
Freeze option: Cover and freeze the unbaked casseroles for up to 3 months. To use, partially thaw in refrigerator overnight. Remove from refrigerator 30 minutes before cooking. Cover and microwave on high for 10-12 minutes or until heated through and a thermometer inserted in the center of the casserole reads 165°, stirring twice.

TOP TIP

MEASURE, THEN MELT
When melted butter is called for in a recipe, it's measured first, then melted. The markings on the wrappers make it easy to slice off the amount you need and melt it.

LEMONY CHICKEN & RICE

I couldn't say who loves this recipe best, because every time I serve it, it gets raves! Occasionally I even get a call or an email from a friend requesting the recipe, and it's certainly a favorite for my grown children and 15 grandchildren.

—MARYALICE WOOD LANGLEY, BC

PREP: 15 MIN. + MARINATING
BAKE: 55 MIN.
MAKES: 2 CASSEROLES (4 SERVINGS EACH)

- 2 **cups water**
- ½ **cup reduced-sodium soy sauce**
- ¼ **cup lemon juice**
- ¼ **cup olive oil**
- 2 **garlic cloves, minced**
- 2 **teaspoons ground ginger**
- 2 **teaspoons pepper**
- 16 **bone-in chicken thighs, skin removed (about 6 pounds)**
- 2 **cups uncooked long grain rice**
- 4 **tablespoons grated lemon peel, divided**
- 2 **medium lemons, sliced**

1. In a large resealable plastic bag, combine the first seven ingredients. Add chicken; seal bag and turn to coat. Refrigerate for 4 hours or overnight.
2. Preheat oven to 325°. Spread 1 cup of rice into each of two greased 13x9-in. baking dishes. Top each with 1 tablespoon lemon peel, 8 chicken thighs and half of the marinade. Top with sliced lemons.
3. Bake, covered, for 40 minutes. Uncover and bake 15-20 minutes longer or until a thermometer inserted in chicken reads 180°. Sprinkle with remaining lemon peel.

ITALIAN SAUSAGE-STUFFED ZUCCHINI

I've always had to be creative when getting my family to eat vegetables, so I decided to make stuffed zucchini using the pizza flavors that everyone loves. It worked! We like to include sausage for a main dish but it could be a meatless side dish, too.

—DONNA-MARIE RYAN TOPSFIELD, MA

PREP: 35 MIN. • **BAKE:** 20 MIN.
MAKES: 6 SERVINGS

- 6 **medium zucchini (about 8 ounces each)**
- 1 **pound Italian turkey sausage links, casings removed**
- 2 **medium tomatoes, seeded and chopped**
- 1 **cup panko (Japanese) bread crumbs**
- ⅓ **cup grated Parmesan cheese**
- ⅓ **cup minced fresh parsley**
- 2 **tablespoons minced fresh oregano or 2 teaspoons dried oregano**
- 2 **tablespoons minced fresh basil or 2 teaspoons dried basil**
- ¼ **teaspoon pepper**
- ¾ **cup shredded part-skim mozzarella cheese**

1. Preheat oven to 350°. Cut each zucchini lengthwise in half. Scoop out pulp, leaving a ¼-in. shell; chop pulp. Place zucchini shells in a microwave-safe dish. In batches, microwave, covered, on high for 2-3 minutes or until crisp-tender.
2. In a large skillet, cook the sausage and zucchini pulp over medium heat 6-8 minutes or until sausage is no longer pink, breaking the sausage into crumbles; drain. Stir in tomatoes, bread crumbs, Parmesan cheese, herbs and pepper. Spoon into the zucchini shells.
3. Place in two ungreased 13x9-in. baking dishes. Bake, covered, for 15-20 minutes or until the zucchini is tender. Sprinkle with mozzarella cheese. Bake, uncovered, 5-8 minutes longer or until the cheese is melted.
Per 2 stuffed zucchini halves: 206 cal., 9g fat (3g sat. fat), 39mg chol., 485mg sod., 16g carb. (5g sugars, 3g fiber), 17g pro.
Diabetic Exchanges: 2 lean meat, 2 vegetable, ½ starch.

TURKEY CORDON BLEU CASSEROLE

We love everything about traditional Cordon Bleu, and this variation is so easy to make. It's a delicious way to eat Thanksgiving leftovers.

—KRISTINE BLAUERT WABASHA, MN

PREP: 20 MIN. • **BAKE:** 25 MIN.
MAKES: 8 SERVINGS

- 2 **cups uncooked elbow macaroni**
- 2 **cans (10¾ ounces each) condensed cream of chicken soup, undiluted**
- ¾ **cup 2% milk**
- ¼ **cup grated Parmesan cheese**
- 1 **teaspoon prepared mustard**
- 1 **teaspoon paprika**
- ½ **teaspoon dried rosemary, crushed**
- ¼ **teaspoon garlic powder**
- ⅛ **teaspoon rubbed sage**
- 2 **cups cubed cooked turkey**
- 2 **cups cubed fully cooked ham**
- 2 **cups shredded part-skim mozzarella cheese**
- ¼ **cup crushed Ritz crackers**

1. Preheat oven to 350°. Cook macaroni according to package directions.
2. Meanwhile, whisk together the soup, milk, Parmesan cheese, mustard and seasonings. Stir in the turkey, ham and mozzarella cheese.
3. Drain the macaroni; add to the soup mixture and toss to combine. Transfer to a greased 13x9-in. baking dish or eight greased 8-oz. ramekins. Sprinkle with crushed crackers. Bake, uncovered, until bubbly, 25-30 minutes.
Freeze option: Cover and freeze unbaked dish or ramekins. To use, partially thaw in refrigerator overnight. Remove from refrigerator 30 minutes before baking. Preheat oven to 350°. Bake as directed, increasing time as necessary to heat through and for a thermometer inserted in center to read 165°.

TURKEY CORDON BLEU CASSEROLE

MAPLE-ROASTED
CHICKEN & ACORN
SQUASH

MAPLE-ROASTED CHICKEN & ACORN SQUASH

When I became a new mother, my mom helped me find comforting recipes to have on hand. This terrific roast chicken is a happy discovery.

—**SARA EILERS** SURPRISE, AZ

PREP: 15 MIN. • **BAKE:** 35 MIN.
MAKES: 6 SERVINGS

- 1 medium acorn squash
- 4 medium carrots, chopped (about 2 cups)
- 1 medium onion, cut into 1-inch pieces
- 6 bone-in chicken thighs (about 2¼ pounds)
- ½ cup maple syrup
- 1 teaspoon salt
- ½ teaspoon coarsely ground pepper

1. Preheat oven to 450°. Cut squash lengthwise in half; remove and discard seeds. Cut each half crosswise into ½-in. slices; discard ends. Place squash, carrots and onion in a greased 13x9-in. baking pan; top with chicken, skin side down. Roast 10 minutes.
2. Turn chicken over; drizzle with maple syrup and sprinkle with salt and pepper. Roast 25-30 minutes longer or until a thermometer inserted in chicken reads 170°-175° and the vegetables are tender.
Per serving: 363 cal., 14g fat (4g sat. fat), 81mg chol., 497mg sod., 36g carb. (23g sugars, 3g fiber), 24g pro.
Diabetic Exchanges: 3 lean meat, 2 starch, 1 vegetable.

BRUSCHETTA-TOPPED CHICKEN & SPAGHETTI

I'm always on the lookout for healthy recipes for my family. If you find yourself craving Italian food, this delicious 30-minute meal hits the spot.

—**SUSAN WHOLLEY** FAIRFIELD, CT

START TO FINISH: 30 MIN.
MAKES: 4 SERVINGS

- 8 ounces uncooked whole wheat spaghetti
- 4 boneless skinless chicken breast halves (5 ounces each)
- ½ teaspoon pepper
- 1 cup prepared bruschetta topping
- ⅓ cup shredded Italian cheese blend
- 2 tablespoons grated Parmesan cheese

1. Preheat broiler. Cook spaghetti according to package directions; drain. Pound chicken breasts with a meat mallet to ½-in. thickness. Sprinkle with pepper. In a large nonstick skillet coated with cooking spray, cook the chicken over medium heat 5-6 minutes on each side or until no longer pink.
2. Transfer to an 8-in. square baking pan. Spoon bruschetta topping over chicken; sprinkle with cheeses. Broil 3-4 in. from heat 5-6 minutes or until cheese is golden brown. Serve with spaghetti.
Test Kitchen Note: Look for bruschetta topping in the pasta aisle or your grocer's deli case.
Per 1 chicken breast half with 1 cup cooked spaghetti : 431 cal., 10g fat (4g sat. fat), 87mg chol., 641mg sod., 47g carb. (4g sugars, 8g fiber), 40g pro.
Diabetic Exchanges: 4 lean meat, 3 starch, ½ fat.

TURKEY POTPIE CUPS

My children look forward to turkey or chicken leftovers because they know this recipe will make an appearance. Refrigerated flaky biscuits make perfect individual potpie crusts.

—**KAREN WOODARD** MUSTANG, OK

PREP: 25 MIN. • **BAKE:** 20 MIN.
MAKES: 8 SERVINGS

- 1 tube (16.3 ounces) large refrigerated flaky biscuits
- 3 cups cubed cooked turkey
- 3 cups turkey gravy
- 2¼ cups frozen mixed vegetables
- ½ teaspoon salt
- ½ teaspoon pepper
- 1 cup french-fried onions
- 2¼ cups mashed potatoes
- ⅓ cup 2% milk
- ½ cup shredded cheddar cheese

1. On a lightly floured surface, roll each biscuit into an 8-in. circle. Press onto the bottoms and up the sides of eight greased 8-oz. ramekins.
2. In a large saucepan, combine turkey, gravy, vegetables, salt and pepper. Bring to a boil. Reduce heat; simmer, uncovered, for 5 minutes. Sprinkle onions into the ramekins; top with the turkey mixture. In a small bowl, combine potatoes and milk; spread over tops. Sprinkle with cheese.
3. Bake at 375° for 18-22 minutes or until golden brown.

TOP TIP

GREASING A PAN

When it comes to greasing a pan for a savory dish or a casserole, the most economical choices are the traditional ones—shortening, butter, reserved bacon grease or canola oil. To cut down on the mess of applying these standbys, slide your hand into a plastic sandwich bag, then apply the grease by hand. When you're done, peel off the plastic bag so that it turns inside out, and discard it. Most of the time, you won't even have to wash your hands when you're done!

SALSA VERDE CHICKEN CASSEROLE

This is a rich and surprisingly tasty rendition of many Tex-Mex dishes molded into one packed, beautiful casserole. Best of all, it's ready in no time!

—**JANET McCORMICK** PROCTORVILLE, OH

START TO FINISH: 30 MIN.
MAKES: 6 SERVINGS

- 2 **cups shredded rotisserie chicken**
- 1 **cup sour cream**
- 1½ **cups salsa verde, divided**
- 8 **corn tortillas (6 inches)**
- 2 **cups chopped tomatoes**
- ¼ **cup minced fresh cilantro**
- 2 **cups shredded Monterey Jack cheese**

Optional toppings: avocado slices, thinly sliced green onions and fresh cilantro leaves

1. Combine chicken, sour cream and ¾ cup salsa in a small bowl. Spread ¼ cup salsa on the bottom of a greased 8-in. square baking dish.
2. Layer with half the tortillas and chicken mixture; sprinkle with tomatoes, minced cilantro and half of the cheese. Repeat the layers with the remaining tortillas, chicken mixture and cheese.
3. Bake, uncovered, at 400° for 20-25 minutes or until bubbly. Serve with remaining salsa and, if desired, optional toppings.

SALSA VERDE CHICKEN CASSEROLE

GINGER-CASHEW CHICKEN SALAD

I revamped an Asian-style chicken salad recipe to create this gingery, crunchy salad. It's a huge success whenever I serve it at ladies' luncheons.

—**SHELLY GRAMER** LONG BEACH, CA

PREP: 20 MIN. + MARINATING
BROIL: 10 MIN.
MAKES: 8 SERVINGS

- ½ **cup cider vinegar**
- ½ **cup molasses**
- ⅓ **cup canola oil**
- 2 **tablespoons minced fresh gingerroot**
- 2 **teaspoons reduced-sodium soy sauce**
- 1 **teaspoon salt**
- ⅛ **teaspoon cayenne pepper**
- 4 **boneless skinless chicken breast halves (6 ounces each)**

SALAD
- 8 **ounces fresh baby spinach (about 10 cups)**
- 1 **can (11 ounces) mandarin oranges, drained**
- 1 **cup shredded red cabbage**
- 2 **medium carrots, shredded**
- 3 **green onions, thinly sliced**
- 2 **cups chow mein noodles**
- ¾ **cup salted cashews, toasted**
- 2 **tablespoons sesame seeds, toasted**

1. In a small bowl, whisk the first seven ingredients until blended. Pour ¾ cup marinade into a large resealable plastic bag. Add chicken; seal bag and turn to coat. Refrigerate at least 3 hours. Cover and refrigerate the remaining marinade.
2. Preheat broiler. Drain the chicken, discarding the marinade in bag. Place the chicken in a 15x10x1-in. baking pan. Broil 4-6 in. from heat for 4-6 minutes on each side or until a thermometer reads 165°. Cut chicken into strips.
3. Place spinach on a serving platter. Arrange chicken, oranges, cabbage, carrots and green onions. Sprinkle with chow mein noodles, cashews and sesame seeds. Stir the reserved marinade; drizzle over the salad and toss to coat. Serve immediately.

Test Kitchen Note: To toast nuts, bake in a shallow pan in a 350° oven for 5-10 minutes or cook in a skillet over low heat until lightly browned, stirring occasionally.

GINGER-CASHEW CHICKEN SALAD

EFFORTLESS
ALFREDO PIZZA

Per 1 slice: 302 cal., 10g fat (4g sat. fat), 45mg chol., 756mg sod., 33g carb. (1g sugars, 1g fiber), 20g pro.
Diabetic Exchanges: 2 starch, 2 lean meat, ½ fat.

ULTIMATE CHICKEN SANDWICHES

After making these sandwiches, you'll never order the fast-food kind again. Marinating the chicken overnight in buttermilk gives it a wonderful taste and tenderness, and the breading is golden and crispy.

—**GREGG VOSS** EMERSON, NE

PREP: 10 MIN. + MARINATING
BAKE: 20 MIN.
MAKES: 6 SERVINGS

- 6 **boneless skinless chicken breast halves (4 ounces each)**
- 1 **cup buttermilk**
- ½ **cup reduced-fat biscuit/baking mix**
- ½ **cup cornmeal**
- 1½ **teaspoons paprika**
- ¾ **teaspoon salt**
- ¾ **teaspoon poultry seasoning**
- ½ **teaspoon garlic powder**
- ½ **teaspoon pepper**
- ¼ **teaspoon cayenne pepper**
- 6 **onion or kaiser rolls, split**
- 6 **lettuce leaves**
- 12 **tomato slices**

1. Flatten chicken to ½-in. thickness. Pour buttermilk into a large resealable plastic bag; add the chicken. Seal the bag and turn to coat; refrigerate for 8 hours or overnight.

2. In a shallow bowl, combine biscuit mix, cornmeal, paprika, salt, poultry seasoning, garlic powder, pepper and cayenne. Remove the chicken from the bag, one piece at a time, allowing the excess buttermilk to drain off. Discard the buttermilk. Coat chicken with the cornmeal mixture; place in a 13x9-in. baking dish coated with cooking spray.

3. Bake, uncovered, at 400° for 8-12 minutes on each side or until a thermometer inserted into a chicken breast reads 170° and the coating is lightly browned. Serve on rolls with lettuce and tomato.

EAT SMART

EFFORTLESS ALFREDO PIZZA

Here's a lighter, scrumptious twist for pizza night. The recipe makes good use of leftovers and convenience items, so I don't have to spend much time in the kitchen. I often use collard greens instead of spinach.

—**BRITTNEY HOUSE** LOCKPORT, IL

START TO FINISH: 20 MIN.
MAKES: 6 SLICES

- 1 **package (10 ounces) frozen chopped spinach, thawed and squeezed dry**
- 1 **cup shredded cooked turkey breast**
- 2 **teaspoons lemon juice**
- ¼ **teaspoon salt**
- ¼ **teaspoon pepper**
- 1 **prebaked 12-inch pizza crust**
- 1 **garlic clove, peeled and halved**
- ½ **cup reduced-fat Alfredo sauce**
- ¾ **cup shredded fontina cheese**
- ½ **teaspoon crushed red pepper flakes**

1. Preheat oven to 450°. In a large bowl, mix the first five ingredients until blended.

2. Place crust on an ungreased 12-in. pizza pan; rub with cut sides of garlic. Discard garlic. Spread Alfredo sauce over crust. Top with the spinach mixture, cheese and pepper flakes. Bake for 8-12 minutes or until the crust is lightly browned.

CHILI-STUFFED
POBLANO PEPPERS

STUFFED CHICKEN BREASTS

Mushroom-rice stuffing turns plain chicken breasts into a terrific main dish your family will remember.
—**PAT NEU** GAINESVILLE, TX

PREP: 20 MIN. • **BAKE:** 1½ HOURS
MAKES: 6 SERVINGS

- 1½ **cups sliced fresh mushrooms**
- 1⅓ **cups uncooked instant rice**
- ¼ **cup chopped onion**
- ¼ **cup chopped celery leaves**
- ¼ **cup butter**
- 1½ **cups water**
- 1½ **teaspoons salt**
- ½ **teaspoon dried oregano**
- ½ **teaspoon rubbed sage**
- ½ **teaspoon dried thyme**
- ¼ **teaspoon pepper**
- ⅓ **cup chopped pecans, toasted**
- 6 **bone-in chicken breast halves (8 ounces each)**

1. In a large saucepan, saute the mushrooms, rice, onion and celery leaves in butter until the onion is tender. Add water and seasonings; bring to a boil. Reduce heat; cover and simmer for 5-7 minutes or until the rice is tender and the liquid is absorbed. Stir in pecans.
2. Stuff ½ cup of the rice mixture under the skin of each chicken breast half. Place in a greased 13x9-in. baking dish. Bake, uncovered, at 350° for 1½ hours or until a thermometer reads 170°.

CHILI-STUFFED POBLANO PEPPERS

After tasting chiles rellenos, I wanted to make them at home. My husband and I teamed up to create this new favorite.
—**LORRIE GRABCZYNSKI**
COMMERCE TOWNSHIP, MI

START TO FINISH: 30 MIN.
MAKES: 4 SERVINGS

- 1 **pound lean ground turkey**
- 1 **can (15 ounces) chili without beans**
- ¼ **teaspoon salt**
- 1½ **cups shredded Mexican cheese blend, divided**
- 1 **medium tomato, finely chopped**
- 4 **green onions, chopped**
- 4 **large poblano peppers**
- 1 **tablespoon olive oil**

1. Preheat broiler. In a large skillet over medium heat, cook turkey, crumbling meat, until no longer pink, 5-7 minutes; drain. Add chili and salt; heat through. Stir in ½ cup cheese blend, tomato and green onions.
2. Meanwhile, cut peppers lengthwise in half; remove seeds. Place on a foil-lined 15x10x1-in. baking pan, cut side down; brush with oil. Broil 4 in. from heat until the skins blister, about 5 minutes.
3. With tongs, turn the peppers. Fill with the turkey mixture; sprinkle with the remaining cheese. Broil until the cheese is melted, 1-2 minutes longer.
Test Kitchen Note: Wear disposable gloves when cutting hot peppers; the oils can burn skin. Avoid touching your face.

TOP TIP

STUFFING A BONE-IN CHICKEN BREAST

When a recipe calls for stuffing a bone-in chicken breast, the stuffing goes between the meat and the skin. Work your fingers under the skin to loosen it and form a pocket, then lightly fill the pocket with the stuffing mixture.

Pork

HONEY DIJON PORK

HONEY DIJON PORK

I'm fond of honey-mustard salad dressing, so I attempted to duplicate its taste when I created this pork recipe. It's quick and easy to prepare. Sometimes I'll put a sweet potato in the oven to bake at the same time. Then I have a complete meal for two.

—AUDREY THIBODEAU GILBERT, AZ

PREP: 15 MIN. • **BAKE:** 50 MIN.
MAKES: 2 SERVINGS

- 2 **boneless pork loin chops (½ inch thick)**
- ¼ **teaspoon salt**
  Dash pepper
- 1 **tablespoon all-purpose flour**
- ½ **cup orange juice, divided**
- ½ **cup honey**
- 1 **tablespoon Dijon mustard**
- ¼ **teaspoon dried basil**
- 2 **medium carrots, cut into 1-inch pieces**
- 1 **small onion, cut into eighths**
- ½ **small green pepper, cut into squares**
- ½ **small sweet red pepper, cut into squares**

1. Sprinkle pork chops with salt and pepper; place in a heavy ovenproof skillet. In a small bowl, whisk flour and 2 tablespoons orange juice until smooth; whisk in the honey, mustard, basil and remaining orange juice. Pour over chops. Place carrots and onion around chops.
2. Cover skillet and bake at 350° for 30 minutes. Stir in peppers; cover and bake 20 minutes longer or until vegetables are tender and pork is no longer pink.

ITALIAN
SMOTHERED
PORK CHOPS

ITALIAN SMOTHERED PORK CHOPS

My brother and I come from an Italian family, and we designed these pork chops to include Italian staples like fresh mozzarella, roasted red peppers and broccoli rabe.

—SHANA LEWIS TOTOWA, NJ

START TO FINISH: 30 MIN.
MAKES: 4 SERVINGS

- ½ **pound broccoli rabe**
- 4 **boneless pork loin chops (¾ inch thick and 6 ounces each)**
- 1 **teaspoon salt**
- 1 **teaspoon garlic powder**
- ½ **teaspoon pepper**
- 1 **tablespoon canola oil**
- ½ **cup sliced roasted sweet red pepper**
- 4 **ounces fresh mozzarella cheese, sliced**

1. Preheat broiler. Trim ½ in. off ends of broccoli rabe; discard any coarse leaves.
2. In a large saucepan, bring 4 cups water to a boil. Add broccoli rabe; cook, uncovered, 4-5 minutes or just until crisp-tender. Remove and immediately drop into ice water. Drain and pat dry.

3. Sprinkle pork chops with seasonings. In a broiler-safe skillet, heat oil over medium-high heat. Add pork chops; cook 3-4 minutes on each side or until a thermometer reads 145°. Remove from the heat.
4. Layer chops with red pepper, broccoli rabe and cheese. Broil 4 in. from heat 1-2 minutes or until cheese is melted.

FREEZE IT
FRENCH CANADIAN TOURTIERES

This recipe comes from my big sister. Each fall, we get together and make about 20 of these pies to serve at Christmas, give as gifts, or save in the freezer for unexpected company.

—PAT MENEE CARBERRY, MB

PREP: 1¼ HOURS • **BAKE:** 40 MIN.
MAKES: 4 PIES (8 SERVINGS EACH)

- 4 **celery ribs**
- 4 **medium carrots**
- 2 **large onions**
- 2 **garlic cloves, peeled**
- 4 **pounds ground pork**
- 2 **pounds ground veal**
- 2 **pounds bulk pork sausage**
- 1 **can (14½ ounces) chicken broth**
- ½ **cup minced fresh parsley**
- 1 **tablespoon salt**
- 1 **teaspoon pepper**
- 1 **teaspoon dried basil**
- 1 **teaspoon dried rosemary, crushed**
- 1 **teaspoon cayenne pepper**
- 1 **teaspoon ground mace**
- 1 **teaspoon ground cloves**
- 1 **cup dry bread crumbs**
  Pastry for four double-crust pies (9 inches)

1. Coarsely chop the celery, carrots and onions; place in a food processor with garlic. Cover and process until finely chopped; set aside.
2. In a stockpot or two Dutch ovens, cook vegetables, pork, veal and sausage until meat is no longer pink; drain. Stir in broth, parsley and seasonings. Cover and cook over low heat for 20 minutes. Stir in bread crumbs.
3. Preheat oven to 400°. Line four 9-in. pie plates with bottom crusts; trim pastry even with edges. Fill each with about 4 cups filling. Roll out remaining pastry to fit tops of pies; place over filling. Trim, seal and flute edges. Cut slits in pastry.
4. Cover edges of pies loosely with foil. Bake for 25 minutes. Reduce heat to 350°; remove foil and bake for 15-20 minutes longer or until the crusts are golden brown.

Freeze option: Cover and freeze unbaked pies. To use, remove from freezer 30 minutes before baking (do not thaw). Preheat oven to 400°. Place pie on a baking sheet; cover edges loosely with foil. Bake 25 minutes. Reduce heat to 350°. Remove foil and bake pie 50-60 minutes longer or until crust is golden brown and a thermometer inserted in center reads 165°.

READER RAVE

"Fantastic! I did not use mace, but kept the recipe the same otherwise. I cut the recipe in half for 2 pies and gave one to a neighbor. Will definitely make again!"

—PSCHUBE TASTEOFHOME.COM

HAM & SWISS
BAKED PENNE

FONTINA HAM STROMBOLI

Pesto seasons these savory meat- and cheese-stuffed slices that my family and friends love. The loaves freeze well—baked or unbaked.

—**NANCY PIANO** NEVADA CITY, CA

PREP: 40 MIN. • **BAKE:** 30 MIN.
MAKES: 2 LOAVES (8 SERVINGS EACH)

- 1 large onion, chopped
- 1 tablespoon olive oil
- 1 garlic clove, minced
- 2 loaves (1 pound each) frozen bread dough, thawed
- ½ cup prepared pesto, divided
- 2 teaspoons dried basil
- ½ pound sliced deli ham
- ½ pound thinly sliced prosciutto or additional deli ham
- ½ pound sliced fontina cheese
- ¼ cup grated Parmesan cheese

1. In a large skillet, saute onion in oil until tender. Add garlic; cook 1 minute longer.
2. On two greased baking sheets, roll each loaf of dough into a 16x10-in. rectangle. Spread 2 tablespoons pesto over each; sprinkle with onion mixture and basil. Arrange the ham, prosciutto and fontina cheese over each rectangle to within ½ in. of edges.
3. Roll up jelly-roll style, starting with a long side; pinch seams to seal and tuck ends under.
4. Brush with remaining pesto and sprinkle with Parmesan cheese. Bake at 350° for 30-35 minutes or until golden brown. Cool for 5 minutes before slicing.

> **READER RAVE**
>
> "Awesome! Perfect cold-day lunch with a nice bowl of soup. And it is so easily adapted to your preference—I made it once with all ingredients suggested, once with salami and American, and then with meatballs and Parmesan cheese. All were top-notch!"
>
> —**AUG2295** TASTEOFHOME.COM

HAM & SWISS BAKED PENNE

As a kid I loved to eat the hot ham and Swiss sandwiches at a local fast-food restaurant. With its melty, gooey goodness, this casserole makes me think of them.

—**ALLY BILLHORN** WILTON, IA

START TO FINISH: 30 MIN.
MAKES: 6 SERVINGS

- 2⅓ cups uncooked penne pasta
- 3 tablespoons butter
- 3 tablespoons all-purpose flour
- 2 cups 2% milk
- 1 cup half-and-half cream
- 1½ cups shredded Swiss cheese
- ½ cup shredded Colby cheese
- 2 cups cubed fully cooked ham

TOPPING
- ¼ cup seasoned bread crumbs
- ¼ cup grated Parmesan cheese
- 2 tablespoons butter, melted

1. Preheat oven to 375°. Cook pasta according to package directions for al dente; drain.
2. Meanwhile, in a large saucepan, melt 3 tablespoons butter over medium heat. Stir in flour until smooth; gradually whisk in milk and cream. Bring to a boil, stirring constantly; cook and stir 1-2 minutes or until thickened. Gradually stir in Swiss and Colby cheeses until melted. Add ham and pasta; toss to coat.
3. Transfer to a greased 11x7-in. baking dish. In a small bowl, mix the topping ingredients; sprinkle over pasta. Bake, uncovered, 15-20 minutes or until bubbly.

PINEAPPLE-GLAZED PORK ROAST

Some recipes are so versatile you can serve them for both family dinners and for company. This is the one that gets the most "oohs" and "aahs."

—**NANCY WHITFORD** EDWARDS, NY

PREP: 10 MIN. • **BAKE:** 50 MIN. + STANDING
MAKES: 10 SERVINGS

- 1 boneless pork loin roast (2½ pounds)
- ¾ teaspoon salt
- ¼ teaspoon pepper
- ⅓ cup pineapple preserves
- 2 tablespoons stone-ground mustard
- ¼ teaspoon dried basil
- 1 can (20 ounces) unsweetened pineapple tidbits, drained

1. Preheat oven to 350°. Place roast on a rack in a shallow roasting pan, fat side up. Sprinkle with salt and pepper. Roast 25 minutes.
2. Meanwhile, for the glaze, in a small bowl, whisk preserves, mustard and basil; brush half of mixture over roast. Add pineapple to roasting pan. Roast 25-35 minutes longer or until a thermometer reads 145°.
3. Remove roast from oven and brush with remaining glaze; tent loosely with foil. Let stand 10 minutes before slicing. Using a slotted spoon, serve pineapple with pork.
Per 3 ounces cooked pork with 1 tablespoon pineapple: 195 cal., 5g fat (2g sat. fat), 56mg chol., 271mg sod., 14g carb. (12g sugars, 1g fiber), 22g pro.
Diabetic Exchanges: 3 lean meat, ½ starch.

PINEAPPLE-GLAZED PORK ROAST

ASPARAGUS-STUFFED PORK TENDERLOIN

Fresh asparagus looks amazing tucked inside a rolled pork tenderloin. A homemade seasoning mix dresses up this eye-catching entree you'll be proud to serve any time.

—**TONYA FARMER** IOWA CITY, IA

PREP: 20 MIN. • **BAKE:** 25 MIN.
MAKES: 4 SERVINGS

- ¼ teaspoon each onion powder, garlic powder, chili powder, salt, seasoned salt and poultry seasoning
- ⅛ teaspoon cayenne pepper
- 1 pork tenderloin (1 pound)
- 1 cup water
- 8 to 10 fresh asparagus spears, trimmed

1. In a small bowl, combine seasonings; set aside. Cut a lengthwise slit down the center of pork tenderloin to within ½ in. of the bottom. Open so meat lies flat; cover with plastic wrap. Flatten to ¼-in. thickness. Remove plastic; sprinkle ½ teaspoon seasoning mix over the meat.
2. In a large skillet, bring water to a boil. Add the asparagus; cover and cook for 2 minutes. Drain the asparagus and immediately place in ice water; drain and pat dry. Arrange the asparagus lengthwise over tenderloin.
3. Fold meat over asparagus, starting with a long side, and secure with kitchen string. Sprinkle with remaining seasoning.
4. Place on a rack in a shallow baking pan coated with cooking spray. Bake at 425° for 25-30 minutes or until a thermometer reads 160°. Let stand for 5 minutes before slicing.
Per serving: 201 cal., 6g fat (2g sat. fat), 90mg chol., 299mg sod., 2g carb. (0 sugars, 1g fiber), 33g pro.
Diabetic Exchanges: 3 lean meat, 1 vegetable.

ORANGE-GLAZED
PORK LOIN

ORANGE-GLAZED PORK LOIN

This is one of the best pork recipes I've ever tried. My family looks forward to the roast for dinner, and guests always want the recipe. The flavorful rub and a glaze sparked with orange juice are also outstanding on pork chops.

—**LYNNETTE MIETE** ALNA, ME

PREP: 10 MIN.
BAKE: 1 HOUR 20 MIN. + STANDING
MAKES: 16 SERVINGS

- 1 teaspoon salt
- 1 garlic clove, minced
- ¼ teaspoon dried thyme
- ¼ teaspoon ground ginger
- ¼ teaspoon pepper
- 1 boneless pork loin roast (5 pounds)

GLAZE
- 1 cup orange juice
- ¼ cup packed brown sugar
- 1 tablespoon Dijon mustard
- ⅓ cup water
- 1 tablespoon cornstarch

1. Preheat oven to 350°. Combine the first five ingredients; rub over roast. Place fat side up on a rack in a shallow roasting pan. Bake, uncovered, for 1 hour.
2. Meanwhile, in a saucepan over medium heat, combine orange juice, brown sugar and mustard. In a small bowl, mix water and cornstarch until smooth. Add to orange juice mixture. Bring to a boil; cook and stir 2 minutes. Reserve 1 cup glaze for serving; brush half of remaining glaze over roast.
3. Bake until a thermometer reads 145°, about 20-40 minutes longer, brushing occasionally with remaining glaze. Let stand 10 minutes before slicing. Reheat reserved glaze; serve with roast.
Per 4 ounces cooked pork with 1 tablespoon glaze: 199 cal., 7g fat (2g sat. fat), 71mg chol., 212mg sod., 6g carb. (5g sugars, 0 fiber), 28g pro.
Diabetic Exchanges: 4 lean meat, ½ starch.

FARMHOUSE PORK & APPLE PIE

I have always loved pork and apples together, and this recipe combines them nicely to create a comforting main dish. My family and I agree that the wonderful flavor makes it worth the extra effort.

—**SUZANNE STROCSHER** BOTHELL, WA

PREP: 70 MIN. • **BAKE:** 2 HOURS
MAKES: 10 SERVINGS

- 1 pound sliced bacon, cut into 2-inch pieces
- 3 medium onions, chopped
- 3 pounds boneless pork, cut into 1-inch cubes
- ¾ cup all-purpose flour
  Canola oil, optional
- 3 medium tart apples, peeled and chopped
- 1 teaspoon rubbed sage
- ½ teaspoon ground nutmeg
- 1 teaspoon salt
- ¼ teaspoon pepper
- 1 cup apple cider
- ½ cup water
- 4 medium potatoes, peeled and cubed
- ½ cup milk
- 5 tablespoons butter, divided
  Additional salt and pepper

1. In a large ovenproof skillet, cook bacon over medium heat until crisp, stirring occasionally. Remove with a slotted spoon; drain on paper towels. Discard all but 2 tablespoons drippings. Increase heat to medium-high. Add onions to drippings; cook until tender, 5-7 minutes. Remove with a slotted spoon; drain. Reduce heat to medium.
2. Preheat oven to 350°. Toss pork with flour. Working in batches, brown pork in drippings, adding oil if needed. Remove with a slotted spoon; drain. Remove skillet from heat; discard drippings. Return pork to pan. Add bacon, onions, apples and seasonings. Stir in cider and water.
3. Bake, covered, until pork is tender, about 2 hours. Meanwhile, place potatoes in a large saucepan; add water to cover. Bring to a boil. Reduce heat; cook until tender, 10-15 minutes.
4. Preheat broiler. Drain potatoes. Mash, gradually adding 3 tablespoons butter, enough milk to reach desired consistency and salt and pepper. Spread potatoes over pork mixture. Melt remaining butter; brush over potatoes. Broil 6 in. from heat until topping is browned, about 5 minutes.

FARMHOUSE
PORK & APPLE PIE

QUICK HAWAIIAN PIZZA

BACON-CHEESE STUFFED SHELLS

I make these rich, bacony shells for parties or to give to friends. The dish is guaranteed to please.

—**REBECCA ANDERSON** DRIFTWOOD, TX

PREP: 45 MIN. • **BAKE:** 40 MIN.
MAKES: 12 SERVINGS

- 24 uncooked jumbo pasta shells
- 1 cup chopped fresh mushrooms
- 1 cup finely chopped onion
- 1 tablespoon plus ¼ cup butter, divided
- 1½ cups ricotta cheese
- 1 package (8 ounces) cream cheese, softened, divided
- 1½ cups shredded Asiago cheese, divided
- 1 cup shredded Parmesan cheese
- 1 cup crumbled cooked bacon
- 2 tablespoons minced fresh parsley, divided
- ½ teaspoon garlic salt
- ½ teaspoon ground nutmeg
- ¼ teaspoon pepper
- 2 tablespoons all-purpose flour
- 2 cups heavy whipping cream
- ½ cup chicken broth
- ½ cup 2% milk
- 2 cups shredded Romano cheese
- 1½ cups shredded part-skim mozzarella cheese

1. Cook pasta according to package directions.
2. Meanwhile, in a large skillet, saute mushrooms and onion in 1 tablespoon butter until tender.
3. In a large bowl, beat ricotta and 4 ounces cream cheese until blended. Stir in ½ cup Asiago cheese, Parmesan cheese, bacon, 1 tablespoon parsley, garlic salt, nutmeg, pepper and mushroom mixture. Spoon into shells; place in a greased 13x9-in. baking dish.
4. Preheat oven to 350°. In a large saucepan, melt remaining butter. Stir in flour until smooth; gradually add cream, broth and milk. Bring to a boil; cook and stir 1-2 minutes or until thickened. Stir in Romano cheese and the remaining cream cheese, Asiago and parsley.
5. Pour over shells. Sprinkle with mozzarella cheese. Cover and bake 30 minutes. Uncover; bake 10-15 minutes longer or until bubbly.

QUICK HAWAIIAN PIZZA

Our family never quite liked the taste of canned pizza sauce, so I tried mixing BBQ sauce into spaghetti sauce to add some sweetness. I've made my pizzas with this special and easy sauce ever since, and my family loves it.

—**TONYA SCHIELER** CARMEL, IN

START TO FINISH: 25 MIN.
MAKES: 6 SLICES

- 1 prebaked 12-inch thin whole wheat pizza crust
- ½ cup marinara sauce
- ¼ cup barbecue sauce
- 1 medium sweet yellow or red pepper, chopped
- 1 cup cubed fresh pineapple
- ½ cup chopped fully cooked ham
- 1 cup shredded part-skim mozzarella cheese
- ½ cup shredded cheddar cheese

1. Preheat oven to 425°. Place crust on a baking sheet. Mix marinara and barbecue sauces; spread over crust.
2. Top with remaining ingredients. Bake until crust is browned and cheeses are melted, 10-15 minutes.
Per 1 slice: 290 cal., 10g fat (5g sat. fat), 29mg chol., 792mg sod., 36g carb. (11g sugars, 5g fiber), 16g pro.
Diabetic Exchanges: 2 starch, 2 lean meat, ½ fat.

SWEET-AND-SOUR PORK CHOPS

Pineapple chunks and pepper rings accent this baked rendition of an American comfort-food classic.

—**SHIRLEY HESTON** PICKERINGTON, OH

PREP: 20 MIN. • **BAKE:** 40 MIN.
MAKES: 4 SERVINGS

- ½ cup all-purpose flour
- ½ teaspoon salt
- 4 bone-in pork loin chops (7 ounces each)
- 2 tablespoons canola oil
- 1 can (20 ounces) unsweetened pineapple chunks, drained
- 1 small green pepper, cut into rings
- 1 cup sugar
- 2 tablespoons cornstarch
- 1 cup chicken broth
- 1 cup cider vinegar
- ⅓ cup ketchup
- ¼ cup cold water
  Hot cooked rice

1. In a large resealable plastic bag, combine the flour and salt. Add pork chops, one at a time, and shake to coat. In a large skillet, brown chops in oil on both sides. Transfer to a greased 13x9-in. baking dish. Top with pineapple and green pepper; set aside.
2. In a small saucepan, combine the sugar, cornstarch, broth, vinegar, ketchup and water until smooth. Bring to a boil over medium heat; cook and stir for 2 minutes or until thickened. Pour over chops. Bake, uncovered, at 325° for 40-45 minutes or until a thermometer reads 160°. Serve over rice.

TOP TIP

GET CREATIVE

Sugar, cider vinegar and ketchup create a classic flavor combination that's both sweet and sour. The sauce would also be tasty with smoked kielbasa, popcorn chicken or frozen meatballs.

ZIPPY BREADED PORK CHOPS

ZIPPY BREADED PORK CHOPS

Need a perky update for pork chops? These chops with ranch dressing and a light breading will bring a delightful zing to your dinner table.

—**ANN INGALLS** GLADSTONE, MO

START TO FINISH: 25 MIN.
MAKES: 6 SERVINGS

- ⅓ cup prepared ranch salad dressing
- 1 cup seasoned bread crumbs
- 2 tablespoons grated Parmesan cheese
- 6 bone-in pork loin chops (8 ounces each)

1. Preheat oven to 425°. Place salad dressing in a shallow bowl. In a separate shallow bowl, mix bread crumbs and cheese. Dip pork chops in dressing, then in crumb mixture, patting to help the coating adhere.
2. Place on a rack in an ungreased 15x10x1-in. baking pan. Bake 15-20 minutes or until a thermometer reads 145°. Let stand 5 minutes before serving.

HAM WITH APPLE-RAISIN SAUCE

Since I ran across this recipe several years ago, I've used it often for special dinners. What I really like is the ease of preparation. You don't have a lot of cleanup because everything is done right there in the bag.

—**SANDY OLBERDING** SPENCER, IA

PREP: 10 MIN. • **BAKE:** 2 HOURS
MAKES: 16 SERVINGS

- 1 tablespoon all-purpose flour
- 1 large oven roasting bag
- 4 medium tart apples, peeled and chopped
- 2 cups apple juice
- 1 cup raisins
- ½ cup packed brown sugar
- 1 teaspoon ground cinnamon
- 1 boneless fully cooked ham (about 6 pounds)

1. Shake flour in the oven roasting bag. Place in an ungreased 13x9-in. baking pan. Place the apples, apple juice, raisins, brown sugar and cinnamon in the bag; mix well. Place ham in bag. Close bag. Cut six ½-in. slits in top of bag.
2. Bake ham at 350° for 2 to 2¼ hours or until a thermometer reads 140°. Serve with sauce.

PAN-ROASTED
PORK CHOPS
& POTATOES

PAN-ROASTED PORK CHOPS & POTATOES

A shortcut marinade gives pork chops plenty of flavor, and a crumb coating packs on the crunch.

—CHAR OUELLETTE COLTON, OR

PREP: 20 MIN. + MARINATING
BAKE: 40 MIN.
MAKES: 4 SERVINGS

- 4 boneless pork loin chops (6 ounces each)
- ½ cup plus 2 tablespoons reduced-fat Italian salad dressing, divided
- 4 small potatoes (about 1½ pounds)
- ½ pound fresh Brussels sprouts, trimmed and halved
- ½ cup soft bread crumbs
- 1 tablespoon minced fresh parsley
- ¼ teaspoon salt
- ⅛ teaspoon pepper
- 2 teaspoons butter, melted

1. Place pork and ½ cup salad dressing in a large resealable plastic bag; seal bag and turn to coat. Chill 8 hours or overnight. Refrigerate remaining dressing.
2. Preheat oven to 400°. Cut each potato lengthwise into 12 wedges. Arrange potatoes and Brussels sprouts in a 15x10x1-in. baking pan coated with cooking spray. Drizzle vegetables with remaining salad dressing; toss to coat. Roast 20 minutes.
3. Drain pork, discarding marinade. Pat the pork dry with paper towels. Stir vegetables; place pork chops over top. Roast 15-20 minutes longer or until a thermometer inserted in pork reads 145°. Preheat broiler.
4. Combine bread crumbs, parsley, salt and pepper; stir in butter. Top pork with crumb mixture. Broil 4-6 in. from heat for 1-2 minutes or until bread crumbs are golden brown. Let stand 5 minutes.
Test Kitchen Note: To make soft bread crumbs, tear bread into pieces and place in a food processor or blender. Cover and pulse until crumbs form. One slice of bread yields ½ to ¾ cup crumbs.
Per 1 pork chop with 1 cup vegetables: 451 cal., 16g fat (5g sat. fat), 87mg chol., 492mg sod., 38g carb. (3g sugars, 5g fiber), 38g pro.
Diabetic Exchanges: 5 lean meat, 2½ starch, 2 fat.

OVERNIGHT TERIYAKI PORK

BAKED FETTUCINE & HAM

My family enjoys this recipe, and it's a great way to use up leftover ham. Although it's a meal all on its own, I often serve a tossed green salad alongside.

—CATHY NEVE YAKIMA, WA

PREP: 15 MIN. • **BAKE:** 25 MIN.
MAKES: 5 SERVINGS

- ¼ cup dry bread crumbs
- ¼ teaspoon dried parsley flakes
- 3 tablespoons butter, divided
- 2 tablespoons all-purpose flour
- 2 cups milk
- 1½ cups sharp white cheddar cheese, shredded
- 2 cups cubed fully cooked ham
- 1½ cups cooked fettuccine
- 1 cup frozen peas

1. In a small skillet, cook bread crumbs and parsley in 1 tablespoon butter over medium heat for 4-5 minutes or until golden brown. Remove from the pan; set aside.
2. In a large skillet, melt the remaining butter. Stir in flour until smooth; gradually add the milk. Bring to a boil; cook and stir for 2 minutes or until thickened. Stir in cheese; cook 2-3 minutes longer or until melted. Stir in the ham, fettuccine and peas.
3. Transfer to a greased 11x7-in. baking dish; sprinkle with bread crumb mixture.
4. Cover casserole and bake at 350° for 20 minutes. Uncover; bake 5-10 minutes longer or until bubbly.

OVERNIGHT TERIYAKI PORK

I use teriyaki, rosemary and wine to marinate meaty bone-in chops. It takes time, so plan ahead. The chops are excellent with noodles tossed in parsley.

—JANE WHITTAKER PENSACOLA, FL

PREP: 10 MIN. + MARINATING
BAKE: 20 MIN.
MAKES: 4 SERVINGS

- 1 cup reduced-sodium teriyaki sauce
- ¾ cup sweet white wine
- ¼ cup packed brown sugar
- 2 tablespoons minced fresh rosemary or 2 teaspoons dried rosemary, crushed
- 4 bone-in pork loin chops (1 inch thick and 10 ounces each)

1. In a 13x9-in. baking dish, mix teriyaki sauce, wine, brown sugar and rosemary until blended. Add pork; turn to coat. Refrigerate, covered, at least 4 hours.
2. Remove from refrigerator 30 minutes before baking. Preheat oven to 350°.
3. Bake 20-25 minutes or until a thermometer reads 145°. Let stand for 5 minutes before serving.

SPINACH
POTATO PIE

FREEZE IT

BACON TORTELLINI BAKE

PREP: 25 MIN. • **BAKE:** 15 MIN.
MAKES: 6 SERVINGS

- 1 **package (20 ounces) refrigerated cheese tortellini**
- 3 **cups small fresh broccoli florets**
- ½ **pound bacon strips, cut into 1-inch pieces**
- 2 **garlic cloves, minced**
- 1 **tablespoon all-purpose flour**
- 1 **teaspoon dried basil**
- ½ **teaspoon salt**
- ⅛ **teaspoon coarsely ground pepper**
- 2 **cups 2% milk**
- ¾ **cup shredded part-skim mozzarella cheese, divided**
- ¾ **cup grated Parmesan cheese, divided**
- 2 **teaspoons lemon juice**

1. Preheat oven to 350°. Cook tortellini according to package directions, adding broccoli during the last 2 minutes; drain.
2. Meanwhile, in a large skillet, cook bacon over medium heat until crisp, stirring occasionally. Remove with a slotted spoon; drain on paper towels. Discard drippings, reserving 1 tablespoon in the pan.
3. Reduce heat to medium-low. Add garlic to drippings in pan; cook and stir 1 minute. Stir in flour, basil, salt and pepper until blended; gradually whisk in milk. Bring to a boil, stirring constantly; cook and stir 3-5 minutes or until slightly thickened. Remove from heat.
4. Stir in ½ cup mozzarella cheese, ½ cup Parmesan cheese and lemon juice. Add tortellini mixture and bacon; toss to combine. Transfer to a greased 13x9-in. baking dish; sprinkle with remaining cheeses. Bake casserole, uncovered, 15-20 minutes or until heated through and broccoli is tender.
Freeze option: Sprinkle remaining cheeses over unbaked casserole. Cover and freeze. To use, partially thaw in refrigerator overnight. Remove from refrigerator 30 minutes before baking. Preheat oven to 350°. Bake casserole as directed, increasing time as necessary to heat through and for a thermometer inserted in center to read 165°.

SPINACH POTATO PIE

When we have brunch with relatives, I like to make this crustless quiche with hash browns and spinach. Add a side of fruit and it makes a great weekend brunch.
—**DEANNA PHILLIPS** FERNDALE, WA

PREP: 25 MIN. • **BAKE:** 55 MIN.
MAKES: 6 SERVINGS

- 5 **large eggs, lightly beaten**
- 4 **cups frozen shredded hash brown potatoes**
- 2 **cups chopped fresh spinach**
- ¾ **cup chopped red onion**
- ½ **cup 2% cottage cheese**
- 7 **bacon strips, cooked and crumbled**
- 3 **green onions, chopped**
- 4 **garlic cloves, minced**
- ½ **teaspoon salt**
- ¼ **teaspoon pepper**
- ⅛ **teaspoon hot pepper sauce**
- 3 **plum tomatoes, sliced**
- ½ **cup shredded Parmesan cheese**

1. Preheat oven to 350°. In a large bowl, combine the first 11 ingredients. Pour into a greased 9-in. pie plate.
2. Bake 40 minutes. Arrange tomatoes over top; sprinkle with Parmesan cheese. Bake 15-20 minutes longer or until a knife inserted near the edge comes out clean. Let stand 5 minutes before cutting.

"I stirred up an easy pasta and figured that if my family liked it, others might, too. Broccoli and bacon add fabulous crunch."

—**AMY LENTS** GRAND FORKS, ND

**BACON
TORTELLINI
BAKE**

PORK
CHOPS
OLE

BBQ COUNTRY RIBS

I created this sauce for ribs many years ago when I adapted a recipe I saw in a magazine. I often triple the sauce and keep some in my freezer to use on chicken, beef or pork.

—BARBARA GERRIETS TOPEKA, KS

PREP: 25 MIN. • **BAKE:** 2 HOURS
MAKES: 8 SERVINGS

- 2½ pounds boneless country-style pork ribs
- 2 teaspoons liquid smoke, optional
- ½ teaspoon salt
- 1 cup water

BARBECUE SAUCE

- ⅔ cup chopped onion
- 1 tablespoon canola oil
- ¾ cup each water and ketchup
- ⅓ cup lemon juice
- 3 tablespoons sugar
- 3 tablespoons Worcestershire sauce
- 2 tablespoons prepared mustard
- ½ teaspoon salt
- ½ teaspoon pepper
- ¼ teaspoon liquid smoke, optional

1. Place ribs in an 11x7-in. baking dish coated with cooking spray. Sprinkle with liquid smoke if desired and salt. Add water to pan. Cover and bake at 350° for 1 hour.

2. Meanwhile, in a saucepan, saute onion in oil until tender. Add the remaining sauce ingredients; bring to a boil. Reduce heat; simmer, uncovered, for 15 minutes or until slightly thickened.

3. Drain the ribs; top with half of the barbecue sauce. Cover and bake 1 hour longer or until meat is tender, basting every 20 minutes. Serve ribs with remaining sauce.

Freeze option: Place cooled meat mixture in freezer containers. To use, partially thaw in refrigerator overnight. Microwave, covered, on high in a microwave-safe dish until heated through, gently stirring and adding a little water if necessary.

PORK CHOPS OLE

This recipe is a fun and simple way to give pork chops south-of-the-border flair. The flavorful seasoning, rice and melted cheese make the dish a crowd-pleaser.

—LAURA TURNER CHANNELVIEW, TX

PREP: 15 MIN. • **BAKE:** 1 HOUR
MAKES: 4-6 SERVINGS

- 6 pork loin chops (½ inch thick)
- 2 tablespoons canola oil
  Seasoned salt and pepper to taste
- 1½ cups water
- 1 can (8 ounces) tomato sauce
- ¾ cup uncooked long grain rice
- 2 tablespoons taco seasoning
- 1 medium green pepper, chopped
- ½ cup shredded cheddar cheese

1. In a large skillet, brown pork chops on both sides in oil; sprinkle with seasoned salt and pepper.

2. Meanwhile, in a greased 13x9-in. baking dish, combine the water, tomato sauce, rice and taco seasoning.

3. Arrange chops over rice; top with green pepper. Cover and bake at 350° for 1 hour or until rice and meat are tender. Uncover and sprinkle with cheese.

Freeze option: Omit water and substitute 1 package (8.8 ounces) ready-to-serve long grain rice for the uncooked rice. Assemble casserole as directed. Cool unbaked casserole; cover and freeze. To use, partially thaw in refrigerator overnight. Remove from refrigerator 30 minutes before baking. Preheat oven to 350°. Bake casserole as directed, increasing time as necessary.

BBQ
COUNTRY
RIBS

SUNDAY BEST
STUFFED
PORK CHOPS

SUNDAY BEST STUFFED PORK CHOPS

When we're having our favorite stuffed pork chops for Sunday dinner, we pass around potatoes, a green salad and steamed broccoli on the side.

—LORRAINE SMITH CARPENTER, WY

PREP: 30 MIN. **• COOK:** 35 MIN.
MAKES: 8 SERVINGS

- 1 **package (6 ounces) pork stuffing mix**
- ¾ **teaspoon seasoned salt**
- ½ **teaspoon garlic powder**
- ½ **teaspoon coarsely ground pepper**
- 1 **can (10¾ ounces) condensed cream of mushroom soup, undiluted**
- ¼ **cup 2% milk**
- 1 **cup shredded smoked Gouda cheese**
- 1 **small apple, finely chopped**
- ½ **cup chopped pecans, toasted**
- 8 **boneless pork loin chops (6 ounces each)**
- 2 **tablespoons olive oil, divided Minced fresh chives or parsley, optional**

1. Prepare stuffing according to package directions; cool slightly. In a small bowl, mix seasonings. In another bowl, whisk soup and milk until blended.

2. Stir cheese, apple and pecans into cooled stuffing. Cut a pocket horizontally in the thickest part of each chop. Fill with stuffing mixture. Brush outsides of chops with 1 tablespoon oil; sprinkle with seasoning mixture.

3. In a Dutch oven, heat remaining oil over medium heat. Stand pork chops in pan, stuffing side up and spacing evenly.

Pour soup mixture around chops; bring to a boil. Reduce heat; simmer, covered, 35-40 minutes or until pork is no longer pink and a thermometer inserted in stuffing reads 165°.

4. Remove pan from the heat; let stand 5 minutes. Transfer chops to a serving dish. Spoon sauce over top. If desired, sprinkle with chives.

Test Kitchen Note: To toast nuts, bake in a shallow pan in a 350° oven for 5-10 minutes or cook in a skillet over low heat until lightly browned, stirring occasionally.

CREAMY HAM & CHEESE CASSEROLE

Here's a comfort-food classic: egg noodle casserole that is creamy, cheesy and simply delicious. I was really proud when I came up with the recipe!

—BETSY L. HOWARD KIRKWOOD, MO

PREP: 15 MIN. **• BAKE:** 20 MIN.
MAKES: 6 SERVINGS

- 8 **ounces uncooked wide egg noodles**
- 1 **can (10¾ ounces) condensed cream of chicken soup, undiluted**
- 1 **carton (8 ounces) spreadable cream cheese**
- 1 **cup plus 2 tablespoons 2% milk**
- ½ **teaspoon garlic-herb seasoning blend**
- ¼ **teaspoon pepper**
- 3 **cups cubed fully cooked ham**
- 2 **cups shredded Monterey Jack cheese**

1. Cook noodles according to package directions. Meanwhile, combine soup, cream cheese, milk and seasonings; add ham. Drain noodles. Add to ham mixture and mix well.

2. Transfer to a 13x9-in. baking dish coated with cooking spray and sprinkle with cheese.

3. Bake, uncovered, at 350° for 20-25 minutes or until heated through.

SAUERKRAUT
HOT DISH

SAUERKRAUT HOT DISH

We often serve this hearty dish at family gatherings, and the men especially seem to enjoy it. My sister gave me the recipe about 15 years ago. It's been a favorite ever since. The unusual blend of ingredients is a pleasant surprise.

—NEDRA PARKER DUNBAR, WI

PREP: 15 MIN. • **BAKE:** 1½ HOURS
MAKES: 8 SERVINGS

- 1 tablespoon canola oil
- 1½ pounds pork stew meat
- 1 medium onion, chopped
- 2 celery ribs, chopped
- 1 can (14 ounces) sauerkraut, undrained
- 8 ounces egg noodles, cooked and drained
- 1 can (10½ ounces) condensed cream of mushroom soup, undiluted
- 1 jar (4½ ounces) whole mushrooms, drained
  Salt and pepper to taste

1. Preheat the oven to 350°. In a large skillet, heat oil over medium heat. Brown pork. Add onion and celery; cook until vegetables are crisp-tender. Stir in the sauerkraut, noodles, soup and mushrooms; sprinkle with salt and pepper.

2. Spoon into a greased 2-qt. baking dish. Bake, covered, stirring occasionally, until meat is tender, about 1½ hours.

HEARTY SAUSAGE-STUFFED LOAF

My family devours this French bread loaf every time I make it. The best part? It's so simple to put together!

—JUDY LEARNED BOYERTOWN, PA

PREP: 20 MIN. • **BAKE:** 20 MIN.
MAKES: 6 SERVINGS

- ¾ pound bulk pork sausage
- 1 tube (11 ounces) refrigerated crusty French loaf
- 2 cups shredded cheddar cheese
- 1 package (10 ounces) frozen chopped spinach, thawed and squeezed dry
- 1 tablespoon butter, melted
- 1 tablespoon grated Parmesan cheese
  Pizza sauce, optional

1. In a small skillet, cook sausage over medium heat until no longer pink; drain. Unroll dough and pat into a 14-in. x 12-in. rectangle. Sprinkle the sausage, cheddar cheese and spinach lengthwise down the center of the dough. Bring edges of dough to the center over filling; pinch seam to seal.

2. Place seam side down on a greased baking sheet. Brush top with butter; sprinkle with Parmesan cheese. Bake at 350° for 20-25 minutes or until golden brown. Serve warm with pizza sauce if desired.

PORK TENDERLOINS WITH WILD RICE

Apricots say sweet things to earthy herbs in this gravy-licious pork dinner. Remember this recipe—it's worthy of a weekend celebration.

—*TASTE OF HOME* TEST KITCHEN

PREP: 25 MIN. • **BAKE:** 25 MIN. + STANDING
MAKES: 6 SERVINGS

- 2 **pork tenderloins (1 pound each)**
- 1 **package (8.8 ounces) ready-to-serve whole grain brown and wild rice medley**
- 1¾ **cups frozen broccoli, carrots and water chestnuts, thawed and coarsely chopped**
- ½ **cup chopped dried apricots**
- ½ **cup minced fresh parsley**
- ½ **teaspoon salt**
- ½ **teaspoon garlic powder**
- ½ **teaspoon dried thyme**
- ½ **teaspoon dried sage leaves**
- ¼ **teaspoon pepper**

GRAVY

- 1 **cup water**
- 1 **envelope pork gravy mix**
- 1 **tablespoon Dijon mustard**
- ¼ **teaspoon dried sage leaves**
- 1 **tablespoon minced fresh parsley**

1. Make a lengthwise slit down the center of each tenderloin to within ½ in. of bottom. Open tenderloins so they lie flat; cover with plastic wrap. Flatten to ¾-in. thickness.

2. Prepare rice according to package directions. In a small bowl, combine the rice, vegetables, apricots, parsley and seasonings.

3. Remove plastic; spread rice mixture over meat. Close tenderloins; tie with kitchen string. Place in an ungreased 15x10x1-in. baking pan. Bake, uncovered, at 425° for 15 minutes.

4. Meanwhile, in a small saucepan, combine the water, gravy mix, mustard and sage. Bring to a boil; cook and stir for 2 minutes or until thickened. Stir in the parsley.

5. Brush 2 tablespoons gravy over tenderloins. Bake 10-15 minutes longer or until a meat thermometer reads 160°. Let stand for 15 minutes. Discard string; cut each tenderloin into nine slices. Serve with remaining gravy.

MANGO CHUTNEY
PORK ROAST

MANGO CHUTNEY PORK ROAST

Bright mango and red bell pepper really liven up this roast. The tropical fruit chutney packs a nice punch. You might consider making an extra batch for tacos the next night.

—**PAMELA VITTI KNOWLES**
HENDERSONVILLE, NC

PREP: 15 MIN. • **BAKE:** 1 HOUR + STANDING
MAKES: 6 SERVINGS (2 CUPS CHUTNEY)

- 1 **tablespoon butter**
- 1 **boneless pork loin roast (2 to 3 pounds)**
- ½ **teaspoon each salt, pepper and ground ginger**

MANGO CHUTNEY

- 2 **medium mangoes, peeled and cubed**
- ¼ **cup finely chopped red onion**
- ¼ **cup finely chopped sweet red pepper**
- 1 **jalapeno pepper, seeded and minced**
- 2 **tablespoons white vinegar**
- 1 **tablespoon grated fresh gingerroot**
- ⅛ **teaspoon each salt, ground turmeric and ground cloves**

1. In a large skillet, heat butter over medium-high heat. Brown pork roast on all sides. Sprinkle with the salt, pepper and ginger.

2. Place on a rack in a shallow roasting pan. Bake at 350° for 1 to 1½ hours or until a thermometer reads 145°. Remove roast from oven; tent with foil. Let stand for 10 minutes before slicing.

3. Meanwhile, in a large saucepan, combine all chutney ingredients. Cook, uncovered, over medium heat for 8-10 minutes to allow flavors to blend, stirring occasionally. Serve with pork.

Per 4 ounces cooked pork with ⅓ cup chutney: 256 cal., 9g fat (4g sat. fat), 80mg chol., 305mg sod., 13g carb. (11g sugars, 2g fiber), 30g pro.
Diabetic Exchanges: 4 lean meat, 1 fruit, ½ fat.

JALAPENO POPPER QUESADILLAS

Jalapeno popper-inspired quesadillas are a simple solution when you're too busy to cook. If you like heat, this one's for you.

—REBECCA NISEWONDER RICHMOND, IN

START TO FINISH: 25 MIN.
MAKES: 4 SERVINGS

- 8 flour tortillas (8 inches)
- 1 carton (8 ounces) spreadable cream cheese
- ½ pound bacon strips, cooked and crumbled
- 5 jalapeno peppers, seeded and finely chopped
- 2 cups shredded cheddar cheese

1. Preheat oven to 400°. Place half of the tortillas on two greased baking sheets. Spread with cream cheese; sprinkle with bacon, jalapeno and cheese. Top with remaining tortillas.
2. Bake 8-10 minutes or until golden brown and cheese is melted.

BEST-EVER PEPPERONI PIZZA

You'll love working with the homemade dough, the cheesy surprise inside the crust, and the jazzed-up sauce in this pie.

—SCOTTIE ORR-WEDEVEN GRAND RAPIDS, MI

PREP: 40 MIN. • **BAKE:** 10 MIN.
MAKES: 8 SLICES

- 1 package (¼ ounce) quick-rise yeast
- 1 cup warm water (120° to 130°)
- 2 tablespoons sugar
- ½ teaspoon salt
- 2 tablespoons plus 2 teaspoons olive oil, divided
- 2½ to 3 cups all-purpose flour
- 4 pieces string cheese
- ½ teaspoon Italian seasoning

SAUCE
- 1 can (8 ounces) tomato sauce
- 1 teaspoon sugar
- 1 teaspoon olive oil
- ¼ teaspoon salt
- ¼ teaspoon garlic powder
- ¼ teaspoon dried oregano
- ¼ teaspoon lemon juice
- ⅛ teaspoon dried thyme
- ⅛ teaspoon dried basil
- ⅛ teaspoon cayenne pepper

TOPPINGS
- 1 package (3 ounces) sliced pepperoni
- 2 cups shredded Italian cheese blend

1. In a large bowl, dissolve yeast in warm water. Add the sugar, salt, 2 tablespoons oil and 2½ cups flour. Beat until smooth. Stir in enough remaining flour to form a soft dough (dough will be sticky).
2. Turn onto a lightly floured surface; knead until smooth and elastic, about 6-8 minutes. Cover and let rest 10 minutes.
3. On a lightly floured surface, roll dough into a 15-in. circle. Transfer to a greased 14-in. pizza pan, letting dough drape over the edge. Cut string cheese pieces in half lengthwise; place around edge of pan. Fold dough over the string cheese and pinch to seal.
4. Prick dough thoroughly with a fork. Brush with remaining oil; sprinkle with Italian seasoning. Bake at 425° for 10-12 minutes or until golden brown.
5. In a small saucepan, combine the sauce ingredients. Bring to a boil. Reduce heat; simmer, uncovered, for 15 minutes. Spread over crust. Arrange pepperoni over top; sprinkle with Italian cheese blend. Bake for 10-15 minutes or until cheese is melted.

JALAPENO POPPER QUESADILLAS

TOP TIP

FAKE A HOMEMADE CRUST

"To make a delicious herbed pizza crust, I add 1 teaspoon each of basil and oregano to a boxed pizza crust mix. It's an excellent way to give a little added zip to homemade pizza."

—MICHELLE D. GREGORY, MI

Fish & Seafood

STUFFED WALLEYE

Walleye is the top game fish in the Midwest. It's a thrill to catch and tastes great, too. This recipe, created by my husband, is a favorite of my family.

—**KIM LEONARD** KALAMAZOO, MI

PREP: 20 MIN. • **BAKE:** 20 MIN.
MAKES: 4 SERVINGS

- 4 **bacon strips, halved**
- ¼ **cup chopped onion**
- 2 **celery ribs, finely chopped**
- 1 **can (6 ounces) crabmeat, drained, flaked and cartilage removed or 1 cup imitation crabmeat, flaked**
- ¼ **cup butter, cubed**
- 4 **cups crushed seasoned stuffing**
- 1½ **cups boiling water**
- ½ **teaspoon salt**
- ⅛ **teaspoon pepper**
- ⅛ **teaspoon cayenne pepper**
- 4 **walleye fillets (about 8 ounces each)**

1. In a large skillet, cook bacon over medium heat until crisp; remove to paper towels; drain. In the same skillet, saute the onion, celery and crab in butter until vegetables are tender. Transfer to a large bowl; add the stuffing, water, salt, pepper and cayenne; toss to moisten.
2. Place fillets in a greased 15x10x1-in. baking pan. Spoon stuffing mixture over fillets; top each with two pieces of bacon. Bake fillets, uncovered, at 425° for 20-25 minutes or until the fish flakes easily with a fork.

MAPLE SALMON WITH MUSHROOM COUSCOUS

This tantalizing glaze was inspired by a chicken dish I enjoyed in Vermont. I decided to try it with salmon...and it's just as good!

—**TRISHA KRUSE** EAGLE, ID

START TO FINISH: 20 MIN.
MAKES: 2 SERVINGS

- 2 **tablespoons maple syrup**
- 2 **tablespoons reduced-sodium soy sauce**
- 1 **garlic clove, minced**
- 2 **salmon fillets (4 ounces each)**
- 1 **cup reduced-sodium chicken broth**
- ½ **cup sliced fresh mushrooms**
- ⅛ **teaspoon pepper**
- ½ **cup uncooked couscous**

1. Line a small baking pan with foil; coat the foil with cooking spray. In a small bowl, combine the syrup, soy sauce and garlic. Place fillets skin side down on prepared pan. Brush half of the syrup mixture over salmon. Broil 6 in. from the heat for 7 minutes. Brush with remaining syrup mixture. Broil 6-8 minutes longer or until fish flakes easily with fork.
2. Meanwhile, in a small saucepan, bring the broth, mushrooms and pepper to a boil. Reduce heat; cover and simmer for 5-6 minutes or until mushrooms are tender. Return to a boil and stir in the couscous. Cover and remove from the heat; let stand for 5 minutes. Fluff with a fork. Serve with salmon.

CRISPY COD WITH VEGGIES

Take the chill off brisk evenings and warm the body and soul with this light but nourishing entree. Round out the meal with a loaf of crusty bread.

—*TASTE OF HOME* TEST KITCHEN

PREP: 15 MIN. • **BAKE:** 25 MIN.
MAKES: 2 SERVINGS

- 2 **cups broccoli coleslaw mix**
- ½ **cup chopped fresh tomato**
- 4 **teaspoons chopped green onion**
- 2 **garlic cloves, minced**
- 2 **cod fillets (6 ounces each)**
  Pepper to taste
- ¼ **cup crushed potato sticks**
- 3 **tablespoons seasoned bread crumbs**
- 2 **tablespoons grated Parmesan cheese**
- 4 **teaspoons butter, melted**

1. In a large bowl, combine the coleslaw mix, tomato, onion and garlic; spread into an 11x7-in. baking pan coated with cooking spray. Top with cod fillets; sprinkle with pepper.
2. Combine potato sticks, bread crumbs, cheese and butter; sprinkle over fillets. Bake the fillets, uncovered, at 450° for 25-30 minutes or until fish flakes easily with a fork.

OVEN-FRIED
FISH NUGGETS

SALMON WITH CREAMY DILL SAUCE

There's nothing like fresh salmon, and my mom bakes it just right so it nearly melts in your mouth. The sour cream sauce is subtly seasoned with dill and horseradish so that it doesn't overpower the delicate salmon flavor.

—SUSAN EMERY EVERETT, WA

START TO FINISH: 30 MIN.
MAKES: 6 SERVINGS

- 1 **salmon fillet (about 2 pounds)**
- 1 **to 1½ teaspoons lemon-pepper seasoning**
- 1 **teaspoon onion salt**
- 1 **small onion, sliced and separated into rings**
- 6 **lemon slices**
- ¼ **cup butter, cubed**

DILL SAUCE
- ⅓ **cup sour cream**
- ⅓ **cup mayonnaise**
- 1 **tablespoon finely chopped onion**
- 1 **teaspoon lemon juice**
- 1 **teaspoon prepared horseradish**
- ¾ **teaspoon dill weed**
- ¼ **teaspoon garlic salt**
  Pepper to taste

1. Line a 15x10x1-in. baking pan with heavy-duty foil; grease lightly. Place salmon skin side down on foil. Sprinkle with lemon-pepper and onion salt. Top with onion and lemon. Dot with butter. Fold foil around salmon; seal tightly.
2. Bake at 350° for 20 minutes. Open foil carefully, allowing steam to escape. Broil the salmon 4-6 in. from the heat for 8-12 minutes or until it flakes easily with a fork.
3. Combine the sauce ingredients. Serve with salmon.

OVEN-FRIED FISH NUGGETS

My husband and I love fried fish, but we're both trying to cut back on dietary fat. I made up this recipe and it's a hit with us both. He says he likes it as much as deep-fried fish, and that's saying a lot!

—LADONNA REED PONCA CITY, OK

START TO FINISH: 25 MIN.
MAKES: 4 SERVINGS

- ⅓ **cup seasoned bread crumbs**
- ⅓ **cup crushed cornflakes**
- 3 **tablespoons grated Parmesan cheese**
- ½ **teaspoon salt**
- ¼ **teaspoon pepper**
- 1½ **pounds cod fillets, cut into 1-inch cubes**
  Butter-flavored cooking spray

1. In a shallow bowl, combine the bread crumbs, cornflakes, Parmesan cheese, salt and pepper. Coat fish with butter-flavored spray, then roll in crumb mixture.
2. Place on a baking sheet coated with cooking spray. Bake at 375° for 15-20 minutes or until fish flakes easily with a fork.

 Freeze option: Cover and freeze unbaked fish nuggets on a waxed paper-lined baking sheet until firm. Transfer to a resealable plastic freezer bag; return to freezer. To use, preheat oven to 375°. Bake nuggets on a rack on a greased baking sheet 15-20 minutes or until fish flakes easily with a fork.
Oven-Fried Chicken Nuggets: Substitute cubed boneless skinless chicken breasts for the cod. Bake as directed until chicken is no longer pink.
Per 9 pieces: 171 cal., 2g fat (1g sat. fat), 66mg chol., 415mg sod., 7g carb. (1g sugars, 0 fiber), 29g pro.
Diabetic Exchanges: 5 lean meat, ½ starch.

TOP TIP

GO WILD
Wild salmon is 20 percent leaner than farm-raised and is higher in heart-healthy omega-3 fatty acids. Some prefer its flavor over farm-raised fish, too. It is available fresh from May to October, as the different species travel upstream to spawn.

BAKED COCONUT SHRIMP & APRICOT SAUCE

SWEET & TANGY SALMON WITH GREEN BEANS

I'm always up for new ways to cook salmon. In this dish, a sweet sauce gives the fish and green beans some down-home barbecue tang. Even our kids love it.
—ALIESHA CALDWELL ROBERSONVILLE, NC

PREP: 20 MIN. • **BAKE:** 15 MIN.
MAKES: 4 SERVINGS

- 4 **salmon fillets (6 ounces each)**
- 1 **tablespoon butter**
- 2 **tablespoons brown sugar**
- 2 **tablespoons reduced-sodium soy sauce**
- 2 **tablespoons Dijon mustard**
- 1 **tablespoon olive oil**
- ½ **teaspoon pepper**
- ⅛ **teaspoon salt**
- 1 **pound fresh green beans, trimmed**

1. Preheat oven to 425°. Place fillets on a 15x10x1-in. baking pan coated with cooking spray. In a small skillet, melt butter; stir in brown sugar, soy sauce, mustard, oil, pepper and salt. Brush half of the mixture over salmon.
2. Place green beans in a large bowl; drizzle with remaining brown sugar mixture and toss to coat. Arrange green beans around fillets.
3. Roast 14-16 minutes or until fish just begins to flake easily with a fork and green beans are crisp-tender.
Per 1 fillet with ¾ cup green beans: 394 cal., 22g fat (5g sat. fat), 93mg chol., 661mg sod., 17g carb. (10g sugars, 4g fiber), 31g pro.
Diabetic Exchanges: 5 lean meat, 1½ fat, 1 vegetable, ½ starch.

BAKED COCONUT SHRIMP & APRICOT SAUCE

Coconut and panko crumbs give this spicy baked shrimp its crunch. It's great for an appetizer or for your main meal.
—DEBI MITCHELL FLOWER MOUND, TX

PREP: 25 MIN. • **BAKE:** 10 MIN.
MAKES: 6 SERVINGS

- 1½ **pounds uncooked large shrimp**
- 1½ **cups flaked coconut**
- ½ **cup panko (Japanese) bread crumbs**
- 4 **large egg whites**
- 3 **dashes Louisiana-style hot sauce**
- ¼ **teaspoon salt**
- ¼ **teaspoon pepper**
- ½ **cup all-purpose flour**

SAUCE
- 1 **cup apricot preserves**
- 1 **teaspoon cider vinegar**
- ¼ **teaspoon crushed red pepper flakes**

1. Preheat oven to 425°. Place a wire rack on each of two baking sheets; coat racks with cooking spray. Peel and devein shrimp, leaving tails on.
2. In a shallow bowl, toss the coconut with bread crumbs; remove half of the mixture and reserve. In another shallow bowl, whisk egg whites, hot sauce, salt and pepper. Place the flour in a third shallow bowl.
3. Dip shrimp in flour to coat lightly; shake off excess. Dip in the egg white mixture, then in coconut mixture, patting to help coating adhere. Refresh coconut mixture in the bowl with reserved mixture as needed.
4. Place shrimp on racks of prepared pans. Bake 5-6 minutes on each side or until coconut is lightly browned and shrimp turn pink.
5. Meanwhile, combine the sauce ingredients in a small saucepan; cook and stir over medium-low heat until preserves are melted. Serve shrimp with sauce.

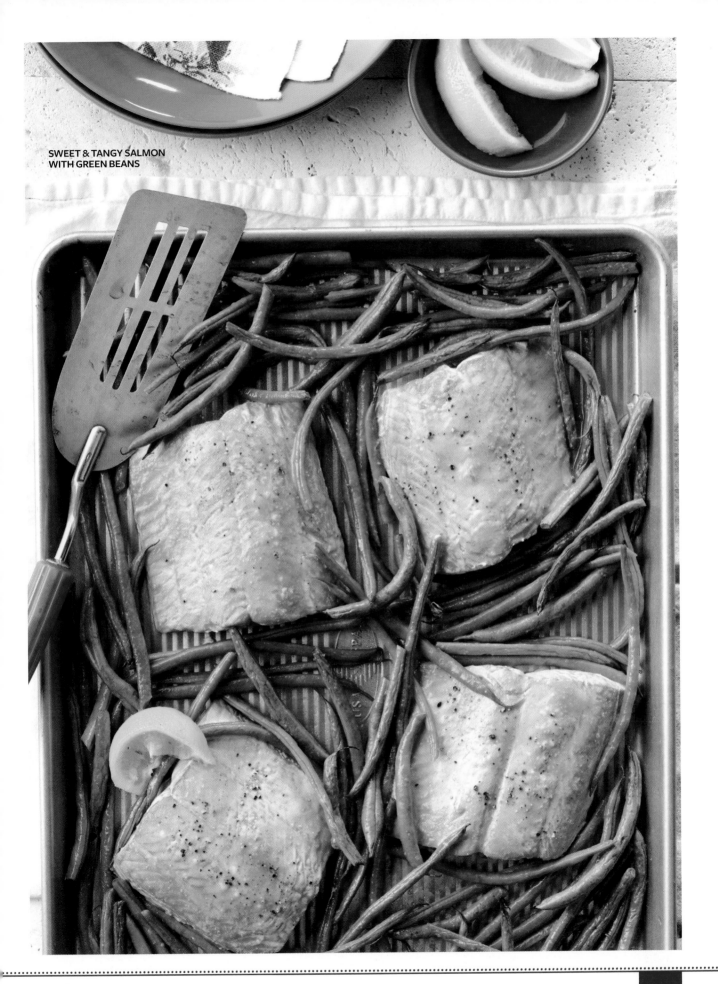

SWEET & TANGY SALMON
WITH GREEN BEANS

EAT SMART

CRISPY FISH & CHIPS

Dial up the flavor in this classic British pub favorite by adding some horseradish, Worcestershire and panko. Try it with any white fish like cod, haddock and flounder.
—**LINDA SCHEND** KENOSHA, WI

START TO FINISH: 30 MIN.
MAKES: 4 SERVINGS

- 4 cups frozen steak fries
- 4 salmon fillets (6 ounces each)
- 1 to 2 tablespoons prepared horseradish
- 1 tablespoon grated Parmesan cheese
- 1 tablespoon Worcestershire sauce
- 1 teaspoon Dijon mustard
- ¼ teaspoon salt
- ½ cup panko (Japanese) bread crumbs
- Cooking spray

1. Preheat oven to 450°. Arrange steak fries in a single layer on a baking sheet. Bake on lowest oven rack 18-20 minutes or until light golden brown.

2. Meanwhile, place the salmon on a foil-lined baking sheet coated with cooking spray. In a small bowl, mix the horseradish, cheese, Worcestershire sauce, mustard and salt; stir in panko. Press mixture onto fillets. Spritz the tops with cooking spray.

3. Bake salmon on middle oven rack for 8-10 minutes or until fish just begins to flake easily with a fork. Serve with fries.

Per 1 fillet with ¾ cup fries: 419 cal., 20g fat (4g sat. fat), 86mg chol., 695mg sod., 26g carb. (2g sugars, 2g fiber), 32g pro.

Diabetic Exchanges: 5 lean meat, 1½ starch.

EAT SMART

SALMON WITH HONEY PECAN SAUCE

I love the explosion of sweet and buttery flavors in every bite of this dish. In summer, sauteed zucchini makes the perfect side dish.
—**ALICE STANKO** WARREN, MI

START TO FINISH: 30 MIN.
MAKES: 4 SERVINGS

- 4 salmon fillets (4 ounces each)
- ½ teaspoon seasoned salt
- ¼ teaspoon pepper
- ¼ cup finely chopped pecans, toasted
- ¼ cup honey
- 3 tablespoons reduced-fat butter

1. Place salmon skin side down on a broiler pan; sprinkle with seasoned salt and pepper. Broil 3-4 in. from the heat for 7-9 minutes or until fish flakes easily with a fork.

2. Meanwhile, in a small saucepan, cook pecans, honey and butter over medium heat for 8-10 minutes or until bubbly. Serve with salmon.

Test Kitchen Note: This recipe was tested with Land O'Lakes light stick butter.

Per 1 fillet with 2 tablespoons sauce: 330 cal., 20g fat (5g sat. fat), 68mg chol., 319mg sod., 19g carb. (18g sugars, 1g fiber), 20g pro. **Diabetic Exchanges:** 3 lean meat, 2½ fat, 1 starch.

TOP TIP

LIGHTEN UP

Light stick butter contains about half the fat, calories and cholesterol of regular salted butter. Using it in this recipe saves about 40 calories, 5g fat and 12mg cholesterol per serving.

CRISPY FISH & CHIPS

SHRIMP ENCHILADAS
WITH GREEN SAUCE

COMFORTING TUNA CASSEROLE

My mother gave me the recipe for this wonderful casserole 20 years ago. Sometimes I use sliced stuffed olives instead of pimientos.

—DOROTHY COLEMAN HOBE SOUND, FL

PREP: 15 MIN. • **BAKE:** 20 MIN.
MAKES: 2 SERVINGS

- 1¾ **cups uncooked wide egg noodles**
- 6 **teaspoons reduced-fat butter, divided**
- 4 **teaspoons all-purpose flour**
- ¼ **teaspoon salt**
  Dash pepper
- ¾ **cup 2% milk**
- 3 **ounces reduced-fat cream cheese**
- 1 **pouch (2½ ounces) albacore white tuna in water**
- 2 **tablespoons diced pimientos**
- 2 **teaspoons minced chives**
- 2 **slices Muenster cheese (¾ ounce each)**
- 2 **tablespoons soft bread crumbs**

1. Cook the egg noodles according to package directions. Meanwhile, in a small saucepan over medium heat, melt 5 teaspoons butter. Stir in the flour, salt and pepper until blended; gradually add milk. Bring to a boil over medium heat; cook and stir for 1-2 minutes or until thickened. Reduce heat to medium-low; add the cream cheese, tuna, pimientos and chives. Cook and stir until the cheese is melted.

2. Drain noodles. Spread ¼ cup tuna mixture into a 3-cup baking dish coated with cooking spray. Layer with half of the noodles, ½ cup tuna mixture and one slice of cheese. Repeat layers.

3. Microwave remaining butter on high, stirring every 30 seconds; stir in bread crumbs. Sprinkle mixture over top of casserole. Bake, uncovered, at 350° for 20-25 minutes or until bubbly.

SHRIMP ENCHILADAS WITH GREEN SAUCE

I started making these enchiladas last year during the Lenten season. It allows my family to observe Lent and still enjoy Mexican food. When I brought it to school, my co-workers couldn't get enough of it.

—MARI ACEDO CHANDLER, AZ

PREP: 35 MIN. • **BAKE:** 25 MIN.
MAKES: 8 SERVINGS

- ½ **cup plus 1 tablespoon olive oil, divided**
- 16 **corn tortillas (6 inches)**
- 2 **medium tomatoes, chopped**
- 2 **medium onions, finely chopped**
- 4 **garlic cloves, minced**
- ½ **teaspoon ground cumin**
- 1½ **pounds uncooked small shrimp, peeled and deveined**
- 2 **packages (10 ounces each) frozen chopped spinach, thawed and squeezed dry**
- 2 **cups shredded part-skim mozzarella cheese, divided**
- 2 **cans (10 ounces each) green enchilada sauce**

1. Preheat oven to 350°. In a skillet, heat ½ cup oil over medium-high heat. In batches, fry tortillas 10 seconds on each side or until pliable (do not allow to crisp). Drain on paper towels. Cover with foil to keep warm and softened.

2. In a large skillet, heat remaining oil over medium-high heat. Add tomatoes, onions, garlic and cumin; cook and stir 3-4 minutes or until onions are tender. Add shrimp; cook 3-4 minutes or until shrimp turn pink, stirring occasionally. Stir in spinach; heat through.

3. Place ¼ cup shrimp mixture off center on each tortilla; top with 1 tablespoon cheese. Roll up and place in a greased 13x9-in. baking dish, seam side down. Top with enchilada sauce; sprinkle with remaining cheese.

4. Bake, uncovered, 25-30 minutes or until heated through and the cheese is melted.

"As a military spouse living overseas, I got the chance to try many styles of cooking. Here's a Mediterranean-inspired recipe that we still love today."
—**STACEY BOYD** SPRINGFIELD, VA

GREEK
FISH BAKE

GREEK FISH BAKE

START TO FINISH: 30 MIN.
MAKES: 4 SERVINGS

- 4 **cod fillets (6 ounces each)**
- 2 **tablespoons olive oil**
- ¼ **teaspoon salt**
- ⅛ **teaspoon pepper**
- 1 **small green pepper, cut into thin strips**
- ½ **small red onion, thinly sliced**
- ¼ **cup pitted Greek olives, sliced**
- 1 **can (8 ounces) tomato sauce**
- ¼ **cup crumbled feta cheese**

1. Preheat oven to 400°. Place cod in a greased 13x9-in. baking dish. Brush with oil; sprinkle with salt and pepper. Top with green pepper, onion and olives.
2. Pour tomato sauce over top; sprinkle with cheese. Bake until fish just begins to flake easily with a fork, 15-20 minutes.

Per 1 fillet with toppings: 246 cal., 12g fat (2g sat. fat), 68mg chol., 706mg sod., 6g carb. (2g sugars, 2g fiber), 29g pro.
Diabetic Exchanges: 4 lean meat, 1½ fat, 1 vegetable.

HERBED TUNA SANDWICHES

Give tuna salad an upgrade in a flash. Herbs and cheese make this sandwich a standout! It's perfect for lunch.

—**MARIE CONNOR** VIRGINIA BEACH, VA

START TO FINISH: 20 MIN.
MAKES: 4 SERVINGS

- 1 **can (12 ounces) light tuna in water, drained and flaked**
- 2 **hard-cooked large eggs, chopped**
- ⅓ **cup fat-free mayonnaise**
- ¼ **cup minced chives**
- 2 **teaspoons minced fresh parsley**
- ½ **teaspoon dried basil**
- ¼ **teaspoon onion powder**
- 8 **slices whole wheat bread, toasted**
- ½ **cup shredded reduced-fat cheddar cheese**

1. Combine the first seven ingredients. Place four slices of toast on an ungreased baking sheet; top with tuna mixture and sprinkle with cheese.
2. Broil 3-4 in. from the heat for 1-2 minutes or until cheese is melted. Top with remaining toast.

LEMON-PARSLEY
BAKED COD

LEMON-PARSLEY BAKED COD

This is the first fish recipe that got two thumbs up from the picky meat-only eaters at my table. The tangy lemon gives the cod some oomph.

—**TRISHA KRUSE** EAGLE, ID

START TO FINISH: 30 MIN.
MAKES: 4 SERVINGS

- 3 **tablespoons lemon juice**
- 3 **tablespoons butter, melted**
- ¼ **cup all-purpose flour**
- ½ **teaspoon salt**
- ¼ **teaspoon paprika**
- ¼ **teaspoon lemon-pepper seasoning**
- 4 **cod fillets (6 ounces each)**
- 2 **tablespoons minced fresh parsley**
- 2 **teaspoons grated lemon peel**

1. Preheat oven to 400°. In a shallow bowl, mix lemon juice and butter. In a separate shallow bowl, mix flour and seasonings. Dip fillets in lemon juice mixture, then in flour mixture to coat both sides; shake off excess.
2. Place fillets in a 13x9-in. baking dish coated with cooking spray. Drizzle with remaining lemon juice mixture. Bake 12-15 minutes or until fish just begins to flake easily with a fork. Mix parsley and lemon peel; sprinkle over fish.

Per 1 fillet: 232 cal., 10g fat (6g sat. fat), 87mg chol., 477mg sod., 7g carb. (0 sugars, 0 fiber), 28g pro.
Diabetic Exchanges: 4 lean meat, 2 fat, ½ starch.

GARLIC BREAD
TUNA MELTS

SEAFOOD CREPES BEARNAISE

This family favorite is an inviting treat on chilly nights. It's warming and has so much flavor in every bite. I like to serve it with a tossed salad and rolls.

—**KRISTY BARNES-ARMSTRONG**

MARYSVILLE, WA

PREP: 30 MIN. + CHILLING
BAKE: 10 MIN.
MAKES: 5 SERVINGS

- 1 cup 2% milk
- 3 large eggs
- 3 tablespoons butter, melted
- ¾ cup all-purpose flour
- ¼ teaspoon salt

FILLING

- 2 envelopes bearnaise sauce
- ½ pound bay scallops
- 2 teaspoons butter
- ½ pound cooked small shrimp, peeled, deveined and chopped
- 1 cup imitation crabmeat
- 1 cup (4 ounces) shredded cheddar cheese

GARLIC BREAD TUNA MELTS

There's something extra comforting about a tuna melt on a chilly day. Take it up a few notches with garlic, cheese and tomatoes.

—**AIMEE BACHMANN** NORTH BEND, WA

START TO FINISH: 20 MIN.
MAKES: 4 SERVINGS

- ¼ cup butter, cubed
- 3 garlic cloves, minced
- 4 French rolls or hoagie buns, split
- 2 cans (one 12 ounces, one 5 ounces) albacore white tuna in water, drained and flaked
- ¼ cup reduced-fat mayonnaise
- 1¼ teaspoons dill weed, divided
- 8 slices cheddar cheese
- 8 slices tomato

1. Preheat broiler. In a microwave, melt butter with garlic. Place rolls on a baking sheet, cut side up; brush with butter mixture. Broil 2-3 in. from heat for 2-3 minutes or until lightly browned.
2. In a small bowl, mix tuna, mayonnaise and 1 teaspoon dill. Layer roll bottoms with tuna mixture and cheese. Broil 1-2 minutes or until cheese is melted. Top with tomato; sprinkle with remaining dill. Replace tops; serve immediately.

TOMATO WALNUT TILAPIA

Tomato, bread crumbs and crunchy walnuts dress up tilapia fillets in this delightful main dish. I often serve it with cooked green beans and julienned carrots.

—**PHYL BROICH-WESSLING** GARNER, IA

START TO FINISH: 20 MIN.
MAKES: 4 SERVINGS

- 4 tilapia fillets (4 ounces each)
- ¼ teaspoon salt
- ¼ teaspoon pepper
- 1 tablespoon butter
- 1 medium tomato, thinly sliced

TOPPING

- ½ cup soft bread crumbs
- ¼ cup chopped walnuts
- 2 tablespoons lemon juice
- 1½ teaspoons butter, melted

1. Sprinkle fillets with salt and pepper. In a large skillet coated with cooking spray, cook fillets in butter over medium-high heat for 2-3 minutes on each side or until lightly browned.
2. Transfer fish to a broiler pan or baking sheet; top with tomato. Combine the topping ingredients; spoon over the tops.
3. Broil 3-4 in. from the heat for 2-3 minutes or until topping is lightly browned and fish flakes easily with a fork.

1. In a small bowl, combine the milk, eggs and butter. Combine flour and salt; add to milk mixture and mix well. Cover and refrigerate for 1 hour.
2. Heat a lightly greased 10-in. nonstick skillet over medium heat; pour ¼ cup batter into the center of skillet. Lift and tilt pan to coat bottom evenly. Cook until top appears dry; turn and cook 15-20 seconds longer. Remove to a wire rack. Repeat with remaining batter, greasing skillet as needed. When cool, stack crepes with waxed paper or paper towels in between.
3. Prepare bearnaise sauce according to package directions. Meanwhile, in a large skillet, cook scallops in butter over medium heat for 3-4 minutes or until scallops are firm and opaque. Add the shrimp, crabmeat and bearnaise sauce; heat through. Set aside ½ cup filling.
4. Spread ⅓ cup filling down the center of each crepe; fold sides and ends over filling and roll up. Place in a greased 13x9-in. baking dish. Spoon reserved filling over top; sprinkle with cheese. Bake crepes, uncovered, at 350° for 10-15 minutes or until heated through and cheese is melted.

CAESAR SALMON WITH
ROASTED TOMATOES
& ARTICHOKES

CAESAR SALMON WITH ROASTED TOMATOES & ARTICHOKES

This is my go-to recipe for quick dinners, for family or guests. This dish is colorful, healthy, easy to prepare and absolutely delicious. Hard to believe it uses just six ingredients!

—MARY HAWKES PRESCOTT, AZ

START TO FINISH: 25 MIN.
MAKES: 4 SERVINGS

- 4 **salmon fillets (5 ounces each)**
- 5 **tablespoons reduced-fat Caesar vinaigrette, divided**
- ¼ **teaspoon pepper, divided**
- 2 **cups grape tomatoes**
- 1 **can (14 ounces) water-packed artichoke hearts, drained and quartered**
- 1 **medium sweet orange pepper or yellow pepper, cut into 1-inch pieces**

1. Preheat oven to 425°. Place salmon on one half of a 15x10x1-in. baking pan coated with cooking spray. Brush with 2 tablespoons vinaigrette; sprinkle with ⅛ teaspoon pepper.

2. In a large bowl, combine tomatoes, artichoke hearts and sweet pepper. Add the remaining vinaigrette and pepper; toss to coat. Place tomato mixture on other half of the pan. Roast for 12-15 minutes or until the fish just begins to flake easily with a fork and vegetables are tender.

Per 1 fillet with ¾ cup tomato mixture: 318 cal., 16g fat (3g sat. fat), 73mg chol., 674mg sod., 12g carb. (4g sugars, 2g fiber), 28g pro.

Diabetic Exchanges: 4 lean meat, 1 vegetable, 1 fat.

SEAFOOD-STUFFED RAINBOW TROUT

Here's a special way to serve fresh rainbow trout—stuffed with a mixture of scallops, shrimp, rice, bacon and vegetables. But don't wait for a special occasion. It's surprisingly easy to put together and pop in the oven.

—MYRONIUK TRACY EDMONTON, AB

PREP: 20 MIN. • **BAKE:** 25 MIN.
MAKES: 4 SERVINGS

- 4 **tablespoons butter, melted, divided**
- 1 **tablespoon lemon juice**
- 2 **pan-dressed trout (about 12 ounces each)**
- ¼ **teaspoon pepper**
- ¼ **cup cooked long grain rice**
- 2 **bacon strips, cooked and crumbled**
- 2 **tablespoons chopped onion**
- 2 **tablespoons diced sweet red pepper**
- 15 **frozen cooked salad shrimp, thawed**
- 4 **sea scallops, diced**
- 1 **tablespoon canola oil**
- 1 **to 2 medium lemons, thinly sliced**

1. Combine 2 tablespoons butter and the lemon juice; drizzle over the trout cavities. Sprinkle with pepper; set aside. In a small skillet, saute the rice, bacon, onion, red pepper, shrimp and scallops in oil for 5 minutes or until scallops are firm and opaque. Spoon into fish cavities. Arrange lemon slices on top of fish.

2. Brush remaining butter over a sheet of heavy-duty foil; wrap fish in foil and seal tightly. Place on a baking sheet. Bake at 425° for 25-28 minutes or until fish flakes easily with a fork. Open foil carefully to allow steam to escape.

Bonus: Most Requested

CARAMELIZED HAM & SWISS BUNS

My next-door neighbor shared her version of this recipe with me. You can make it ahead and cook it quickly when company arrives. The combo of poppy seeds, ham and cheese, horseradish and brown sugar makes it simply delicious!

—IRIS WEIHEMULLER BAXTER, MN

PREP: 25 MIN. + CHILLING
BAKE: 30 MIN.
MAKES: 1 DOZEN

- 1 **package (12 ounces) Hawaiian sweet rolls, split**
- ½ **cup horseradish sauce**
- 12 **slices deli ham**
- 6 **slices Swiss cheese, halved**
- ½ **cup butter, cubed**
- 2 **tablespoons finely chopped onion**
- 2 **tablespoons brown sugar**
- 1 **tablespoon spicy brown mustard**
- 2 **teaspoons poppy seeds**
- 1½ **teaspoons Worcestershire sauce**
- ¼ **teaspoon garlic powder**

1. Spread roll bottoms with horseradish sauce. Layer with ham and cheese; replace tops. Arrange in a single layer in a greased 9-in. square baking pan.
2. In a small skillet, heat butter over medium-high heat. Add onion; cook and stir for 1-2 minutes or until tender. Stir in remaining ingredients. Pour over rolls. Refrigerate, covered, several hours or overnight.
3. Preheat the oven to 350°. Bake, covered, for 25 minutes. Bake, uncovered, 5-10 minutes longer or until golden brown.

CARAMELIZED
HAM & SWISS BUNS

CHEESEBURGER
SOUP

WONTON MOZZARELLA STICKS

You won't believe something this easy could taste so fantastic! Crunchy outside, gooey cheese inside, these mozzarella sticks are a treat all ages will love. Kids can help wrap them, too.
—**SHIRLEY WARREN** THIENSVILLE, WI

START TO FINISH: 20 MIN.
MAKES: 1 DOZEN

> 12 **pieces string cheese**
> 12 **large egg roll wrappers (see note)**
> **Oil for frying**
> **Marinara or spaghetti sauce**

1. Place a piece of string cheese near the bottom corner of one egg roll wrapper (keep remaining wrappers covered with a damp paper towel until ready to use). Fold bottom corner over cheese. Roll up halfway; fold sides toward center over cheese. Moisten remaining corner with water; roll up tightly to seal. Repeat with remaining wrappers and cheese.
2. In an electric skillet, heat ½ in. of oil to 375°. Fry sticks, a few at a time, for 30-60 seconds on each side or until golden brown. Drain on paper towels. Serve with marinara sauce.

Test Kitchen Note: Be sure to get wrappers labeled egg roll wrappers and not spring roll wrappers. Egg roll wrappers are soft and bendable while in the package. Spring roll wrappers are usually thin and very firm, and must be dipped in water to soften before using.

CHEESEBURGER SOUP

A local restaurant has a cult following thanks to its cheeseburger soup, a recipe the chef keeps top secret. I made my own version with beef, Velveeta and potatoes.
—**JOANIE SHAWHAN** MADISON, WI

PREP: 45 MIN. • **COOK:** 10 MIN.
MAKES: 8 SERVINGS (2¼ QUARTS)

> ½ **pound ground beef**
> 4 **tablespoons butter, divided**
> ¾ **cup chopped onion**
> ¾ **cup shredded carrots**
> ¾ **cup diced celery**
> 1 **teaspoon dried basil**
> 1 **teaspoon dried parsley flakes**
> 1¾ **pounds (about 4 cups) cubed peeled potatoes**
> 3 **cups chicken broth**
> ¼ **cup all-purpose flour**
> 1 **package (16 ounces) Velveeta process cheese, cubed**
> 1½ **cups whole milk**
> ¾ **teaspoon salt**
> ¼ **to ½ teaspoon pepper**
> ¼ **cup sour cream**

1. In a large saucepan over medium heat, cook and crumble beef until no longer pink; drain and set aside. In same saucepan, melt 1 tablespoon butter over medium heat. Saute onion, carrots, celery, basil and parsley until tender, about 10 minutes. Add potatoes, beef and broth; bring to a boil. Reduce heat; simmer, covered, until potatoes are tender, 10-12 minutes.
2. Meanwhile, in a small skillet, melt remaining butter. Add flour; cook and stir until bubbly, 3-5 minutes. Add to soup; bring to a boil. Cook and stir 2 minutes. Reduce heat to low. Stir in cheese, milk, salt and pepper; cook until cheese melts. Remove from heat; blend in sour cream.

PEA & PEANUT SALAD

PEA & PEANUT SALAD

A friend gave me this easy-peasy salad recipe that contains peanuts, celery and bacon. Even folks who normally push away peas will devour this by the bowlful.

—LAURINDA NELSON PHOENIX, AZ

START TO FINISH: 15 MIN.
MAKES: 4 SERVINGS

- 2½ cups frozen peas (about 10 ounces), thawed
- 1 cup dry roasted peanuts
- 1 cup chopped celery
- 6 bacon strips, cooked and crumbled
- ¼ cup chopped red onion
- ½ cup mayonnaise
- ¼ cup prepared zesty Italian salad dressing

In a large bowl, combine the first five ingredients. In a small bowl, mix mayonnaise and salad dressing; stir into salad. Refrigerate, covered, until serving.

CRISP CUCUMBER SALSA

Here's a fantastic way to use cucumbers. You'll enjoy the creamy, crunchy texture and fresh flavors.

—CHARLENE SKJERVEN HOOPLE, ND

START TO FINISH: 20 MIN.
MAKES: 2½ CUPS

- 2 cups finely chopped seeded peeled cucumber
- ½ cup finely chopped seeded tomato
- ¼ cup chopped red onion
- 2 tablespoons minced fresh parsley
- 1 jalapeno pepper, seeded and chopped
- 4½ teaspoons minced fresh cilantro
- 1 garlic clove, minced
- ¼ cup reduced-fat sour cream
- 1½ teaspoons lemon juice
- 1½ teaspoons lime juice
- ¼ teaspoon ground cumin
- ¼ teaspoon seasoned salt
  Baked tortilla chip scoops

In a small bowl, combine the first seven ingredients. In another bowl, combine the sour cream, lemon juice, lime juice, cumin and seasoned salt. Pour over cucumber mixture and toss gently to coat. Serve immediately with chips.

Test Kitchen Note: Wear disposable gloves when cutting hot peppers; the oils can burn skin. Avoid touching your face.

CHICKEN
CRESCENT
WREATH

FREEZE IT

CHICKEN CRESCENT WREATH

This is an impressive-looking main dish that's a snap to prepare. When my cooking time is limited, I can still serve this delicious wreath if I've stashed a spare in the freezer. The red pepper and green broccoli add a festive touch.

—MARLENE DENISSEN ST. CROIX FALLS, WI

PREP: 15 MIN. • **BAKE:** 20 MIN.
MAKES: 6-8 SERVINGS

- 2 tubes (8 ounces each) refrigerated crescent rolls
- 1 cup shredded Colby-Monterey Jack cheese
- ⅔ cup condensed cream of chicken soup, undiluted
- ½ cup chopped fresh broccoli
- ½ cup chopped sweet red pepper
- ¼ cup chopped water chestnuts
- 1 can (5 ounces) white chicken, drained or ¾ cup cubed cooked chicken
- 2 tablespoons chopped onion

1. Arrange crescent rolls on a 12-in. pizza pan, forming a ring with pointed ends facing the outer edge of pan and wide ends overlapping.

2. Combine the remaining ingredients; spoon over wide ends of rolls. Fold points over filling and tuck under wide ends (filling will be visible).

3. Bake at 375° for 20-25 minutes or until golden brown.

Freeze option: Securely wrap cooled wreath in plastic and foil before freezing. To use, remove from freezer 30 minutes before reheating. Remove wreath from foil and plastic; reheat on a greased baking sheet in a preheated 325° oven until heated through.

PINEAPPLE ORANGE CAKE

I've been adapting one of my favorite cake recipes for years and now it's almost guilt-free. It's moist and light, yet so satisfying.

—PAM SJOLUND COLUMBIA, SC

PREP: 15 MIN. • **BAKE:** 25 MIN. + CHILLING
MAKES: 15 SERVINGS

- 1 package yellow cake mix (regular size)
- 1 can (11 ounces) mandarin oranges, undrained
- 4 large egg whites
- ½ cup unsweetened applesauce

TOPPING

- 1 can (20 ounces) crushed pineapple, undrained
- 1 package (1 ounce) sugar-free instant vanilla pudding mix
- 1 carton (8 ounces) reduced-fat whipped topping

1. In a large bowl, beat the cake mix, oranges, egg whites and applesauce on low speed for 2 minutes. Pour into a 13x9-in. baking dish coated with cooking spray.

2. Bake at 350° for 25-30 minutes or until a toothpick inserted near the center comes out clean. Cool on a wire rack.

3. In a bowl, combine the pineapple and pudding mix. Fold in whipped topping just until blended. Spread over cake. Refrigerate for at least 1 hour before serving.

PINEAPPLE ORANGE CAKE

AMISH BREAKFAST CASSEROLE

I enjoyed a hearty breakfast bake during a visit to an Amish inn. When I asked for the recipe, one of the ladies told me the ingredients right off the top of her head. I modified it to create this version my family loves. Try breakfast sausage in place of bacon.

—BETH NOTARO KOKOMO, IN

PREP: 15 MIN. • **BAKE:** 35 MIN. + STANDING
MAKES: 12 SERVINGS

- 1 pound sliced bacon, diced
- 1 medium sweet onion, chopped
- 6 large eggs, lightly beaten
- 4 cups frozen shredded hash brown potatoes, thawed
- 2 cups shredded cheddar cheese
- 1½ cups 4% cottage cheese
- 1¼ cups shredded Swiss cheese

1. Preheat oven to 350°. In a large skillet, cook bacon and onion over medium heat until bacon is crisp; drain. In a large bowl, combine remaining ingredients; stir in bacon mixture. Transfer to a greased 13x9-in. baking dish.

2. Bake, uncovered, 35-40 minutes or until a knife inserted near the center comes out clean. Let stand 10 minutes before cutting.

Test Kitchen Note: Create a pretty burst of color and fresh flavor by adding a pinch of minced herbs to the egg mixture. Thyme and parsley are perfect candidates; try 1 teaspoon fresh or ¼ teaspoon dried. Assemble the casserole a day in advance, and bake just before serving.

TOP TIP

FOR LIGHT, MOIST CAKE

"Beat in a 12-ounce can of diet soda. Try diet lemon-lime soda with white or yellow cake mix and diet cola with a chocolate cake mix. Once baked, top each piece with 2 tablespoons of fat-free whipped topping instead of icing."

—DEBBIE M. OWENSBORO, KY

CAULIFLOWER
SOUP

CAULIFLOWER SOUP

Cauliflower and carrots share the stage in this cheesy soup that's sure to warm you up on the chilliest nights. We like it with hot pepper sauce; however, it can be omitted with equally tasty results.
—**DEBBIE OHLHAUSEN** CHILLIWACK, BC

START TO FINISH: 30 MIN.
MAKES: 8 SERVINGS (ABOUT 2 QUARTS)

- 1 **medium head cauliflower, broken into florets**
- 1 **medium carrot, shredded**
- ¼ **cup chopped celery**
- 2½ **cups water**
- 2 **teaspoons chicken or 1 vegetable bouillon cube**
- 3 **tablespoons butter**
- 3 **tablespoons all-purpose flour**
- ¾ **teaspoon salt**
- ⅛ **teaspoon pepper**
- 2 **cups 2% milk**
- 1 **cup shredded cheddar cheese**
- ½ **to 1 teaspoon hot pepper sauce, optional**

1. In a Dutch oven, combine the cauliflower, carrot, celery, water and bouillon. Bring to a boil. Reduce heat; cover and simmer for 12-15 minutes or until vegetables are tender (do not drain).
2. In another large saucepan, melt butter. Stir in the flour, salt and pepper until smooth. Gradually add milk. Bring to a boil over medium heat; cook and stir for 2 minutes or until thickened. Reduce heat. Stir in the cheese until melted. Add hot pepper sauce if desired. Stir into the cauliflower mixture.

PUMPKIN LASAGNA

Even friends who aren't big fans of pumpkin are surprised by this delectable lasagna. Canned pumpkin and no-cook noodles make it a cinch to prepare.
—**TAMARA HURON** NEW MARKET, AL

PREP: 25 MIN. • **BAKE:** 55 MIN. + STANDING
MAKES: 6 SERVINGS

- ½ **pound sliced fresh mushrooms**
- 1 **small onion, chopped**
- ½ **teaspoon salt, divided**
- 2 **teaspoons olive oil**
- 1 **can (15 ounces) solid-pack pumpkin**
- ½ **cup half-and-half cream**
- 1 **teaspoon dried sage leaves Dash pepper**
- 9 **no-cook lasagna noodles**
- 1 **cup reduced-fat ricotta cheese**
- 1 **cup shredded part-skim mozzarella cheese**
- ¾ **cup shredded Parmesan cheese**

1. In a small skillet, saute mushrooms, onion and ¼ teaspoon salt in oil until tender; set aside. In a small bowl, combine the pumpkin, cream, sage, pepper and remaining salt.
2. Spread ½ cup pumpkin sauce in an 11x7-in. baking dish coated with cooking spray. Top with three noodles (noodles will overlap slightly). Spread ½ cup pumpkin sauce to edges of noodles. Top with half of mushroom mixture, ½ cup ricotta, ½ cup mozzarella and ¼ cup Parmesan cheese. Repeat layers. Top with remaining noodles and sauce.
3. Cover and bake at 375° for 45 minutes. Uncover; sprinkle with remaining Parmesan cheese. Bake 10-15 minutes longer or until cheese is melted. Let stand for 10 minutes.
Freeze option: Cover and freeze unbaked lasagna. To use, partially thaw in refrigerator overnight. Remove from refrigerator 30 minutes before baking. Preheat oven to 375°. Bake as directed, increasing time as necessary to heat through and for a thermometer inserted in the center to read 165°.
Per piece: 310 cal., 12g fat (6g sat. fat), 36mg chol., 497mg sod., 32g carb. (7g sugars, 5g fiber), 17g pro.
Diabetic Exchanges: 2 starch, 2 fat, 1 lean meat.

CREAMY WHITE CHILI

I got this wonderful recipe from my sister-in-law, who made a big batch and served a crowd one night. It was a hit. Plus, it's easy and quick, which is helpful since I'm a college student. In all my years of 4-H cooking, I've never had another dish get so many compliments.
—LAURA BREWER LAFAYETTE, IN

PREP: 10 MIN. • **COOK:** 40 MIN.
MAKES: 7 SERVINGS

- 1 pound boneless skinless chicken breasts, cut into ½-inch cubes
- 1 medium onion, chopped
- 1½ teaspoons garlic powder
- 1 tablespoon canola oil
- 2 cans (15½ ounces each) great northern beans, rinsed and drained
- 1 can (14½ ounces) chicken broth
- 2 cans (4 ounces each) chopped green chilies
- 1 teaspoon salt
- 1 teaspoon ground cumin
- 1 teaspoon dried oregano
- ½ teaspoon pepper
- ¼ teaspoon cayenne pepper
- 1 cup (8 ounces) sour cream
- ½ cup heavy whipping cream
  Tortilla chips, optional
  Shredded cheddar cheese, optional
  Sliced seeded jalapeno pepper, optional

1. In a large saucepan, saute the chicken, onion and garlic powder in oil until chicken is no longer pink. Add the beans, broth, chilies and seasonings. Bring to a boil. Reduce heat; simmer, uncovered, for 30 minutes.
2. Remove from the heat; stir in sour cream and heavy whipping cream. If desired, top with tortilla chips, cheese and jalapenos.
Test Kitchen Note: You can make this using half-and-half cream instead of heavy cream with great success.

FREEZE IT
RUSTIC ITALIAN TORTELLINI SOUP

This is my favorite soup recipe. It's full of healthy, tasty ingredients. It originally called for spicy sausage links, but I've found that turkey sausage, or even ground turkey breast, is just as good.
—TRACY FASNACHT IRWIN, PA

PREP: 20 MIN. • **COOK:** 20 MIN.
MAKES: 6 SERVINGS (2 QUARTS)

- ¾ pound Italian turkey sausage links, casings removed
- 1 medium onion, chopped
- 6 garlic cloves, minced
- 2 cans (14½ ounces each) reduced-sodium chicken broth
- 1¾ cups water
- 1 can (14½ ounces) diced tomatoes, undrained
- 1 package (9 ounces) refrigerated cheese tortellini
- 1 package (6 ounces) fresh baby spinach, coarsely chopped
- 2¼ teaspoons minced fresh basil or ¾ teaspoon dried basil
- ¼ teaspoon pepper
  Dash crushed red pepper flakes
  Shredded Parmesan cheese, optional

1. Crumble sausage into a Dutch oven; add onion. Cook and stir over medium heat until meat is no longer pink. Add garlic; cook for 1 minute longer. Stir in the broth, water and tomatoes. Bring to a boil.
2. Add tortellini; return to a boil. Cook for 5-8 minutes or until almost tender, stirring occasionally. Reduce heat; add the spinach, basil, pepper and red pepper flakes. Cook for 2-3 minutes longer or until spinach is wilted and tortellini are tender. Serve with cheese if desired.
Freeze option: Place individual portions of cooled soup in freezer containers and freeze. To use, partially thaw in refrigerator overnight. Heat through in a saucepan, stirring occasionally and adding a little broth if necessary.
Rustic Italian Ravioli Soup: Substitute ravioli for the tortellini.

SPECIAL BANANA NUT BREAD

PREP: 25 MIN.
BAKE: 1 HOUR + COOLING
MAKES: 2 LOAVES (12 SLICES EACH)

- ¾ cup butter, softened
- 1 package (8 ounces) cream cheese, softened
- 2 cups sugar
- 2 large eggs
- 1½ cups mashed ripe bananas (about 4 medium)
- ½ teaspoon vanilla extract
- 3 cups all-purpose flour
- ½ teaspoon baking powder
- ½ teaspoon baking soda
- ½ teaspoon salt
- 2 cups chopped pecans, divided

ORANGE GLAZE
- 1 cup confectioners' sugar
- 3 tablespoons orange juice
- 1 teaspoon grated orange peel

1. Preheat oven to 350°. Cream butter, cream cheese and sugar until light and fluffy. Add eggs, one at a time, beating well after each addition. Beat in bananas and vanilla. In another bowl, combine flour, baking powder, baking soda and salt; gradually add to creamed mixture. Fold in 1 cup pecans.
2. Transfer to two greased 8x4-in. loaf pans. Sprinkle with remaining pecans. Bake loaves, covering with foil if they darken too rapidly, until a toothpick inserted in the center comes out clean, 1-1¼ hours. Cool for 10 minutes before removing to wire racks.
3. While loaves are still slightly warm, whisk glaze ingredients. Drizzle over loaves, using a baking pan or parchment paper under racks to catch excess. Cool completely.

"Make a wonderful gift for friends and neighbors with this extra-special banana bread. The recipe makes two loaves, so I serve one and keep one in the freezer so I have a last-minute gift on hand."

—**BEVERLY SPRAGUE** BALTIMORE, MD

SPECIAL
BANANA NUT
BREAD

MAMA'S
POTATO SALAD

GRILLED HULI HULI CHICKEN

When I lived in Hawaii, I got this recipe for chicken marinated in a ginger-soy sauce from a friend. Huli means turn in Hawaiian and refers to turning the meat on the grill.
—SHARON BOLING SAN DIEGO, CA

PREP: 15 MIN. + MARINATING
GRILL: 15 MIN.
MAKES: 12 SERVINGS

  1 cup packed brown sugar
  ¾ cup ketchup
  ¾ cup reduced-sodium soy sauce
  ⅓ cup sherry or chicken broth
 2½ teaspoons minced fresh gingerroot
 1½ teaspoons minced garlic
 24 boneless skinless chicken thighs (about 5 pounds)

1. In a small bowl, mix the first six ingredients. Reserve 1⅓ cups for basting; cover and refrigerate. Divide remaining marinade between two large resealable plastic bags. Add 12 chicken thighs to each; seal bags and turn to coat. Refrigerate for 8 hours or overnight.
2. Drain and discard marinade from chicken. Moisten a paper towel with cooking oil; using long-handled tongs, lightly coat the grill rack.
3. Grill chicken, covered, over medium heat for 6-8 minutes on each side or until no longer pink; baste occasionally with reserved marinade during the last 5 minutes.

> **TOP TIP**
>
> ### GINGERROOT FACTS
> Fresh gingerroot is available in your grocer's produce section. It should have a smooth skin. If wrinkled and cracked, the root is dry and past its prime. When stored in a heavy-duty resealable plastic bag, unpeeled gingerroot can be frozen for up to 1 year. When needed, simply peel and grate.

MAMA'S POTATO SALAD

Mama made this old-fashioned potato salad without a lot of ingredients, the way her mother did, and that's the way I still make it today. Try it and see if it isn't one of the best-tasting potato salads you have ever eaten!
—SANDRA ANDERSON NEW YORK, NY

START TO FINISH: 30 MIN.
MAKES: 12 SERVINGS

  3 to 3½ pounds potatoes (about 10 medium)
  6 hard-cooked eggs
  1 medium onion, finely chopped
  ½ cup mayonnaise
  ½ cup evaporated milk
  3 tablespoons white vinegar
  2 tablespoons prepared mustard
  ¼ cup sugar
  1 teaspoon salt
  ¼ teaspoon pepper
     Additional hard-cooked eggs, sliced
     Paprika

1. In a large kettle, cook potatoes in boiling salted water until tender. Drain and cool. Peel potatoes; cut into chunks. Separate egg yolks from whites. Set yolks aside. Chop whites and add to potatoes with onion.
2. In a small bowl, mash yolks. Stir in mayonnaise, milk, vinegar, mustard, sugar, salt and pepper. Pour over potatoes; toss well. Adjust seasonings if necessary. Spoon into a serving bowl. Garnish with egg slices and paprika. Chill until serving.

SAVORY PARTY BREAD

COMPANY MAC & CHEESE

I'm not usually a fan of homemade macaroni and cheese, but when a friend served this, I had to have the recipe. This is by far the creamiest, tastiest and most special macaroni and cheese I have ever tried. Since it's simple to make and well received, it's a terrific potluck dish.

—CATHERINE OGDEN MIDDLEGROVE, NY

START TO FINISH: 30 MIN.
MAKES: 6-8 SERVINGS

- 1 package (7 ounces) elbow macaroni
- 6 tablespoons butter, divided
- 3 tablespoons all-purpose flour
- 2 cups milk
- 1 package (8 ounces) cream cheese, cubed
- 2 cups shredded cheddar cheese
- 2 teaspoons spicy brown mustard
- ½ teaspoon salt
- ¼ teaspoon pepper
- ¾ cup dry bread crumbs
- 2 tablespoons minced fresh parsley

1. Preheat oven to 400°. Cook macaroni according to the package directions. Meanwhile, melt 4 tablespoons butter in a large saucepan. Stir in flour until smooth. Gradually add milk. Bring to a boil; cook and stir for 2 minutes.
2. Reduce heat; add cheeses, mustard, salt and pepper. Stir until cheese is melted and sauce is smooth. Drain macaroni; add to cheese sauce and stir to coat.
3. Transfer to a greased shallow 3-qt. baking dish. Melt remaining butter; toss with bread crumbs and parsley. Sprinkle over macaroni. Bake, uncovered, 15-20 minutes or until golden brown.

SAVORY PARTY BREAD

It's impossible to stop nibbling on warm pieces of this cheesy, oniony loaf. The bread fans out for a fun presentation.

—KAY DALY RALEIGH, NC

PREP: 10 MIN. • **BAKE:** 25 MIN.
MAKES: 8 SERVINGS

- 1 unsliced round loaf sourdough bread (1 pound)
- 1 pound Monterey Jack cheese
- ½ cup butter, melted
- ½ cup chopped green onions
- 2 to 3 teaspoons poppy seeds

1. Preheat oven to 350°. Cut bread widthwise into 1-in. slices to within ½ in. of bottom of loaf. Repeat cuts in opposite direction. Cut cheese into ¼-in. slices; cut slices into small pieces. Place cheese in cuts.
2. In a small bowl, mix butter, green onions and poppy seeds; drizzle over bread. Wrap in foil; place on a baking sheet. Bake for 15 minutes. Unwrap; bake 10 minutes longer or until cheese is melted.
Test Kitchen Note: The bread can be sliced and filled a day ahead. Right before company comes, melt the butter and add the green onions and poppy seeds.

BAKE-SALE LEMON BARS

The recipe for these tangy lemon bars comes from my cousin Bernice, a farmer's wife who is famous for cooking up delicious feasts.

—MILDRED KELLER ROCKFORD, IL

PREP: 25 MIN. • **BAKE:** 20 MIN. + COOLING
MAKES: 4 DOZEN

- ¾ cup butter, softened
- ⅔ cup confectioners' sugar
- 1½ cups plus 3 tablespoons all-purpose flour, divided
- 3 large eggs
- 1½ cups sugar
- ¼ cup lemon juice
  Additional confectioners' sugar

1. Preheat oven to 350°. In a large bowl, beat butter and confectioners' sugar until blended. Gradually beat in 1½ cups flour. Press onto bottom of a greased 13x9-in. baking pan. Bake for 18-20 minutes or until golden brown.
2. Meanwhile, in a small bowl, whisk eggs, sugar, lemon juice and remaining flour until frothy; pour over hot crust.
3. Bake for 20-25 minutes or until lemon mixture is set and lightly browned. Cool completely on a wire rack. Dust with additional confectioners' sugar. Cut into bars. Refrigerate leftovers.

TASTY
LENTIL TACOS

TASTY LENTIL TACOS

My husband has to watch his cholesterol. This is a dish I found that's healthy for him and yummy for our five children.
—**MICHELLE THOMAS** BANGOR, ME

PREP: 15 MIN. • **COOK:** 40 MIN.
MAKES: 6 SERVINGS

- 1 teaspoon canola oil
- 1 medium onion, finely chopped
- 1 garlic clove, minced
- 1 cup dried lentils, rinsed
- 1 tablespoon chili powder
- 2 teaspoons ground cumin
- 1 teaspoon dried oregano
- 2½ cups vegetable or reduced-sodium chicken broth
- 1 cup salsa
- 12 taco shells
- 1½ cups shredded lettuce
- 1 cup chopped fresh tomatoes
- 1½ cups shredded reduced-fat cheddar cheese
- 6 tablespoons fat-free sour cream

1. In a large nonstick skillet, heat oil over medium heat; saute onion and garlic until tender. Add lentils and seasonings; cook and stir for 1 minute. Stir in broth; bring to a boil. Reduce heat; simmer, covered, until lentils are tender, 25-30 minutes.
2. Cook, uncovered, until mixture is thickened, 6-8 minutes, stirring occasionally. Mash lentils slightly; stir in salsa and heat through. Serve in taco shells. Top with remaining ingredients.
Per 2 tacos: 365 cal., 12g fat (5g sat. fat), 21mg chol., 777mg sod., 44g carb. (5g sugars, 6g fiber), 19g pro.
Diabetic Exchanges: 2½ starch, 2 lean meat, 1 vegetable, 1 fat.

"I'm always looking to switch it up with some meatless options for dinner. These lentil tacos were amazing! I use this lentil filling just as often as I make ground beef filling now. Definitely a 5-star recipe!"
—**SHANNONDOBOS**
TASTEOFHOME.COM

HERB & CHEESE-STUFFED BURGERS

HERB & CHEESE-STUFFED BURGERS

Tired of the same old ground-beef burgers? This quick-fix alternative, with its creamy cheese filling, will definitely wake up your taste buds.
—**SHERRI COX** LUCASVILLE, OH

START TO FINISH: 30 MIN.
MAKES: 4 SERVINGS

- ¼ cup shredded cheddar cheese
- 2 tablespoons cream cheese, softened
- 2 tablespoons minced fresh parsley
- 3 teaspoons Dijon mustard, divided
- 2 green onions, thinly sliced
- 3 tablespoons dry bread crumbs
- 2 tablespoons ketchup
- ½ teaspoon salt
- ½ teaspoon dried rosemary, crushed
- ¼ teaspoon dried sage leaves
- 1 pound lean ground beef (90% lean)
- 4 hamburger buns, split
  Optional toppings: lettuce leaves and tomato slices

1. In a small bowl, mix cheddar cheese, cream cheese, parsley and 1 teaspoon mustard. In another bowl, mix green onions, bread crumbs, ketchup, seasonings and remaining mustard. Add beef; mix lightly but thoroughly.

2. Shape mixture into eight thin patties. Spoon cheese mixture onto the center of four patties; top with remaining patties, pressing edges firmly to seal.
3. Grill burgers, covered, over medium heat or broil 4 in. from heat for 4-5 minutes on each side or until a thermometer reads 160°. Serve on buns with toppings as desired.

STRAWBERRY SPRITZER

Three simple ingredients are all you need to create this fresh and fruity summer beverage. It's bound to become a warm-weather favorite.
—**KRISTA COLLINS** CONCORD, NC

START TO FINISH: 10 MIN.
MAKES: 2½ QUARTS

- 1 package (10 ounces) frozen sweetened sliced strawberries, thawed
- 2 liters lemon-lime soda, chilled
- 1 can (12 ounces) frozen pink lemonade concentrate, thawed

Place the strawberries in a blender; cover and process until pureed. Pour into a large pitcher; stir in the soda and pink lemonade concentrate. Serve immediately.

ZUCCHINI PARMESAN

You'll knock their socks off with this easy-to-prep side that's absolutely delicious. My favorite time to make it is when the veggies are fresh out of the garden.

—SANDI GUETTLER BAY CITY, MI

START TO FINISH: 25 MIN.
MAKES: 6 SERVINGS

- 4 medium zucchini, cut into ¼-inch slices
- 1 tablespoon olive oil
- ½ to 1 teaspoon minced garlic
- 1 can (14½ ounces) Italian diced tomatoes, undrained
- 1 teaspoon seasoned salt
- ¼ teaspoon pepper
- ¼ cup grated Parmesan cheese

1. In a large skillet, saute zucchini in oil until crisp-tender. Add garlic; cook for 1 minute longer.
2. Stir in the tomatoes, seasoned salt and pepper. Simmer, uncovered, for 9-10 minutes or until liquid is evaporated. Sprinkle with Parmesan cheese. Serve with a slotted spoon.

TUSCAN-STYLE ROASTED ASPARAGUS

This recipe is especially wonderful when locally grown asparagus is in season, and it is so easy for celebrations because you can serve it hot or cold.

—JANNINE FISK MALDEN, MA

PREP: 20 MIN. • **BAKE:** 15 MIN.
MAKES: 8 SERVINGS

- 1½ pounds fresh asparagus, trimmed
- 1½ cups grape tomatoes, halved
- 3 tablespoons pine nuts
- 3 tablespoons olive oil, divided
- 2 garlic cloves, minced
- 1 teaspoon kosher salt
- ½ teaspoon pepper
- 1 tablespoon lemon juice
- ⅓ cup grated Parmesan cheese
- 1 teaspoon grated lemon peel

1. Preheat oven to 400°. Place the asparagus, tomatoes and pine nuts on a foil-lined 15x10x1-in. baking pan. Mix 2 tablespoons oil, garlic, salt and pepper; add to asparagus and toss to coat.

2. Bake for 15-20 minutes or just until asparagus is tender. Drizzle with remaining oil and the lemon juice; sprinkle with cheese and lemon peel. Toss to combine.

Per serving: 95 cal., 8g fat (2g sat. fat), 3mg chol., 294mg sod., 4g carb. (2g sugars, 1g fiber), 3g pro.
Diabetic Exchanges: 1½ fat, 1 vegetable.

SCRAMBLED EGG MUFFINS

After enjoying scrambled egg muffins at a local restaurant, I came up with this savory version that my husband likes even better. Freeze the extras to reheat on busy mornings.

—CATHY LARKINS MARSHFIELD, MO

START TO FINISH: 30 MIN.
MAKES: 1 DOZEN

- ½ pound bulk pork sausage
- 12 large eggs
- ½ cup chopped onion
- ¼ cup chopped green pepper
- ½ teaspoon salt
- ¼ teaspoon garlic powder
- ¼ teaspoon pepper
- ½ cup shredded cheddar cheese

1. Preheat oven to 350°. In a large skillet, cook sausage over medium heat until no longer pink; drain.
2. In a large bowl, beat eggs. Add onion, green pepper, salt, garlic powder and pepper. Stir in sausage and cheese.
3. Spoon by ⅓ cupfuls into muffin cups coated with cooking spray. Bake for 20-25 minutes or until a knife inserted near the center comes out clean.

Freeze option: Cool baked egg muffins. Cover and place on waxed paper-lined baking sheets and freeze until firm. Transfer to resealable plastic freezer bags; return to freezer. To use, place in greased muffin pan, cover loosely with foil, and reheat in a preheated 350° oven until heated through. Or, microwave each muffin on high for 30-60 seconds or until heated through.

ZUCCHINI PARMESAN

CHOCOLATE CHIP
CHEESE BALL

DELICIOUS TOMATO PIE

How about pie for dinner? This savory staple is a wonderful way to accentuate summer's abundance of tomatoes from the garden or from a farm stand.

—EDIE DESPAIN LOGAN, UT

PREP: 15 MIN. • **BAKE:** 30 MIN.
MAKES: 8 SERVINGS

- 1¼ **pounds tomatoes (5 large), cut into ½-inch slices, seeded**
- 1 **pastry shell (9 inches), baked**
- ½ **cup thinly sliced green onions**
- 2 **tablespoons minced fresh basil**
- ¼ **teaspoon salt**
- ¼ **teaspoon pepper**
- ½ **cup reduced-fat mayonnaise**
- ½ **cup shredded reduced-fat cheddar cheese**
- 2 **bacon strips, cooked and crumbled**
- 2 **tablespoons shredded Parmesan cheese**

1. Place half of the tomatoes in pastry shell. Top with onions and remaining tomatoes. Sprinkle with the basil, salt and pepper. Combine mayonnaise and cheddar cheese; spread over tomatoes, leaving 1½ in. around the edge. Sprinkle with bacon and Parmesan cheese.
2. Bake at 350° for 30-35 minutes or until tomatoes are tender.

CHOCOLATE CHIP CHEESE BALL

Your guests are in for a sweet surprise when they try this unusual cheese ball...it tastes just like cookie dough! The chip-studded spread is wonderful on regular or chocolate graham crackers. I especially like it because it can be assembled in a wink.

—KELLY GLASCOCK SYRACUSE, MO

PREP: 15 MIN. + CHILLING
MAKES: 16 SERVINGS
(2 TABLESPOONS EACH)

- 1 **package (8 ounces) cream cheese, softened**
- ½ **cup butter, softened**
- ¼ **teaspoon vanilla extract**
- ¾ **cup confectioners' sugar**
- 2 **tablespoons brown sugar**
- ¾ **cup miniature semisweet chocolate chips**
- ¾ **cup finely chopped pecans Graham crackers**

1. Beat cream cheese, butter and vanilla until smooth; beat in sugars just until blended. Stir in chocolate chips. Refrigerate, covered, until firm enough to shape, about 2 hours.
2. Place mixture on a large sheet of plastic wrap; shape into a ball. Refrigerate, wrapped, at least 1 hour.
3. To serve, roll cheese ball in pecans. Serve with graham crackers.

> **TOP TIP**
>
> This indulgent spread can be made with reduced-fat cream cheese, but it will be too soft to shape into a ball. Instead, serve in a shallow dish and sprinkle with the chips and pecans—still completely delicious (but with fewer calories and less fat).

COOKIE DOUGH TRUFFLES

The filling at the center of these candies tastes like genuine chocolate chip cookie dough—without raw eggs.

—**LANITA DEDON** SLAUGHTER, LA

PREP: 1 HOUR + CHILLING
MAKES: 5½ DOZEN

- ½ cup butter, softened
- ¾ cup packed brown sugar
- 1 teaspoon vanilla extract
- 2 cups all-purpose flour
- 1 can (14 ounces) sweetened condensed milk
- ½ cup miniature semisweet chocolate chips
- ½ cup chopped walnuts
- 1½ pounds dark chocolate candy coating, coarsely chopped

1. In a large bowl, cream the butter and brown sugar until light and fluffy. Beat in vanilla. Gradually add flour, alternately with milk, beating well after each addition. Stir in chocolate chips and walnuts.

2. Shape into 1-in. balls; place on waxed paper-lined baking sheets. Loosely cover and refrigerate for 1-2 hours or until firm.

3. In a microwave, melt candy coating; stir until smooth. Dip balls in coating; allow excess to drip off. Place on waxed paper-lined baking sheets. Refrigerate until firm, about 15 minutes. If desired, remelt the remaining candy coating and drizzle over candies. Store in the refrigerator.

Test Kitchen Note: Eating raw or uncooked flour may cause food-borne illnesses.

GRILLED THREE-CHEESE POTATOES

While this is delicious grilled, I've also cooked it in the oven at 350° for an hour. Add cubed ham to it and you can serve it as a full-meal main dish.

—**MARGARET RILEY** TALLAHASSEE, FL

PREP: 15 MIN. • **GRILL:** 35 MIN.
MAKES: 6-8 SERVINGS

- 6 large potatoes, sliced ¼ inch thick
- 2 medium onions, chopped
- ⅓ cup grated Parmesan cheese
- 1 cup shredded sharp cheddar cheese, divided
- 1 cup shredded part-skim mozzarella cheese, divided
- 1 pound sliced bacon, cooked and crumbled
- ¼ cup butter, cubed
- 1 tablespoon minced chives
- 1 to 2 teaspoons seasoned salt
- ½ teaspoon pepper

1. Divide the potatoes and onions equally between two pieces of heavy-duty foil (about 18 in. square) that have been coated with cooking spray.

2. Combine Parmesan cheese and ¾ cup each cheddar and mozzarella; sprinkle over potatoes and onions. Top with bacon, butter, chives, seasoned salt and pepper. Bring opposite ends of foil together over filling and fold down several times. Fold unsealed ends toward filling and crimp tightly.

3. Grill, covered, over medium heat for 35-40 minutes or until potatoes are tender. Remove from the grill. Open foil carefully and sprinkle with remaining cheeses.

BLUEBERRY FRENCH TOAST

Luscious blueberries are tucked into this French toast and in the sauce that goes over the top. With the cream cheese and berry combination, this dish reminds me of dessert. A local blueberry grower shared the recipe.

—**PATRICIA AXELSEN** AURORA, MN

PREP: 30 MIN. + CHILLING • **BAKE:** 55 MIN.
MAKES: 8 SERVINGS (1¾ CUPS SAUCE)

- 12 slices day-old white bread, crusts removed
- 2 packages (8 ounces each) cream cheese
- 1 cup fresh or frozen blueberries
- 12 large eggs, lightly beaten
- 2 cups 2% milk
- ⅓ cup maple syrup or honey

SAUCE

- 1 cup sugar
- 1 cup water
- 2 tablespoons cornstarch
- 1 cup fresh or frozen blueberries
- 1 tablespoon butter

1. Cut bread into 1-in. cubes; place half in a greased 13x9-in. baking dish. Cut cream cheese into 1-in. cubes; place over bread. Top with blueberries and remaining bread cubes.

2. Whisk the eggs, milk and syrup in a large bowl. Pour over bread mixture. Cover and refrigerate for 8 hours or overnight.

3. Remove from the refrigerator 30 minutes before baking. Cover and bake at 350° for 30 minutes. Uncover; bake 25-30 minutes longer or until a knife inserted in center comes out clean.

4. Combine the sugar, water and cornstarch until smooth in a small saucepan. Bring to a boil over medium heat; cook and stir until thickened, 3 minutes. Stir in blueberries; bring to a boil. Reduce heat and simmer until berries burst, 8-10 minutes. Remove from heat; stir in butter. Serve with French toast.

Test Kitchen Note: If using frozen blueberries, do not thaw.

TOP TIP

USES FOR FROZEN BLUEBERRIES

Frozen blueberries work great in many sweets, sauces and baked goods. They are especially nice in pancakes, muffins, pies, cobblers, coffee cakes, tea breads and many baked desserts. Because frozen blueberries give off more juice than fresh berries, be sure to reduce the liquid and increase the thickener when you use them in dessert fillings, such as when making pies, tarts and cobblers. For best results, do not thaw before using.

BLUEBERRY
FRENCH TOAST

General Recipe Index

Alphabetical Recipe Index